ON AIR
A History of BBC Transmission

Compiled and edited by
Norman Shacklady and Martin Ellen

"A high power wireless station is such a lovely thing. The process is silent, there is no gas or smell or fussy reciprocation; no sound except a purposeful humming. One is conscious of power contained and controlled......"

P.P. Eckersley, the BBC's first Chief Engineer

© Norman Shacklady and Martin Ellen 2003
ON AIR – A History of BBC Transmission

ISBN 0 9544077 1 7 *(Paperback)*
      0 9544077 0 9 *(Hardback)*

Published by Wavechange Books
94 Goddington Lane
Orpington
Kent BR6 9DY
England

The right of Norman Shacklady and Martin Ellen to be identified as authors of this work has been asserted by them in accordance with the Copyright, Designs and Patents Act 1988.

All rights reserved. No part of this publication may be produced in any form or by any means – graphic, electronic or mechanical including photocopying, recording, taping or information storage and retrieval systems – without the prior permission, in writing, of the publisher.

Design & production co-ordinated by:
The Better Book Company Ltd
Havant
Hampshire
PO9 2XH

Printed in England.

Cover photograph:
The BBC Tower at Crystal Palace in south London

FOREWORD

BBC Transmission was an integral and important part of that complex organisation 'The BBC', which benefited hugely from the progress made by Transmission and the other elements of BBC Engineering identified in the history as supporting the development and harnessing of transmission technology. They strove to ensure ever increasing high efficiency - pioneering the operation of high power RF equipment; developing monitoring and control systems at a time when those needed to be produced 'in house' before such systems became as common place as they are today.

I began my BBC career as a Technical Assistant at Daventry in 1956 and carried throughout my time some unfading memories. One in particular was the recognition that provided you did the job when it had to be done and did it well then any personal idiosyncrasy was accepted. As you will see from the anecdotes in the text, many diverse personalities contributed to the success of BBC Transmission and they were indeed one of its great strengths. Any history such as presented in this volume is as much a reflection of those writing the history as of the events themselves.

It was always interesting to ask an individual what was his occupation; the answer would be "a BBC engineer" – not many organisations could have such a pride held by their staff. BBC Transmission engineers at remote transmitting sites were also the public's first and main contact with the BBC and they acted as mini ambassadors.

I hope that when you read this history you will derive pleasure from the many human memories and identify all that BBC Transmission achieved in its long and illustrious career and the contribution made to the BBC's development.

Bill Dennay

BBC Director of Engineering 1987-1993

CONTENTS

PREFACE	*i*
ACKNOWLEDGEMENTS	*iii*
INTRODUCTION	*v*
SECTION 1 THE BEGINNING	1
The British Broadcasting Company	1
The British Broadcasting Corporation	4
SECTION 2 MF, LF & VHF RADIO TRANSMISSION	5
The Regional Scheme	5
The War Years	8
The European Service	10
The War Reporting Unit 1944/1945	12
Home, Light and Third Programmes	13
Mast collapse	13
Bombs	14
MF unattended operation	14
Local Radio	15
MF Efficiency Improvement	17
LF Radio Data	19
The start of VHF/FM broadcasting	19
Radio 1, Radio 2 and Local Radio	21
Stereo	21
NICAM for radio distribution	22
Radio Data Service	22
VHF/FM Re-engineering	23
Digital Broadcasting	23
SECTION 3 HF TRANSMISSION	24
The war years	28
Post-War HF Reconstruction	30
HF Automation	32
HF Efficiency Improvement	33
The closure of Daventry as an HF station	33
Overseas Relay Stations	34

SECTION 4 TELEVISION TRANSMISSION	50
Post War Extension of the Band I Television Service	51
Temporary Low Power Television Stations	54
Alexandra Palace Replacement	60
Low Power Band I Relay Stations	61
Colour Television	61
The introduction of UHF transmission	62
Mast collapse	65
Sound-in-Syncs	65
Teletext	66
NICAM stereo sound for television	66
Low Power UHF TV Relay Stations	66
Valves, klystrons and transistors	67
Digital Broadcasting	68
SECTION 5 AUTOMATION	69
Unattended Operation	69
Mobile Maintenance Teams	71
Increase in efficiency	73
Mobile Team Transport	73
SECTION 6 ASSOCIATED DEPARTMENTS	77
The early days	77
Research Department	79
Designs Department	88
Equipment Department	91
Communications Department	91
Engineering Training Department	92
Transmitter Capital Projects Department	92
SECTION 7 REMINISCENCES	96
Growing up with Broadcasting, R. A. Herbert	97
The Phantom Winch Winder, Bill Skelton	117
A visit to Stagshaw, Peter Pearson	119
MF Stations, Derek Hearn	133
The War Reporting Unit 1944/1945, E C P Metcalfe	134

The "Singing Arc", Bob Crawford	140
Installing Kirk o'Shotts – and "The Ladies Stocking Factory", Dennis Surridge	141
Sound Studio and Control Room engineering, 1929-1971, L G Smith	142
A Scottish Threat to the Coronation Broadcast, Dai Thomas	151
Life in Lines Department, 1944-1979, Geoff Martin	151
Atlantic Relay Station & the Falklands War, Norman Shacklady	166
Crystal Palace and the Rockets, Ian Blanthorn	170
It all began with "What's my Line", Tim Burrell	170
Sender 3 and "The Apiezion Q", Dick Skyrme	171
New blood and ideas were needed, John Packman	174
Snowtracs, DE's muddy shoes and windy sites, Roy Dalrymple	179
Bagpipes, Grallaching and Goliath, Syd Garrioch	182
"The Quality Street Gang", Jim McPherson	185
Crossed lines, Power, Christmas trees, Spiders & Diesels, Peter Condron	188
Life on a Maintenance Team & in TCPD, Roy Sharp	190
Rigging Services: a brief history and some memories, Clive Hosken	192
Daventry remembered, Norman Tomlin	195
Spanner in the rigging, Rex Boys	204
Fareham and the Electricity Board, Dick Stibbons	206
Starting with the BBC in 1941, Don Bowman	207
Finishing with the BBC in 1997, Martin Ellen	214
Index	218

PREFACE

The BBC's services were broadcast by its own transmitters from 1922 until 1997 — a lifetime.

Thousands of people were involved in the process of researching, planning, designing, specifying, acquiring, making, operating, maintaining and managing the facilities needed to broadcast the programmes and hundreds of millions of people benefited through the information, education and entertainment that they received.

This book celebrates a lifetime of achievement and includes many anecdotes from the lives of people involved. It does not aim to be the definitive history of BBC Transmission, but the initial chapters give an overview and record some of the most relevant information. The definitive history for the first 50 years is in Edward Pawley's excellent book "BBC Engineering 1922-1972".

The idea for *A History of BBC Transmission* arose at the time of privatisation, because an era was ending and it was a natural point for reflection on what had been achieved. The people of Transmission were geographically spread, but there was a tremendous sense of community and the unusual aspects of the work generated many stories. These stories are best told over a pint of beer and this was often the case, but many people felt that it would be worth trying to get some of the anecdotes into a book, so here it is.

It can often be difficult to get busy people, working or retired, to actually sit down and write something, so I would like to pay tribute to Norman Shacklady who has encouraged and cajoled potential contributors for over four years in order to make this book a reality. Notices have been in Ariel and Prospero, and numerous phone calls have taken place to spread the word that this book is being written, so hopefully all those who wished to contribute have done so. If not, another book is always possible! Very many thanks to all those who have contributed.

The legacy of BBC Transmission lives on in two successful companies. Crown Castle International now operates the BBC home transmission services and Merlin Communications now operates the BBC world transmission services, having purchased the assets for £244m and £30m respectively.

- Crown Castle has over 15,000 towers in the United Kingdom, United States and Australia as a result of subsequent acquisitions. In the UK, it built and now operates the world's first large scale digital terrestrial television networks; it built the mobile phone network for One-2-One in Northern Ireland; it's preparing for third generation mobile telecoms (where mobile and the Internet converge); and there are numerous other contracts, as well as all the traditional domestic BBC services.

- Merlin, which was purchased through a management buy-out, has added about 60 customers to its portfolio since inception and, through exclusive partnerships around the world, has reinforced its position as the leading global provider of short wave capacity. Merlin has won two major contracts, one with the BBC to design, build and maintain a new medium wave and short wave relay station in Oman worth £30 million and one with the Ministry of Defence for the provision of naval communications services worth more than £100 million over the period of the contract. Other projects include the completion of earth stations at Fareham and in Cyprus and taking a leading role in the development of DRM as a founder member of the Digital Radio Mondiale consortium.

Many of the BBC staff remain in the new organisations and there is a general feeling of pride at having worked for BBC Transmission, but there are very few regrets because advances in technology and developments in the worlds of broadcasting and telecommunications meant that privatisation was a very natural and positive step forward into the future.

Martin Ellen
BBC 1966 – 1997
Crown Castle International 1997 – 2002

ACKNOWLEDGEMENTS

Many thanks are due to the contributors listed below and to the BBC, Crown Castle International and Merlin Communications for their support.

Paul Abernethy	Jim McPherson
Ee Chai Beng	John Packman
Ian Blanthorn	Peter Pearson
Don Bowman	George Pryde
Rex Boys	Colin Richardson
Tim Burrell	David Russell
Jeff Cant	David Savage
Peter Chamerlain	Roy Sharp
Chua Cheng Boon	John Shelley
Peter Condron	Bill Skelton
Bob Crawford	Dick Skyrme
Alex Cruickshank	Graham Smith
Roy Darlymple	L G Smith
Mark Evans	Dick Stibbons
Derek Hearn	Noel Sudbury
Syd Garrioch	Dennis Surridge
John Goodall	Dai Thomas
Chris Gregory	Peter Tingey
Roy Hatton	Norman Tomalin
R Allen Herbert	Ivor Tupper
Pete Hodgskin	Ian Vickers
Clive Hosken	John White
Ron Johnson	Duncan Whittle
Peter Lamb	Mike Whyman
Steve Lee	J C Williams
Cindy Leo	David Wilson
Mike Littlewood	John Winrow
Norman Marsden	Ken Worden
Geoff Martin	

Edward Pawley's excellent book "BBC Engineering 1922-1972 (published by the BBC, ISBN 0 563 12127 0)" has been a significant source of reference. Information extracted for this book on BBC Transmission is duly acknowledged.

The photographs have kindly been made available by Crown Castle, Merlin Communications, the BBC, Graham Phillips (rear cover) and News Team International (Picture 1).

INTRODUCTION

BBC Transmission was part of the nation's heritage. It was transmitters that provided the key technology which led to the creation of broadcasting and the formation of the BBC. The result was a major change in the culture of the nation. News, education and entertainment reached millions of people for seven decades from the engineering systems of BBC Transmission. From its very earliest days it was dedicated to two particular aims, the maintenance of the highest technical standards, and providing the maximum possible coverage to all areas.

It gained an international reputation of the highest order, and throughout its existence it contributed considerably to that arena in every aspect of broadcast engineering. The BBC's World Services, which are held in much regard throughout many parts of the world, have over the years depended upon the dedication and enterprise of an engineering department second to none.

A department actually called "BBC Transmission" only existed from 1987 to 1996, but the term is used throughout this book to cover the relevant activities previously undertaken by departments with different names. For instance in 1935, the equivalent was "Station Design and Installation Department", "Lines Department" and part of the "Operations and Maintenance Department" which for many years was known as "Transmitter Department".

SECTION 1 THE BEGINNING

By 1922 there was considerable activity in public broadcasting both in Europe and the USA, with several countries already operating regular services in one form or another. In Great Britain, a number of companies which included Marconi, Metropolitan Vickers and Western Electric, had been granted permits by the Post Office to operate a number of experimental MF transmitters with such famous call signs as 2LO, 2MT, 2ZY, 2WP etc. Initially there were considerable constraints on these transmissions, which largely stemmed from fears of interference with aircraft and other essential services. Gradually however, the restrictions eased and in May 1922, 2LO began operating a regular daily service from Marconi House in London.

At about this time the government decided that for public broadcasting Great Britain should be divided into eight areas, each to be served by one or more broadcasting stations. The stations serving these areas were to be in London, Cardiff, Plymouth (later changed to Bournemouth), Birmingham, Manchester, Newcastle, Glasgow or Edinburgh and Aberdeen. At a later date Belfast was added. A meeting was held at the GPO in London attended by representatives of 28 companies interested in broadcasting, and they were asked to formulate a plan to create one or more organisations to give effect to the proposals. Two further meetings followed, both held at the I.E.E.[1] and the final decision was to create a single company.

THE BRITISH BROADCASTING COMPANY

So it was that the British Broadcasting Company was formed. Six major companies provided the main investment, and guaranteed to finance a service for two years.

They were:-
                The Marconi Company
           The Metropolitan Vickers Company
             The Western Electric Company

---

[1] Institution of Electrical Engineers

The Radio Communications Company
The General Electric Company
The British Thompson-Houston Company

A number of smaller investors, receiver manufacturers and retailers, were also represented.

The Company was authorised to install and operate nine 1.5kW MF main stations in the designated areas, plus smaller relay stations as necessary. It took over 2LO in London, 2ZY in Manchester and 5IT in Birmingham, each with a range of about 25 miles during daylight hours, and began its operations on the 14 November 1922. J.C.W. Reith was appointed General Manager, later to become Sir John Reith, and subsequently Lord Reith. His influence on British broadcasting was to become legendary, and his insistence on the highest professional standards set a trend which is still felt to this day. The income of the Company was from a half share of the ten shilling (50 pence) receiving licence fee, which had been introduced on 1 November 1922, and a further element from royalties paid on the sale of receivers.

In the space of only two years, the company had installed all the required main stations and a further eleven 100W relay stations. These latter stations were of BBC design, because no suitable low power MF transmitters were available. The total coverage at this time was estimated to be about 65% of the population, on the assumption that most listeners used crystal sets (although valved receivers were becoming popular). At this point the BBC's annual income from the licence fee had risen to about £500,000. Without the excellent programmes that the BBC had started to make, the demand for the service would not have existed, but it is worth noting that BBC Transmission played a vital role in securing more income each year for the programme makers. This contribution continued throughout its existence.

MF transmitting stations in operation by December 1924
(closing dates in brackets):-

Main Stations:-

London	2LO (5/4/25)	Glasgow	5SC (12/6/32)
Manchester	2ZY (17/5/31)	Aberdeen	2BD (9/9/38)
Birmingham	5IT (21/8/27)	Bournemouth	6BM (14/6/39)
Newcastle	5NO (19/10/37)	Belfast	2BE (20/3/36)
Cardiff	5WA (28/5/33)		

Relay Stations:-

Sheffield	6FL	Hull	6KH
Plymouth	5PY	Nottingham	5NG
Edinburgh	2EH	Dundee	2DE
Liverpool	6LV	Stoke-on-Trent	6ST
Leeds	2LS	Bradford (Bradford relayed Leeds)	2LS

By the end of 1924 there were 110 engineering staff, 21 of whom were designated Engineer-in-Charge. On 1 January 1925 the BBC's share of the licence fee was increased to 7s. 6d. (an additional $12^{1}/_{2}$ pence) and the royalty payments discontinued.

In 1923 Captain P.P. Eckersley was appointed the BBC's first Chief Engineer. From the very beginning he felt that total coverage of the United Kingdom was paramount, and where possible with a second 'national' programme. Owing to the limited number of available wavelengths, and lack of resoursez, he was drawn to the idea of setting up a single high power LF (or long wave as it was then known) station in the centre of England. It had been shown for some time that stations operating in this waveband on quite modest power levels were capable of broadcasting very long distances, and he was convinced that a high power station would cover most of the country. Eventually the idea was considered viable, and following a period of successful experimental transmissions in 1924 from the Marconi works at Chelmsford, it was decided to look for a permanent site.

The result was the purchase of the site at Daventry in Northamptonshire, and the building of a station to become famously known as Daventry 5XX. It was the world's first high power low frequency station designed exclusively for broadcasting, and it commenced operation in July 1925 on 187.5kHz. The highly successful result was a coverage of some 85% of the population, and with it the ability to provide an alternative programme, for those within range of a medium wave station. Due to initial complaints from the Services, the output power was restricted to 25kW, but nevertheless was at that time claimed to be the world's most powerful transmitter. When later it was apparent that a higher power was needed, 5XX was replaced in 1934 with the 200kHz Droitwich station operating at 150kW.

In April 1925 the 2LO transmitter at Marconi House was closed down, and the service transferred to a new 2kW transmitter mounted on the roof of Selfridges store in Oxford Street. A much improved coverage was achieved, and this transmitter remained in service until 1929, when the high power station at Brookmans Park opened.

The British Broadcasting Corporation

The Company's licence was due to expire on 31 December 1926, and in the previous year a government committee sat to consider the future. It recommended that the Company should be replaced with a public authority, and to be independent of commercial and political pressures. The committee's recommendation was accepted, and on 1 January 1927 the Company became the British Broadcasting Corporation, in the charge of a Board of Governors. John Reith was made the first Director General, a post he would hold for eleven years, and on that same day Reith received a Knighthood. At this stage there were some two million licence holders, and the Company had established the firm foundations of a public broadcasting service.

SECTION 2 MF, LF & VHF RADIO TRANSMISSION

The Regional Scheme

With the formation of the Corporation in January 1927, P P Eckersley remained as Chief Engineer. In his desire to achieve total coverage of the United Kingdom, and to provide listeners with a choice of two programmes, he had previously proposed a high power MF 'Regional Scheme'. His idea was to build a series of high power MF stations, each radiating two services, a regional programme and a national programme. It was calculated that such an arrangement would require a network of transmitters, each rated at some 50kW, and as no MF transmitters of that size had ever been built, the BBC in late 1926 had set about building an experimental installation at Daventry. Within a little over six months they produced Daventry 5GB, which was powered into aerial in May 1927. In August of that year it commenced service for the Midland region operating at 30kW; an altogether remarkable achievement. Sadly, only a short time after the station opened, an engineer was killed whilst leaning over a guard rail to make an adjustment; he had inadvertently touched a high voltage conductor. This was the BBC's first fatality. In those early days it was common to work with exposed high voltage conductors, a practise which today is thankfully outside the law – safety standards have improved dramatically since those days.

Following the success of 5GB at Daventry, the various approvals for the regional scheme to go ahead were in place by April 1928, and the construction of the first station at Brookmans Park was commenced. This was to serve London and the Home Counties, and it came into service in October 1929, with an output power of 70kW radiating the London Regional Programme. At this same time, the London 2LO transmitter was closed down. As there was no national electricity grid, and supplies were not so reliable, the station was powered by four diesel engines driving DC generators which together produced nearly 1MW. The reason for choosing DC was in order to use a battery as a standby supply. This latter was of some 2,000Ah and capable of running the station for a short time in an emergency. The various voltages required for the transmitters were derived using DC-DC rotating converters, and there were about 20 of them.

The design of Brookmans Park set the standard for the Regional Scheme, and in the following ten years a further 9 main stations and 2 relay stations were opened.

Regional Scheme as at September 1939

Transmitter Site	Frequency (kHz)	Power (kW)	Programme	Opened
Brookmans Park	877	70	London Region	Oct. 1929
Brookmans Park	1149	40	National	Mar. 1930
Moorside Edge	668	70	North Region	May 1931
Moorside Edge	1149	40	National	July 1931
Westerglen	767	70	Scottish Region	June 1932
Westerglen	1149	50	National	June 1932
Washford	804	70	West Region	May 1933 (1)
Washford	1149	40	National	July 1933 (2)
Droitwich	200	150	National	Oct. 1934 (3)
Droitwich	1013	70	Midland Region	Feb. 1935 (4)
Lisnagargey	977	100	N. Ireland Region	Mar. 1936
Burghead	767	60	Scottish Region	Oct. 1936
Penmon	804	5	Welsh Region	Feb. 1937
Stagshaw	1122	60	North Region	Oct. 1937
Redmoss	1285	5	Scottish Region	Sep. 1938
Start Point	1050	100	West of England	June 1939
Clevedon	1474	20	West of England	June 1939

(Relay Stations shown in italics)

(1) From July 1937 radiated Welsh Regional Programme

(2) From July 1937 radiated West of England Regional Programme

(3) Replaced Daventry 5XX service

(4) Replaced Daventry 5GB service

A modified design was introduced at Lisnagarvey producing 100kW – then the most powerful MF transmitter in the United Kingdom. A grand opening ceremony was attended by the BBC Chairman and the Director General Sir John Reith, with the station being opened on air by the Northern Ireland Governor, the Duke of Abercorn.

Most of the high power MF transmitter buildings were of a design which reflected their importance in providing the nation's broadcasting system. It is a tribute to the design, installation and maintenance engineers associated with these transmitters that many of them were still capable of operation some 40 years later. All of these sites are still used today for broadcasting medium frequency services.

By the mid-1930's, all the wavelengths allotted to the BBC had been utilised, and further expansion of the high power network depended upon successful synchronisation. Fairly stable drives had been used previously when the 1926 Geneva Plan had required that the low power relay stations should operate on a single frequency, 1040kHz. These were Tuning Fork drives, which had been designed by the BBC's Development Section as early as 1924. Use in the high power situation was of course a much more stringent exercise, and the solution adopted was to send tone derived from the 'Master Station' tuning fork by line to the 'Slave Station', thereby keeping both the drives within acceptable limits. Although requiring fairly constant and skilled attention, the system worked reasonably well, and it was first used by the high power National Programme transmitters at Brookmans Park and Washford sharing 1148kHz. By 1937, drives utilising quartz crystal oscillators were available which could achieve a better carrier frequency stability than the tuning fork drives. The continued development of this type of drive was to play a very important role in the war years ahead.

Broadcasting House in London and the equivalents in several major cities, were of course also vitally important and central elements of the BBC in the 1930s. However the scale of engineering at the transmitting stations was far greater than at the studio centres.

- Physically, all of the BBC's studio equipment could have been fitted inside the main transmitter hall at Brookmans Park alone, and it could have been powered from just one of the four diesels in the building.

- Technically, the studios used state of the art equipment including microphones, audio amplifiers, mixers, switching systems and loudspeakers, all of which was very skilfully controlled. However, all of this technology also existed at transmitting stations - the remnants of a small studio at Brookmans Park were still there in 1978.

- In addition, the transmitting stations had radio frequency systems such as drives, amplifiers and antennas, as well as very large valves, power systems big enough to run small towns, and some of the highest structures in the country.

THE WAR YEARS

Wartime broadcasting had to fulfil two main requirements. The first was to provide an adequate service however bad the conditions might become, and secondly and perhaps more importantly, to ensure that the transmitters could not be used as navigational aids by enemy aircraft. Plans to achieve both these objectives had already been made in 1938, when it was decided to broadcast a single programme from two synchronised groups of four high power MF transmitters. One group operated on 668kHz and the other on 767kHz. In this way, enemy aircraft were denied any direction finding aid until they were within close proximity of a particular station; by then, however, the transmitter would have been closed down under RAF Fighter Command instructions. It was one of the duties of transmission engineers to respond rapidly to orders from Fighter Command and switch off a transmitter, and this happened no less than 8,591 times during 1940 alone.

Shortly after the outbreak of hostilities, a second programme was introduced, 'The Forces Programme'. In 1941 an Italian station operating on 877kHz, the Forces Programme frequency, radiated what became known as the 'Mocking Voice', which took the form of interjections during pauses in the Forces Programme material. To overcome this, arrangements were made to shift the carrier frequency of the Forces Programme transmitters by 1kHz when the Mocking Voice was present; thereby producing a heterodyne note and obscuring the interference. A second and more effective solution adopted was to pick-up the Italian signal at Tatsfield Receiving Station in Kent, route it through a speech inverter at Broadcasting House and then add it to the programme fed to the 877kHz group. This soon resulted in a cessation of the interference.

Initially a 100kW transmitter on 565kHz at Athlone in the Irish Republic posed a particular problem, as this would have been a very useful navigational aid for approaching German aircraft. Synchronising equipment was installed at Clevedon, Penmon, and Redmoss, and a receiver in Wales passed the Athlone programme by land line to each station. One observer mentions speculation in Aberdeen and district on the reason for the increase of Athlone's signal strength! Subsequently, the Irish Athlone, Dublin and Cork transmitters were formed into a synchronised group.

There were times when transmitters in areas under attack were closed down for long periods. In order to meet this situation, and to provide for the transmission of special bulletins and instructions by Regional Commissioners in the event of invasion, it was decided to install a number of low power transmitters in the areas of large population. As a result, a total of sixty-one 100W MF 'Group H' transmitters were hastily produced and commissioned, and the first ten were in operation by November 1940. They were a synchronised group on 1474kHz, and it was agreed that providing they closed down on a local 'RED' alert, they would not be subject to Fighter Command control.

The locations of these stations included many unlikely sites: factories, laundries, brickworks, one was in a museum and another in a mortuary, and so on. Anywhere that could provide basic accommodation, plus a chimney or the side of a building to support a simple aerial was acceptable. Each was run by an Engineer-in-Charge, but a notable aspect was the inclusion for the first time of female shift staff at transmitting stations. Each station had to be manned on a three shift system, and this was impossible to cover with the staff then available. The solution was to recruit Technical Assistants (Female), or 'TAF's' as they were affectionately known. A TAF and a 'Youth in Training' formed the shift complement, and stories of these years, probably embellished with the passage of time and mostly unprintable, are legion. Suffice to say that the TAF's must certainly have brightened up an otherwise very grey and austere time. Several of these stations were damaged by enemy action and one member of staff recalls a truncheon hanging on the wall alongside the transmitter, which in the event of an invasion, was to be used to smash the rows of working and spare valves. Sadly three H group members of staff were killed, although none of the high power transmitting stations were damaged during the war. When after the Battle of Britain and the threat of invasion had diminished, many of the H group stations were closed down, however some 32 stations remained in service until July 1945.

The European Service

At the outbreak of war, three 50kW 'Regionals' were used synchronised on 1149kHz radiating during the hours of darkness. They were Brookmans Park, Moorside Edge and Westerglen, to be joined later by the Droitwich 200kW low frequency transmitter which had been re-engineered for use on MF, and finally Washford. This group was later superseded by Droitwich alone using a horizontally polarised aerial. Although horizontally polarised transmissions were less effective in the far field, this was more than outweighed by the fact that enemy aircraft could not use such a single station as a navigation beacon; the reverse being true for vertically polarised transmissions. The remainder of the group formed yet another group synchronised on 804kHz. In October 1940 the Start Point transmitter operating at 180kW on 1050kHz was added, also with horizontal polarisation.

With the fall of France in June 1940, these services increasingly became subject to enemy jamming. To overcome this, additional transmitters were installed at Brookmans Park (STC 140kW) Moorside Edge (Marconi 150kW) and with the Droitwich 200kW they commenced service in March 1941 synchronised on 804kHz. A further high power transmitter was installed at Droitwich. This had an output power of 400kW, which at that time was quite exceptional, and could only be achieved by using transmitters operating in parallel. Two Marconi 150kW transmitters running at 200kW each were used; the increased power level resulting in a slight increase in distortion. The necessary combining equipment had to be designed, for no such equipment existed at that time. The aerial consisted of two horizontal half wave dipoles supported by two existing 700ft masts. In February 1941 it took over the European Service on 1149kHz, and was known as 'Droitwich HPMW', as well as OSE6 (Overseas Station Extension No. 6).

A low frequency group was formed using Droitwich 5XX (converted back to LF), the original Daventry 5XX (30kW) and a new STC 15kW transmitter at Brookmans Park. A new site for a very high power station was being planned, and this group was to operate until the new station was commissioned.

The new station was situated at Ottringham, East Yorkshire, and was known as OSE5 (Overseas Station Extension No.5). It was capable of producing up to 800kW, which made it the most powerful broadcasting station in the world. Designed to work on LF or MF, it comprised four 200kW transmitters, each installed in individual bomb proof buildings, and controlled from an underground centre. Six 500ft stayed masts were erected (eight were planned but two collapsed during construction) and could operate at 200, 400, 600 or 800kW. It was capable of radiating up to four separate programmes simultaneously, and three 740 bhp diesel alternator sets provided a standby supply. It began service in February 1943 on 200kHz, with an output power of 600kW. The station had a permanent security guard and its whole operation was shrouded in secrecy. Ottringham closed down in 1953 due to lack of broadcast channels and funds, and the transmitters were moved to Droitwich.

From November 1942, the European Service had partial use of a high power transmitter sited at Crowborough, in Sussex. This was a 500kW MF transmitter built for the Political Warfare Executive, and known by the code name 'Aspidistra'. BBC Transmission provided synchronising equipment in order to maintain the carrier frequency stability when operating in a BBC group.

In 1944 additional buildings were constructed at Moorside Edge, Westerglen and Rampisham to house transmitters for the American and Canadian Forces networks (ABSIE-American Broadcasting Station In Europe) and transmissions continued until July 1945.

THE WAR REPORTING UNIT 1944/1945

Experiences during the early years of the war in establishing communication links with the UK for correspondents in the field, led to a decision to form a unit specifically designed for the purpose. Using mobile transmitters it was to be operational with the D-Day landings and the further coverage of the progress of the war in Europe. At the time, radio transmission equipment was in very short supply and a number of transmitters were eventually obtained from a variety of sources. They ranged from a 250W MF/HF unit up to four 7.5kW RCA transmitters. The 250W was mounted in a three ton truck with a second vehicle carrying a 15kVA diesel alternator. Other transmitters were crated and sent to various destinations, including Paris and Rome. They were all assigned call-signs in an MC series. A further requirement was a means of London communicating with the units in the field, and to this end two transmitters capable of telegraphic use were installed in Broadcasting House. The other part of the Reporting Unit was concerned with programme production, mainly that of recording facilities.

The whole venture demanded much work on behalf of Engineering Division, not only the technical aspects, but much liasion with the armed forces and the War Office. It is to the BBC's credit, and particularly it's engineers, that at this time, such a high standard of war reporting was achieved. Although accrediting War Correspondents was an established practice, the same was not so for civilian engineers.

After much debate, BBC Transmitter and Recording Engineers seconded to the WRU were eventually designated 'Engineer Correspondents'. By the beginning of 1945 there were nine units operating in Europe, two in the Mediterranean area and one in South-East Asia. A reminiscence by E P B Metcalfe in section 7 of this book gives a vivid picture of the unit's activities.

HOME, LIGHT AND THIRD PROGRAMMES

After the war, the MF and LF transmitters were re-arranged to establish the BBC's Home and Light programme services, broadcasting from:-

Bartley	Droitwich	Norwich	Stagshaw
Brookmans Park	Lisnagarvey	Penmon	Start Point
Burghead	Londonderry	Redmoss	Washford
Clevedon	Moorside Edge	Redruth	Westerglen

Not all of these transmitters broadcast both programmes and there were several variations of Home Service (which replaced the Regional Programme) – Northern, Scottish, Welsh, Basic, etc. This arrangement started on 29 July 1945.

On 1 June 1946 the 1922 radio licence was doubled to £1 and a £2 combined radio and televsion licence was introduced.

The Third programme started broadcasting on 29 September 1946 from a high power transmitter at Droitwich, as well as 21 of the old Group H transmitters used during the war. On 1 January 1947 the BBC's Royal Charter was renewed.

MAST COLLAPSE

A 500ft mast radiator collapsed at Brookmans Park on 29 September 1956 while contractors were carrying out maintenance work. The service interruption was minimal as a reserve antenna was available and a replacement mast from Ottringham was taken into service on 1 July 1957.

Bombs

On 12 December 1956 a bomb exploded at the Londonderry MF station - fortunately when no staff were on duty - and caused considerable damage to the station. Bomb damage also occurred at Brougher Mountain in County Tyrone on 7 January 1971, but a more tragic incident followed on 9 February, when two members of the transmitter maintenance team based at Divis, together with four contractors, were killed when their vehicle was blown up on the way to the Brougher Mountain station.

MF unattended operation

On 1 December 1947, BBC Transmission opened its first unattended transmitting station. It was at Farnley, four miles south west of Leeds and it broadcast the Third programme at low power on MF. This was the first step towards the present day domestic transmitter network which operates on a completely unattended basis. (see "Automation")

In October 1962 the original regional transmitter of 1929 carrying the Light Programme at Brookmans Park was replaced by a new design of Marconi 50kW transmitter using a high efficiency output amplifier. Around this time, most of the original MF transmitters were replaced with more efficient equipment and from 1965 onwards they were converted to unattended working (e.g. Redmoss 1966, Bartley 1967 and Clevedon 1967).

When considering unattended operation, automatic switching from say a 2kW transmitter to a reserve was unattractive. It would depend on the automatic operation of high power relays switching out the faulty transmitter and switching the reserve transmitter into the complex load of the MF aerial, often via RF circuits combining the outputs of other programme transmitters. Automation could add minutes more programme loss due to the filament warm up delay needed by the valved reserve transmitter.

The Marconi company had developed, for a communications transmitter requirement, an RF bridged-T circuit that could combine two in-phase RF inputs with negligible loss. If one input failed, half the remaining input power continued to the output without any interruption. The system acted as if there was an instant switch to a quarter power reserve. A common RF oscillator was needed for both transmitters, but an oscillator failure could be detected at RF instantly, and at low power a working reserve oscillator could be selected. A star-delta version of the bridged T could combine three 660W MF transmitters to deliver 2kW yet buffer a faulty transmitter. This was what was wanted for unattended operation. At the tender stage Marconi's, with their patented "star/delta hybrid", had a major technical advantage and received the contract. In practical operations the system proved successful and the same spares suited all transmitters.

More low power MF transmitters were needed when Radio 1 was introduced. Transistors could provide reliable low power transmitters but at that time valves were essential at the 1kW or above level. Traditional high level anode modulated transmitters inevitably require at least three valves. Industry offered a transistorised low level modulator followed by a one valve linear amplifier giving a 1kW modulated MF carrier. The most likely valve failure mode was a loss of output level as the filament lost emission rather than a catastrophic fault of a hard driven Class C valve. The one valve linear amplifier had higher electricity costs but at the 1kW level the difference was not great. For unattended operation this was the best solution then available so a number of these transmitters were ordered.

LOCAL RADIO

Local Radio began as a VHF/FM only experiment serving eight towns from new sites. Although unattended and maintained by the mobile transmitter maintenance teams, a near-by studio could monitor the transmission and an engineer would be able to give first aid maintenance. Some later stations were co-sited with existing VHF stations.

The experiment was reviewed in 1969 and it was apparent that Local Radio needed MF transmitters as, in those days, VHF/FM receivers were rare in kitchen portables and in cars. In the morning, the very time when Local Radio had relevant local news to offer, many members of the public did not have the equipment to listen to it.

The Government agreed that the BBC's eight experimental Local Radio stations were successful; they should be increased by another 12 stations and all 20 should also transmit on MF. Research Department's Service Planning Section produced a new plan rearranging the use of the existing UK LF/MF frequencies and negotiated for UK use of some "foreign" frequencies to permit both commercial and BBC Local Radio to transmit on MF.

The Sound Broadcasting Act authorising the changes was not finally effected until 12 July 1972 and the great frequency change took place on the night of 2 September 1972. For the BBC's National MF transmitters it was mostly a change of programme and the re-tuning of reserve VHF receivers. The BBC had to surrender 1151kHz so Stagshaw and Scarborough were re-tuned to 908kHz and Whitehaven to 692kHz.

Public appreciation of local radio grew and by the time that BBC Transmission was privatized there were 238 VHF/FM Local & Regional Radio transmitters and 48 MF Local Radio transmitters.

Major MF changes in 1978

The MF band had continued to suffer growing interference and the Regional International Conferences strived to improve frequency allocations. For the BBC the MF and LF transmitters changed the programme they were to radiate, and many transmitters required their frequencies to be changed. The changes took place on the night of 23 November 1978. In the previous months, Transmitter Department staff working at night re-tuned the affected transmitters and antenna matching units, marking the settings before restoring them to their normal operating frequency. TCPD rewired the MF lines at the PCM transmitter terminals and then patched out the changes at the U-link panels. On the Night the transmitters were re-tuned and the distribution patch cords removed. Slowly the reports came in: "It's OK here", None needed the order "Shut it down". The 1978 BBC

Handbook reported 35 "new" transmitters & 19 "new" aerial systems were needed.

MF Efficiency Improvement

In the mid eighties BBC engineers invented a new companding technique whereby the carrier power of a high power MF transmitter is dynamically reduced at high modulation levels. This technique reduces the electricity consumed by the transmitter without affecting the service area, and the effect is enhanced when audio compression is used in the programme fed to the transmitter. Use is made of the receiver AGC to ensure the listener does not notice the reduction in carrier level.

Tests were carried out using the Radio 1 and Radio London transmitters at Brookmans Park. Subsequently all the BBC's high power MF transmitters were modified to use this technique, which saved over 30% of the electricity bill.

MF feeds via PCM (Pulse Code Modulation)

PCM revolutionised the MF transmitter programme feeds. The programmes, carried by PCM to nearby main VHF/FM stations could be fed to the MF stations by relatively short Post Office audio "music" lines. The lines were monitored by 7.6 & 7.8 kHz tones added in London and filtered out at the MF stations. The 7.6 kHz tone was added when the MF programme differed from its VHF version. Then if the line failed the VHF/FM reserve receiver at the MF site would not be used. This prevented the MF transmitter jamming other BBC co-channel MF transmitters with the wrong programme.

Mush Area Problem

Following the 1948 Copenhagen International LW/MW Plan, Britain had exclusive Europe-wide rights to the frequencies used by the UK high power MF and LF stations, but nevertheless interference grew over the years and subsequent conferences addressed this problem.

At the 1974 ITU Geneva Conference many countries including the UK made technically sound proposals based on using 8kHz instead of 9kHz channel spacing. Still in the cold war era, these were rejected. So the Conference met again in 1975 to sort out fresh proposals but unfortunately the UK lost the exclusive use of 200kHz, which meant that the Radio 4 LF Droitwich transmission would not serve even Central Scotland. Experts were forced to improvise on the last day of the Conference and the UK obtained shared rights with a Polish transmitter on 227kHz.

It was hoped that with a new 50kW transmitter on 227kHz at Westerglen and a new 50kW transmitter on 200kHz at Burghead, the R4 LF coverage in Scotland would improve. However nobody knew that an omni-directional LF aerial system sent a stronger signal East to West than in other directions. Many months monitoring of the Polish signal established that interference on 227kHz would be too high for it to be used in Scotland. So Westerglen, Burghead and Droitwich would all have to use 200kHz. There would be a "mush" area on the Scottish Borders, and in Scotland at places roughly equidistant from Burghead and Westerglen.

In a mush area the RF signals add and subtract to produce a standing wave pattern. If the frequencies of the stations remain exactly the same, the pattern does not move and people in the mush areas can often orient their receiver's ferrite aerials to receive a tolerable signal strength. Otherwise the standing wave pattern in the mush area will move at a speed proportional to the carrier difference.

Droitwich was already equipped as a national frequency standard station. With Westerglen and Burghead equipped with rubidium controlled oscillators the mush pattern would move very slowly indeed and an adjustment signalled over a control line every few days could be made to hold the mush area standing wave pattern steady. At Pontop Pike a pair of LF aerials was installed; one nulled on Westerglen and the other on Droitwich, which enabled the relative phase of the LF signal from the two stations to be measured and this provided the information sent over the control line. A similar arrangement at Aberdeen could lock the Scottish mush area.

It is also necessary that the modulation on the two signals arrives in the mush area with equal time delay. Designs Department developed a unit whose delay, valid over the audio band, could be adjusted (pre-set). The PCM system carried the R4 LF signal fairly close to both Scottish LF transmitters and made it possible to adjust and then set the modulation delay to suit the mush areas.

The LF phase monitoring was also carried out by Transmitter Department operational staff. Skelton HF station south of Carlisle is, roughly, on a line from Burghead through Westerglen to Droitwich. If the 200 kHz signal at Skelton was not constant perhaps it was not true that the propagation characteristics of a given LF ground wave path is constant. If so it was suggested, there was no need to bother with the phase lock system. Research Department regarded the Skelton test results summing three transmissions (with some sky wave possibility) as inconclusive. But they were able to negotiate "foreign" MF frequencies for transmissions at Newcastle, Carlisle and Redmoss for the "Long Wave" R4 programme and this provided a preferred solution for the majority of the people in mush areas.

LF Radio Data

LF Radio Data was introduced in 1987 at Droitwich, followed by Burghead and Westerglen, using digital modulation techniques and equipment developed by BBC Research Department. It is mainly used for switching tariffs on electricity meters installed in domestic and business premises throughout the UK.

The start of VHF/FM broadcasting

Serious interference on MF after dark was the main factor leading to the rapid development of sound broadcasting on VHF in the immediate post-war years. The first experiments were carried out by BBC Research Department in 1945 at Alexandra Palace and Moorside Edge, as well as Bagley Croft near Oxford, which was the home of BBC Research Department near the end of the war. The tests were very successful and demonstrated that frequency modulation in the VHF band could provide much better performance than amplitude modulation in the MF band. Horizontal polarisation was found to be somewhat less susceptible to ignition interference, and to distortion caused by multi-path propagation, than vertical polarisation. It also simplified antenna design.

In order to confirm the viability of the new service, a site was acquired in 1949 at Wrotham in Kent, and two 20kW VHF transmitters were installed. Test transmission started in May 1950 with one transmitter frequency modulated and the other amplitude modulated. After extensive comparisons, FM was confirmed as the preferred choice.

The new service would demand a substantial investment by industry in developing and producing new equipment for the transmitting stations, and new receivers for the public. Additional expenditure was required by the BBC in setting up the new network, and also by listeners in buying new receivers. At the time there were still national restrictions on capital expenditure, and the Government did not authorise the start of work until 1953.

In May 1955, Wrotham opened the first regular VHF/FM transmission of the Home, Light and Third Programmes, serving London and the South East. Pontop Pike and a low power station at Penmon followed later in the same year.

The first unattended television and VHF/FM station was built at Llandrindod Wells in 1961, followed by Redruth, Oxford, Morecambe Bay, Ashkirk and Skegness. These sites were manned by an engineer during the daytime who lived in the area and was on-call outside normal office hours. In 1965 all the 'one man' sites were de-staffed and the Transmitter Maintenance Teams (TMT's) took over full responsibility for unattended transmitters.

The VHF/FM station at Rosemarkie (north of Inverness) opened in 1958 and was the first to receive its programme input by rebroadcast link (RBL). An RBL link also fed the new VHF/FM service from Orkney in 1958 and from Bressay (Shetland) in 1964.

By 1955, the BBC domestic services were received in about 14 million homes and a quarter of a million cars. However, the VHF/FM service was slow to gain acceptance and even ten years later, in 1965, only about 30% of listeners had radios capable of receiving the new service.

Between 1955 and 1972, VHF/FM coverage increased from 33% to 99%, from 77 transmitting stations with most radiating three services.

Radio 1, Radio 2 and Local Radio

In 1967, the BBC Light Programme was replaced by two programmes: Radio 1 and Radio 2. Also, in the same year, Local Radio stations were introduced.

Stereo

The first stereophonic broadcast in the UK took place in 1958 using two different VHF/FM transmitters at Wrotham for the left and right channels. In addition, the left and right channels were broadcast on television sound from Crystal Palace and MF radio from Brookmans Park respectively. This use of separate transmitters for each channel was clearly not viable as a full scale service and so the Zenith-GE multiplex pilot tone system was put on trial in 1962 and subsequently adopted throughout the network. A major difficulty was ensuring the performance of the programme distribution. Post Office circuits were, amongst other things, subject to the switching of lines and phase reversals, and the integrity of left and right channels could not be guaranteed. The solution was the use of dedicated SHF links. In July 1966 regular stereophonic transmissions were started from Wrotham, then Sutton Coldfield and Holme Moss in 1968 and Rowridge in 1971. A major chain of radio links was established for this purpose from Swains Lane in North London to Whipsnade, then Wychwood Hill near Chipping Norton, Sutton Coldfield, Tick Hill and Holme Moss. The links to and from Wychwood Hill proved to be too long and caused unacceptable fading, so two new sites were established at Thorpe Lodge and Meriden. The link equipment was actually designed to carry video, but it was used initially to carry the stereo multiplex signal and later it carried 13 Channel PCM. This latter was a BBC designed system of distribution.

NICAM FOR RADIO DISTRIBUTION

In the mid-1970s, standards began to emerge for digital telephone networks and the use of high capacity digital circuits from British Telecom appeared to be a possibility for sound broadcast contribution (to studio centres) and distribution (to transmitters). The most interesting standard bit-rate was 2048kbit/s which, using techniques similar to those employed in the 13 channel PCM system, would have provided five mono channels. Six channels was far more attractive operationally as these could be paired into three stereo channels, and so BBC Research/Designs Departments produced a system which squeezed six high quality mono channels into 2048 kbit/s. In 1976, an engineer in Designs Department gave this system the name Near Instantaneously Companded Audio Multiplex, or NICAM – an acronym which is now familiar to millions of people.

Widespread use of BT's digital circuits did not materialise due to high tariffs, but in 1984 one six channel NICAM system was added to the 13 channel PCM system and now NICAM alone provides a 24 channel backbone for Radio distribution and other applications. Two channel versions are also used for other purposes including Local Radio feeds and Outside Broadcasts.

RADIO DATA SERVICE

Much of the pioneering work for RDS was carried out at BBC Research Department and specialised equipment was produced by BBC Designs Department. Following this work, BBC Transmission in 1988 installed the world's first network RDS service from all its main VHF/FM transmitters and filler stations in all regions of the UK. It overcomes the need for motorists to re-tune as they move between the service areas of different transmitters. It also provides a visual readout of the received station name and includes a travel announcement service that gives motorists local traffic information, regardless of which BBC FM programme they are listening to. This was quite a feat of engineering, given the multiplicity of services broadcast by the BBC, and the spread of FM to even the remotest parts of the land.

VHF/FM RE-ENGINEERING

The FM radio service on VHF had been planned long before the availability of low cost portable radios and the intention was that members of the public should have aerials on their roof or at least in their loft. One consequence of this was that the service used horizontal polarisation which meant that the aerial rods should be horizontal rather than vertical. This was fine for fixed installations, but with the advent of portable radios it was far more natural for the aerial rod to be vertical and this, combined with the typical location of a portable radio inside a building, meant that coverage was not adequate.

The problem was partially overcome in the late seventies and early eighties when antenna re-engineering was required. The original antennas were approaching the end of their useful life and instead of replacing them with similar, horizontally polarised, antennas, they were replaced with mixed polarisation antennas which produced a signal that could be received much better on portable radios. This had the side effect of reducing the signal received by horizontal roof mounted antennas and so the VHF transmitters were also re-engineered with new transmitters of twice the power.

DIGITAL BROADCASTING

Following research and development work carried out by a number of organisations throughout the world, including the BBC, a completely new method of broadcasting emerged and in Septenber 1995 BBC Transmission started the world's first digital audio broadcasting (DAB) service from Crystal Palace, Alexandra Palace, Guildford, Reigate and Bluebell Hill. The start of a new era in broadcasting.

SECTION 3 HF TRANSMISSION

In the beginning, amateur radio operators played a significant part in demonstrating the potential of short wave long distance transmission, and by the early nineteen twenties communication had already been made with the USA, the West Indies and Australasia. With much of the theory still to be established, and consequent poor reliability, both the USA and Holland had nevertheless begun regular overseas broadcasts as early as 1924 and 1926 respectively.

Reith was anxious to broadcast to the Empire, and in 1924 had approached the government, however financial and technical problems delayed any decisions. Then in 1926, the Post Office gave the BBC permission to carry out experimental transmissions. A transmitter with an output power of 8-10kW was rented from Marconi, and transmissions began from Chelmsford in November 1927 with a call sign of G5SW. These experiments eventually led to the setting up of the Empire Station at Daventry, which came into operation in December 1932. Two ST&C transmitters were installed, each with an output power of 10-15kW, and designated Senders 1 & 2. (The title of Sender was used to avoid confusion with 'transmissions' which were periods of broadcasting time during each day.) Directional groups of vertically polarised aerials were employed to provide services to Australasia, India, South and West Africa and Canada. Following reception reports and various tests, it became clear that horizontally polarised aerials would give far better results, and accordingly the aerials were eventually replaced. A third transmitter was deemed necessary, and in 1935, G5SW at Chelmsford was refurbished and transferred to Daventry as Sender 3. It was modified to operate in several wavebands and had a maximum output power of 20kW. Later this was increased to 60kW.

On the 26 February 1935 a notable experiment took place at Daventry, when the possibility of detecting aircraft by means of radio transmission was put to the test. Using the 49m BBC Empire Service transmission, Watson Watt's propagation specialist successfully detected a Heyford bomber flying at 10,000 feet. This was to mark the beginning of the development of British radar.

During the early thirties, many countries were increasing their overseas HF broadcasting, and in particular Germany, with Hitler in power, was transmitting propaganda material to many areas. In response, the BBC obtained approval to extend the facilities at Daventry. In 1937, two ST&C 50-80kW transmitters, Senders 4 & 5, were commissioned, and the following year a 100kW Marconi transmitter, Sender 6, was installed. This was a 'Floating Carrier' design, a form of suppressed carrier during periods of low or no modulation; a power saving technique. In 1940 a fourth transmitter Sender 7, was supplied by ST&C which utilised twin RF channels and a common modulator. Senders 4 to 7 were designated OSE1 (Overseas Station Extension 1). A decision taken in 1937 to allow broadcasts to be made in foreign languages, resulted in the installation of Senders 8, 9, 10 & 11 (OSE2), all Marconi 100kW type SWB18. Together with all the necessary masts, aerials and associated feeders, the whole system was in place by June 1940, and Daventry had become one of the world's major HF transmitting stations.

BBC Transmission's early short wave stations needed a large number of staff to keep them going. Just like the early MF transmitters, they used state-of-the-art technology which was rather temperamental, but there was the added complication that they had to be 'wave changed'. This involved adjusting a number of high and low power tuned circuits, having replaced components necessary for the new operating frequency, some of which, such as large coils could be very heavy to handle and quite hot (see picture 13). This is still the case on many transmitters today.

The Marconi SWB18 transmitters at Daventry used a clever mechanical design in which all of the high power components that needed to be replaced for wave-changing were mounted on a truck which ran on rails. There was a separate truck for each waveband, up to four on each Sender, and when not in use they were put in 'sidings'. A second truck, rubber wheeled and somewhat smaller, was used for the lower powered circuits. It is a tribute to the Marconi design engineers that these transmitters stayed in service for over 30 years with wave changes being carried out half a dozen times a day.

The transmitters were connected to aerials using open wire feeders about 3 metres above the ground. It was necessary to use different aerials according to the time of day, and so there were many places where feeders could be re-routed by hooking them on to a choice of destinations. There were three main positions for feeder routing, selection (to a Sender), bi-furcation and tri-furcation, together providing a pattern of arrays that could be selected at any one time. There was then further switching in the field associated with each curtain array and their driving points.

In the control room, engineers had to make sure that the correct programme feed (or 'chain') was plugged into each transmitter, and it was also necessary to set oscillators (known as "drives") so that the transmitters broadcast on the correct frequencies. Setting the oscillators was quite a tricky process because they were continuously variable and the dials were not accurate enough to be relied upon. The problem was overcome by mixing the output with a comb of frequencies produced from a single, expensive, high stability crystal oscillator and listening to the beat frequency on headphones. The early design of this was remarkably efficient in picking up Radio Luxembourg, and hence became 'affectionately' known as the "Luxembourg machine."

Fifteen minutes was normally allowed between broadcasts for the system to be set up for broadcasting a new programme, on a different frequency, to a different part of the world. So, at the appointed time:-

- One person would switch off the transmitter, open the doors, pull the high power tuning truck into the siding, change the points, push the new tuning truck in, replace the second truck, do any urgent maintenance, close the door and set half a dozen tuning controls to approximately the right position.

- While this was going on, perhaps at 3am on a cold and wet winter's morning, another person will have dressed up in oilskins and wellington boots (not always issued), grabbed a torch lamp, then disappeared into the night, probably on a bicycle and hoping that the torch lamp battery would hold out (frequently it didn't). This was the 'aerial man' who would proceed through the site, sometimes dodging sheep, to carry out whatever feeder switching was required. One needed to know the layout of the aerial field like the back of one's hand. In thick fog, say, identifying an array switch which for some unknown reason had lost its label (not at all unusual) could be something of a nightmare, or to be disoriented in such conditions was a very lonely feeling indeed. The Daventry site was an encampment in Roman times, and one section was supposed to be haunted by Roman Centurions, (or so all newcomers were gleefully told). Imagine those of a nervous disposition in the dead of night and hearing a sheep cough - it can sound remarkably human; many an 'aerial man' has reappeared back at the transmitter building looking somewhat pale! Returning to our intrepid cyclist, he would ascertain by field telephone that all power was off before commencing the switching.

- Using a long wooden pole with a special end-fitting, he would unhook the feeder lines from their original destination and hook them onto the new position. The feeders were held in tension by a large spring anchored to the ground, suitably insulated from the lines of course. It was not unusual for him to have to accomplish more than one switch in the allotted time, and when all was ready he would telephone back to give the all-clear. Whilst all this was going on, a further man was attending to the switching at the selector and bi-furcating positions. To be the aerial man on a winter's night shift was without doubt the most unpopular part of the job. However, on a lovely summer's afternoon, things were quite different!

- In the comfort of the control room another engineer would change the programme feed and set up the drive oscillator.

- With all preparations in place, the Sender engineer would begin the process of 'bringing the Sender up'. Several switches and oil circuit breakers would be operated to select the outputs of large rotating machines and energise a mercury arc rectifier.

- With the main HT raised to about 5,000 Volts, the tuning of the Sender would be adjusted to optimise the performance. If everything seemed OK the main HT would then be increased to 11,000 Volts, and the tuning trimmed. Occasionally, for one reason or another, there would be a problem, and on reaching the final HT voltage a 'flash-over' might occur, which visually and aurally could be quite spectacular. The incoming programme at this stage would be line-up tone, and the depth of modulation would be set to the required level.

- The Sender engineer would check on his headphones that the correct programme was being radiated, usually preceded by the 'Victory' interval signal (the morse code letter "V" played continuously on the Timpani). Then an announcer would say "This is London" – which somehow made it all seem worthwhile!

THE WAR YEARS

At the outbreak of war in 1939, the BBC had eight HF transmitters all of which were based at Daventry; Senders 1-6, 8 and 9. Two Marconi high power transmitters were in the process of being installed (Senders 10 and 11), and Sender 7 (ST&C) would not be commissioned until December of the following year. To have all HF transmitters on the same site, was from a security point of view highly undesirable, and there was an urgent need to provide some form of backup in the event that Daventry was put out of action.

At Start Point, the MF transmitter was converted for use on HF by day and MF at night, and a Marconi SWB18 100kW HF transmitter was installed (Sender 22); the latter came into service in January 1940 and was also designated OSE4. From September of that year, Sender 22 radiated the European Service, and continued to do so throughout the entire period of the war. Also in September 1940, the Clevedon (Bristol) MF was converted to HF operation (15kW), and radiated the European Service. This brought the total of HF transmitters to 14, operating from 3 separate sites. During this time, a new station was being planned to provide a more permanent solution. A site at Rampisham in Dorset was to be equipped with four Marconi SWB18 100kW transmitters, Senders 31 to 34, and 15 masts supporting 29 arrays capable of world wide coverage. The station, known as OSE3, featured a remotely controlled switching tower by which any transmitter could be connected to any of the aerial arrays. The station was also equipped with new variable-frequency drives, designed by the Drive Section of Transmitter Department. A standby supply was provided by two 750 bhp diesel alternator sets and the station entered service in February 1941. Later in the same year, a Marconi SWB18 100kW HF transmitter was installed at Lisnagarvey, Northern Ireland; Sender 51 (OSE7). 1941 also saw a new Drive Room installed at Daventry; this was equipped with 15 of the new drives, replacing a variety of earlier drives. In 1942, Sender 7 (STC) at Daventry began operation as a double channel transmitter using a common modulator.

Then in 1943, there was a major expansion of HF broadcasting and a new site at Skelton, in Cumbria, to be known as OSE8 and OSE9 became the largest short wave transmitting complex in the world, with 18 HF senders. The Skelton site consisted of two independent transmitting stations; OSE8 was equipped with 6 Marconi SWB18 senders (described earlier); OSE9 had 6 ST&C CS8 senders each with two RF channels capable of operating on different bands with a common audio (modulator) channel. These could be operated in single or two channel mode as required, but when in single channel mode, the idle RF unit could be prepared for a new frequency, and the sender changed over from one RF channel to the other in a few seconds - this process, known as 'roll-over', caused many a heart stopping moment for the operator when for one reason or another the new RF channel failed to power up.

Later in 1943 a further six HF senders started broadcasting from a new site at Woofferton in Shropshire (OSE10). These senders were American and they were not designed for rapid wave changing - but this did not deter the transmission staff, who wave changed them nonetheless. These senders were used by the services in 1944 for counter-measure work. Following a crash-landing in Sweden of an experimental German V2 rocket, it was believed that they were fitted with a radio guidance system. The government ordered that the senders at Woofferton be taken out of service and modified in order to jam these devices. The RAF carried out the work and a system was devised to radiate the necessary signals. It was discovered later that the rockets were not fitted with radio guidance and the scheme was discontinued. The senders were restored and returned to normal service.

During the war BBC Transmission engineers played a significant part in providing and operating the master station at Daventry for the eastern chain of the GEE radar system, a navigational aid used by the RAF. These engineers were from the London Television Station at Alexandra Palace which had been closed down at the outbreak of war.

In 1944 additional buildings were constructed at Moorside Edge, Westerglen and Rampisham to house transmitters for the American and Canadian Forces networks (ABSIE-American Broadcasting Station In Europe) and transmissions continued until July 1945.

In 1948 Woofferton was closed down for a short period due to economic problems. However later that year it was re-opened, but financed mainly by the Voice of America (VOA) whose programmes were then relayed from that site.

Due to the Cold War the Communist Bloc began jamming all broadcasts from the West, starting in 1949. It was apparent that in general only the initial part of a transmission was likely to get through unaffected. A system of 'crash starts' was instigated, which took the form of a random selection of HF senders not applying final HT until the very last seconds. 30 seconds to programme the final HT was run up, and if the correct settings had been selected both on the sender and out in the aerial field, a hurried final tuning could just be completed by the opening announcement. An operator's nightmare!

Post-War HF Reconstruction

The first stage of the programme for the post-war re-equipment of H.F. stations was the addition of two 100kW transmitters, senders 35 and 36 at Rampisham in 1960. These were the first post-war designed transmitters and they had features which were to change the operational routines of H.F. stations.

The transmitters had dual H.F. channels, one in operation and the other with access for operational staff to wave-change the channel for the next required frequency.

The change-over of the channels took less than thirty seconds for the E.H.T. modulator and the aerial pneumatic operated switches to function. In comparison, the H.F. transmitters currently in operation required an out-of-service time of fifteen minutes for a similar wave-change.

They were the first transmitters in the B.B.C. to utilise vapour-cooled valves. This feature caused problems during the initial commissioning of the equipment by the manufacturers, Marconi, as there was little experience of the operating peculiarities of this mode of valve cooling. The need for the vapour from the 'boiling' valve to be separated into steam and water had not been appreciated, and it was necessary to provided separators to accomplish this. (The first trial separators were constructed from metal biscuit tins!)

During the early sixties, Woofferton was re-engineered. The original RCA senders (S81-86) were replaced with 6 Marconi 250kW BD272's, Senders 93-98. They began operation in October 1964. These transmitters also employed vapour cooling, which together with the use of high power BY1144 triode valves, produced an output power of 250kW. Wave changing was still accomplished by manually replacing tuning components, the largest being a metal tube 10cms in diameter formed into a loop of one and a half metres diameter and usually quite hot to handle. With an ever increasing need for a stronger voice in the growing congestion of the HF wavebands, these transmitters with more than twice the power of the previous generation were a significant improvement.

HF Automation

The complexity, coupled with the sheer size and high power of the transmitting stations, meant that unattended operation was initially only possible at three sites constructed in the 1990's. However significant staffing reductions were made as a result of changes in working practices and the introduction of automatic control systems.

The first fully automatic control system was installed at Skelton A (Cumbria) in 1971. Solid state memories were not sufficiently advanced at that time and so the system was built around a 168kbit ferrite core, as used in mainframe computers at the time.

Microprocessors became available in the mid-1970's and this permitted the design of a far more advanced automatic control system which was installed at Woofferton, then Skelton A, Skelton B, Rampisham and Daventry. This system used a resilient computer system, produced by Designs Department, that was based on a local area network – some years before LANs were in widespread use.

BBC Transmission's first high power HF transmitters with fully automatic tuning were designed by Marconi and installed at Woofferton in 1981; 300kW B6124 (S81-84). This was a significant advance and it enabled experience to be gained which led to BBC Transmission running the world's first fully automatic high power HF transmitting station in Hong Kong (1987), followed by Seychelles (1988) and Skelton C (1991).

Rampisham was completely re-engineered in the mid 1980's using fully automatic 500kW senders throughout, together with an improved version of the Woofferton/Skelton automatic control system and flexible antenna facilities. It became BBC Transmission's highest power transmitting station and, at 5MW, ranked amongst the highest power transmitting stations in the world. Nevertheless for much of the day it was attended by just two staff, due to the sophisticated automation and good reliability.

As part of the BBC World Service audibility improvement programme it was decided in 1988 to replace Skelton 'B' with a new station on the same site, designed to improve coverage in a number of areas, and unsurprisingly called Skelton 'C'. This station initially comprised four 300kW Marconi transmitters and fifteen antenna arrays, and was phased into operation by BBC Transmission from March to December 1991. Six of the new antennas serve southern Europe and north Africa, seven serve eastern Europe and the Middle East, with the final two broadcasting to the Caribbean region. Skelton 'C' was the first high power HF transmitting station not only to be fully automatic in operation, but to be run as a completely unmanned station, 24 hours a day. (Once Skelton 'C' was in service, the old Skelton 'B' station was demolished).

HF Efficiency Improvement

In 1992 tests carried out on an HF sender at Rampisham using the BBC's AMC[2] system, invented by BBC engineers for use on MF transmitters, proved successful. This is a companding technique whereby the carrier power is dynamically reduced at high modulation levels. This reduces the electricity consumed by the sender without affecting the service area, and the effect is enhanced when audio compression is applied to the programme input. Use is made of the receiver AGC to ensure that the listener does not notice the reduction in carrier level. Subsequently, a programme of modifying HF transmitters in the UK and overseas was started. The use of this technique can save up to 30% of the power consumption.

The closure of Daventry as an HF station

At the end of the Cold War, the requirement for HF transmitters in the UK diminished and this coincided with the time when a great deal of capital would need to have been spent on re-engineering Daventry's masts and antennas. Therefore, after 67 years of broadcasting from this site, the final transmission was made on 29 March 1992. It was an emotional occasion for many BBC staff, including the 400 guests at the closing down ceremony. Although it was somewhat remote from the creative programme makers, there was considerable pride in Daventry's role of delivering these programmes to people around the world. For many years, millions of domestic wireless sets

---

[2] AMC = Amplitude Modulation Companding

had 'Daventry' on their dial, so it was a well-known broadcasting station and its closure really did mark the end of an era.

Daventry became Transmission's strategic store and the centre for specialised maintenance services. Most of the antenna field was sold and only one mast was retained for communication purposes and Digital Audio Broadcasting.

OVERSEAS RELAY STATIONS

Plans were made as early as 1937 to build an HF relay station in the Far East and, around the outbreak of war, a Marconi 100kW HF sender was despatched to Singapore but it was sunk en route by enemy action. A further attempt was made but that was thwarted by the Japanese advance through Malaya.

The BBC in South East Asia

Broadcasting operations commenced in Singapore in 1946, under the title of "The British Far Eastern Broadcasting Service". Live programmes in English and some Asian languages (Burmese, Indonesian, Siamese) originating in local studios in the Cathay Building, were broadcast from 4 HF transmitters sited at Jurong, a station established by the Diplomatic Wireless Service of the Foreign Office - these transmitters were all 10kW Marconi type SWB11, previously used at a station in Ceylon (now Sri Lanka).

In 1949, the Studios and Administration of B.F.E.B.S. moved to Caldecott Hill, Thomson Road, sharing the site with Radio Malaya (Singapore). Operations at Caldecott Hill consisted of live broadcasting in English, Indonesian and Siamese, news editing and monitoring.

In the same year, the transmitting station was moved to Tebrau on the mainland of Malaya, and control of BFEBS was handed over by the Foreign Office to the BBC

Tebrau, Malaya

The Tebrau site consisted of 450 acres of jungle and Japanese ammunition dumps! There were no access roads, let alone any infrastructure, so the transmitting station was made entirely self-sufficient. Initially, there were 26 single-band HF Arrays, 2 towers and 10 stayed masts. Switching transmitters to arrays was accomplished by means of a multi-level motorised switching tower and HT frame. The station was equipped with the 4 SWB11 transmitters from Jurong, and 2 new 100kW Marconi SWB18 transmitters. 3 Mirless 400kW Diesel Generator sets provided the power supply for the transmitters (and also for the Tebrau domestic quarters in the early days), and Transmission from Tebrau commenced on Christmas Day, 1949. The programme source continued to be the Thomson Road studio, until the Woodleigh (Singapore) Receiving Station came into operation in 1951.

The first few years of operations of the Tebrau station coincided with the Malayan Emergency situation when a guerrilla war was being fought in the countryside. The complex was protected by armed security guards, and armed guards accompanied technical assistants whenever they had to go out into the aerial field to carry out array switching operations. It was a requirement that staff be resident on the site, and so there existed a self contained community within the perimeter fence, with housing and recreational facilities.

Woodleigh Receiving Station

The first receiving station was set up in an old bungalow in the compound of the Woodleigh water filtering site in Singapore. Operations commenced in August 1951, and with the relaying of English and Asian programmes from the UK, operations at Thomson Road were reduced to the playing of pre-recorded programmes, and junction and frequency announcements in English only.

Receiving equipment consisted of AR-88 diversity and Mullard ISB type GRF552 receivers, two Racal RA17 receivers with Evershed & Vignoles pen-recorders were used for Signal Strength Measurement, and Tebrau transmit frequencies were checked on a Marconi TME-1. There were 2 Rhombic antennas and a Beverage antenna. Green and Red programmes[3] were relayed, programme being fed to Tebrau by landline, via Thomson Road with a VHF radio backup circuit.

---

[3] All overseas programme networks were identified by colour. Green was the General Overseas Service (in English) later to become the World Service and Red was the Far Eastern Programme network.

In 1960 Woodleigh staff took on the manning of the Thomson Road studio until the BBC Far Eastern Service closed down its studio operations in Singapore in August 1965.

Ulu Tiram

A new receiving station was built at Ulu Tiram in Malaysia at the Johor Jungle Warfare Training School, equipment and staff being transferred from Woodleigh. The transfer was completed in August 1965. (A tragic accident occurred during this transfer when a mast which was being dismantled collapsed and killed the A.R.E.[4]).

The station closed down in October 1975 when the facility was transferred to Singapore.

Tebrau Re-engineering

Re-engineering of the Far Eastern Relay Station at Tebrau commenced in 1970. The transmitter building was extended to accommodate 4 x 250kW Marconi B6122 and 4 x 100kW Marconi B6123 transmitters. The SWB11 transmitters were dismantled, but the 2 SWB 18 transmitters were retained. An additional 100 acres of the site were cleared to provide space for 14 new towers and masts to support 26 250kW arrays, and an RF matrix switch station was provided for the new transmitters. The old switching tower HT frame and associated arrays were retained for use on the SWB18 transmitters. Re-engineering was completed in 1972.

Kranji, Singapore

In 1972, just as re-engineering of Tebrau was completed, the Malaysian Government gave the BBC notice of its intention to terminate the BBC's licence to broadcast with effect from March 1975 - the termination date was later extended to March 1979 to enable the BBC to transfer to a new site. The possibilities of sites at Christmas Island and Brunei were explored, but eventually a 30 acre site at Kranji offered by the Government of Singapore was selected, and building work commenced in 1976.

---

[4] A.R.E. = Assistant Resident Engineer

The site was in a swampy area adjacent to a reservoir, and extensive land filling and piling works were necessary. The B6122 and B6123 transmitters were moved one by one from Tebrau, the first transmitter at Kranji coming into service on 1 February 1978, and the installation was completed in March 1979.

In the antenna field, 17 towers supported 14 Marconi 4-Band Kraus, 4 BBC dual-band and one 4MHz array. An additional tower and 15-21MHz array was added in 1982. An automatic control system was installed which accommodated array selection and slewing, transmitter on/off switching, programme selection and tape machine control. The transmitter complement was increased to 9 in 1987 with the installation of an additional Marconi BD272 250kW transmitter ex Daventry.

Yew Tee Receiving Station

In October 1975 a temporary receiving station was set up at the Yew Tee Army Camp in Singapore. The station was equipped with two new Plessey PRD200, 4 serviced Plessey PRD200 and the Racal RA133A Diversity and bandscanner receivers from Ulu Tiram.

Use was made of one of the signals camp aerials and no BBC aerials were installed. Programme was fed to Tebrau on a UHF link, with a microwave link loaned by the Singapore Broadcasting Corporation as a reserve. Operations at Yew Tee came to an end with the opening of a new receiving station at Punggol on 1 December 1977.

Punggol & Satellite Feeds

The Receiving Station was built on the Punggol river. Only the Receiver building, a Marconi omni-directional antenna and 1 tower were on dry land, the other 7 towers (supporting 4 Rhombic and 2 sloping V aerials) were built in the river estuary, and so were only accessible by boat. The station was equipped with 6 Plessey PRD200, 10 Channel diversity receivers, a Plessey PR2250 search receiver and a Plessey PR2250 adapted for bandscanning, all being capable of being remotely controlled via modems from Kranji. Initially the station became remotely controlled in May 1980. Main & Reserve

Programme circuits were provided between Punggol and Kranji on a PCM system, by cable, and by a radio link via Bukit Timah Hill.

In 1983 programmes from the UK were routed via the Indian Ocean Satellite. Punggol was retained as a backup and to provide search Rx and Bandscanning facilities; It was closed down in August 1990.

Tanglin FM Station

Around 1965 The British Forces Broadcasting Service operated a 5kW Marconi BD321B transmitter, installed in a building at Tanglin Army Camp, and this was handed over to the BBC Far Eastern Service when the British Forces left Singapore. This radiated World Service until the station closed in 1994, when the service was transferred to SIMCOM Bukit Batok transmitting station.

Atlantic Relay Station (A.R.S.) Ascension Island

The Atlantic Relay Station sited on Ascension Island in the South Atlantic Ocean was opened in 1966 to serve areas of Africa and South America. A volcanic outcrop, the terrain gave rise to construction difficulties, particularly with regard to the mast bases and stay blocks. The station was equipped with 4 Marconi BD272 250kW transmitters, 18 dual band aerial arrays and a receiving station for the HF ISB[5] programme feeds from the U.K. A low power MF transmitter provided a source of World Service for staff and their families. Pre-recorded tapes shipped out from Bush House were used whenever possible to ensure the highest quality programme feed.

During the Falklands war in 1982, the British Government, under the terms of the BBC's licence and agreement, requisitioned one of the HF senders in order to transmit programmes to the Argentinean forces on the Falkland Islands. These were non-BBC programmes and were carried under the station name of "Radio Atlantico del Sur". Two periods of transmission were made each day.

In 1985 a satellite programme feed from U.K. was installed which later resulted in the closing down of the receiving station, and in 1988 work commenced on expanding the station. A further two

---

[5] ISB = Independent Sideband

BD272 250kW transmitters were installed, ex-Daventry, and the aerial facilities were increased to include 5 new self supporting towers and 4 x 4 band arrays.

The following extract written in 1973 gives a good description of the early years:-

"...The most desolate barren land (and like a land that God has cursed) that ever my eyes beheld" – That's how Ascension Island looked to the seventeenth-century seafarer, Peter Mundy. Over 300 years later, staff arriving to man the BBC Relay Station could say much the same of this speck of volcanic debris in mid-Atlantic. Seen from the comfort of a modern air-liner, which is the way most people get there nowadays, the first impression is perhaps even more startling. Some forty volcanic craters rise up from dusty plains and grotesquely formed lava flows, coloured in drab reds and browns, and the black of cinders. Adding to the air of unreality, and dominating the island, a 3,000 ft mountain rears into the clouds, densely vegetated and capped with a forest of bamboo.

It was into this unlikely setting that the BBC installed its Atlantic Relay Station, beginning a new chapter in the century and a half of Ascension's human habitation, and in its long association with the business of communications, started in 1899 with the establishment of the Eastern Telegraph Company's Cable station. For the BBC, looking for ways of improving its service to Africa and South America, Ascension Island, lying almost mid-way between the two continents, and about 7° south of the Equator could hardly have been better placed.

In other ways, though, it could hardly have been worse. Very few people lived there; the island had no indigenous population and only the most primitive water and electricity supplies. Passenger ships called at three-monthly intervals, and the only access by air meant flying to Antigua first to pick up an American military flight via Brazil. Such were the formidable problems facing the Ministry of Public Buildings and Works when it started construction work for the BBC in 1964. Construction meant not only building a transmitting station, but the power station to supply it, a desalination plant for fresh water, and, as if that were not enough, the creation of an entire new village to house the staff. The people involved in this most daunting and complex of tasks could take justifiable pride in the fact that, eventually, all the many difficulties were overcome. A work force was flown in from the West Indies, and supplies and equipment arrived by ship from England. For these latter the last half mile or so of the 4,000 mile journey was undoubtedly the most precarious, carried on pontoons to the stone pier head of the old naval station at Georgetown. Ways were found to anchor the 325 ft aerial masts into the loose volcanic rock; to build some 25 miles of road and to install 12 miles of overhead power cable and 8 miles of water mains – all this over rugged terrain of rock and dust, more fitting for the Moon than a tropical island.

For the first of the BBC's operational staff and their families who arrived in April 1966, it was very much a pioneering way of life. Houses in the village were still being built; the noise and dust were all pervading. The village shop had yet to be completed, and a notice about Christmas trading arrangements advised customers that 'Bread will be on sale from the shop van at the site of the BBC milk refrigerator from 0900 to 0930'. The provision of such an everyday item as a petrol pump for private motorists was an event that warranted quite detailed notices setting out the correct procedure. '... give a coupon or coupons of the required value to the pump attendant who will then dispense the appropriate amount of petrol'. Those early settlers survived to tell many a tale of the tribulations and pleasures of the good old days, and the relay station went on the air on 3 July 1966. But that, in many ways, was only a beginning. It was to be another ten months before the full complement of staff was on the island, twenty-five from Great Britain and ten from the neighbouring (800 miles away) island of St. Helena, and not until early 1968 were the thirty aerial arrays all available for transmissions. They are a good example of the engineering know-how and ingenuity that went into the building of the station. The latest 'dual band' design meant that they occupied only half the space of conventional types, and the horseshoe pattern of masts provided easy coverage of the two continents. An aerial which is beamed towards North-West Africa in the early evening has only to be reversed later in the day to cover South America, while in the same way a single aerial can serve, at different times, both southern Africa and Central America. However, they have not been free from problems and difficulties. There was the occasion when the Resident Engineer, taking a boat trip round the island, remarked to his fellow passengers how well the aerials looked from the sea. He arrived home to be greeted with the news that a whole bay of aerials had collapsed, victim of high winds and unexpectedly rapid corrosion of the steel support wires. The half-ton of copper wire which had presented such a pleasing pattern against the sky lay in a tangled mess on the dust and lava, while a few lonely strands swung to and fro in the breeze, challenging the rigging staff whose job it would be to restore order out of chaos.

The heart of the Relay Station is a small, unimposing building, nestling in the eroded remnants of a volcano, called Butt Crater. It is here that special aerials and high-performance receivers, operating in pairs to lessen the effects of fading, pick up transmissions from England for re-broadcasting by the transmitters at English Bay. A natural barrier of hills between the two sites guards against the embarrassing, and technically disastrous possibility of the receivers being swamped by the station's own transmissions. Where programmes can be prepared sufficiently in advance for the tapes to be flown to Ascension, these are broadcast from the receiving station at the same time as the transmission from London, but giving the listener very much better quality for such items as plays, talks and concerts.

As well as radio receivers and tape machines, the small building in Butt Crater also houses a studio used for linking announcements and station identification, and through the not very sound-proof windows of which more than one of the island's donkeys has inadvertently broadcast to the world. Shut away in a back room is the solitary operator's mechanical assistant — the automatic switching unit. A daunting mass of clicking relays and rotary switches, it would be easy to believe that it has a mind of its own, as it starts tape machines and routes programmes in any of five languages (French, English, Hausa, Spanish and Portuguese) to the four transmitters. Timed to the second, and working its way through a schedule of alarming complexity, it has no sympathy for the broadcaster who talks beyond his appointed time. Many is the golden phrase that's been cut in half by the inexorably ticking robot. The engineer working a lonely night shift here will not be entirely without visitors. A passing donkey calling for a bucket of water, or a land crab hopelessly off course in a cable duct demand attention, and a luckless centipede which carelessly stepped across two 50-volt terminals not only contaminated the BBC World Service with a loud hum, but provided an exercise in fault-finding not generally dealt with at training school.

If the well-ordered business of broadcast engineering is affected by the peculiarities of Ascension Island, so too is the life of the staff out of working hours. The island community is probably the smallest and most cosmopolitan in which many of them ever lived, with British, American, South African, West Indian and St. Helenian all represented in a total population of about 1,200. It's a place where people quickly, and of necessity, discover how to provide their own entertainments and amusements, and where the absence of television is seldom, if ever, lamented. In a pleasant climate, where the temperature generally stays around 80°F, outdoor activities flourish. Game fishing in the well stocked coastal waters is a regular attraction; football and cricket are both played with enthusiasm and a high incidence of minor injuries, on iron-hard pitches, the dusty surfaces of which have never seen a blade of grass, and golf on a home-made course which is proudly described, and with some accuracy, as the worst in the world, is as addictive as ever the lush greens and fairways of St. Andrews. An amateur dramatic society plays to a highly appreciative captive audience, and voluntary effort produces a weekly ten-page local newspaper. All of which is not to say that there are no frustrations and anxieties. There is a sense of isolation from the outside world, but here, appropriately enough, radio comes into its own. The BBC operates a low-power medium-wave relay of the World Service for the island, and there is no shortage of amateur disc jockeys to man the local American Forces radio Station 'Volcano Radio'.

Supply lines, though still tenuous, have been much improved. Airmail arrives twice a week, and mail ships on the Southampton-Capetown run call at three-or four-week intervals, but the five direct flights a year from England, bringing not only new faces but also such half-forgotten delicacies as mushrooms, and fresh fruit and vegetables, are great occasions indeed. 'Charter Days' are dates to be ringed in red on the calendar, and mark the progress of the year, much as the seasons would at home.

Visitors to the island are few, and a high proportion of these are drawn to study the wild life, still relatively un-affected by man's intrusion. While many sea birds have retreated to the off-shore rock of Boatswainbird Island, Wideawake Terns come in their thousands to nest on the mainland. Ascension is also one of the main breeding grounds of the Green Turtle, and it's a treat for the children to go to the beaches on a moonlit night to see these great creatures lumbering over the sand to lay their eggs.

Reminders are everywhere of the island's past history as a naval garrison. Paths cut round Green Mountain, which now make a pleasant Sunday afternoon walk, were first used by marine patrols scanning the ocean for would-be rescuers of Napoleon from St. Helena. The museum in Georgetown is housed in an old fort, and near the new village of Two Boats the up-ended halves of a naval cutter still stand by the old road, as shelter for weary travellers.

For an island which spent the first 300 years after its discovery in almost total obscurity, Ascension has come a long way. From naval garrison to cable station, then, during the Second World War, a strategically sited air-strip, and in the last decade a vital link in the NASA Apollo space programme. And, of course, as our listeners in Africa and the Americas are well aware, the Atlantic Relay Station of the BBC.

Now on the air for 24 hours a day, there's no doubt that the station has proved its worth. As a listener in West Africa reported "we now receive BBC programmes as if you were transmitting from the end of the street". [6]

---

[6] From an article entitled "This is the BBC Atlantic Relay Station", part of a BBC publication "How to Listen to the World".

Caribbean Relay Company (C.R.C.) Antigua

Opened in 1975, The Caribbean Relay Company is a joint venture agreement between the German broadcaster Deutsche Welle and the BBC. The station is equipped with four Marconi BD272 250 kW transmitters with Marconi H1100 drivers, and the antennas are of BBC design. Power to the station is supplied by five 1mW Ruston sets, each transmitter has a dedicated engine and the fifth set is held as a spare. The service area covered by the station includes north and central America.

Ex-patriate staff are seconded from both organisations, and are housed in a specially provided compound some 12 miles from the station.

British East Mediterranean Relay Station (B.E.M.R.S.)

The British East Mediterranean Relay Station (Cyprus) has been used for broadcasting BBC programmes since 1957 when it was taken over by the Diplomatic Wireless Service as a result of the Suez crisis. Prior to this it was an Arabic station, (the main entrance doors to the station still have Arabic script engraved in the glass panels), as the following brief history shows.

In 1941 the Near East Arab Broadcasting Station, more commonly known as Sharq-Al-Adna, began broadcasting from Jenin in Northern Palestine using locally produced programmes in Arabic. In 1942, in new premises near Jerusalem, a second programme in various European languages was added for the British War Department. At the end of the war all programmes reverted to Arabic and remained so until 1947 at the close of the British Mandate in Palestine. By early 1948 some of the original equipment and some of the staff had been transported to Cyprus and were operating from a site in Polemidhia near Limassol. Sharq-Al-Adna continued to grow and with four 7.5kW HF transmitters, its antennas strung between 100 ft wooden poles and one tree, and its own resident orchestra, singers and programme staff in adjacent buildings, it was amongst the larger of the stations then operating in the Middle East. In 1955 more powerful transmitters were brought into service at the present site at Zyyi. A year later Sharq-Al-Adna ceased at the time of the Suez

Crisis and the following year the British Diplomatic Wireless Service officially took over responsibility and began transmitting the BBC's Arabic Service as the Voice of Britain. In 1957 the station was renamed the British East Mediterranean Relay Station (B.E.M.R.S.) and BBC External Service programmes began to be relayed by two 100kW MF, two 20kW and two 7.5kW HF transmitters from Zyyi. In 1963 four 100kW HF transmitters were additionally installed and in 1978 two 500kW MF transmitters were introduced into service at a new site at Lady's Mile. In 1983 the two 7.5kW HF transmitters were replaced by four 250kW HF transmitters.

BBC Transmission became responsible for this station in 1985, but the Foreign & Commonwealth Office manager stayed on, and the first BBC EiC did not take up residence until 1987.

Finally the two 20kW transmitters were de-commissioned in 1989 at the end of their useful life, and were replaced in 1990 by two 250kW fully automated transmitters.

In 1991 the control of all transmitters of the two sites was transferred to a BBC designed computer based Automatic Control System. Also in that year two antennas were re-engineered to take the greater power of two transmitters combined in order to effectively increase the number of antennas directed towards the north.

At the end of 1994 the four 100kW HF transmitters were removed and by the end of January 1995 a further four 300 kW fully automatic HF transmitters, formerly installed at Daventry, had been brought into service.

The following is a list of significant events.

1941 Near East Arab Broadcasting Station began broadcasting from Jenin, Palestine.
1948 Near East Arab Broadcasting Transmitting Station transferred to Limassol Cyprus from Palestine.
1955 Station transferred to present site at Zyyi.
100kW Marconi MF 620kHz.
Two 7.5kW Marconi HF.

All programmes in Arabic from studios in Limassol to Zyyi by VHF link.

1956 Near East Arab Broadcasting became Voice of Britain and began re-broadcasting BBC's Arabic service.

1957 Voice of Britain became British East Mediterranean Relay Station. Separate Receiving Site established on adjacent British military base near Zyyi.
Two 20kW Marconi HF.
100kW Marconi MF 719kHz.
First Deltic Standby generator installed.

1958 7.5kW RCA MF 1421 kHz.
7.5kW RCA MF BFBS transmission began.

1963 Four 100kW Marconi HF installed in Annexe.
Dual Band curtain arrays installed in extended antenna field.
Second Deltic Standby generator installed.

1964 50kW Continental MF replaced 7.5 kW RCA MF.
Receiver site relocated at Lady's Mile.

1976 BFBS transmission closed down.

1978 Four F&CO 250kW MF on 719kHz & 638kHz installed on new site at Lady's Mile taking over the services from 100kW Marconi.

1979 Two 100kW Marconi MF paralleled on 1323kHz took over the service from 50kW Continental and were additionally equipped as reserves for the 250kW MF with 50 kW MF becoming reserve for 100kW MF.

1983 Four Marconi HF B6124 300kW transmitters installed.
HF Antenna field re-engineered with 4 Band arrays.

1986 BBC management under a joint F&CO/BBC contract.

1987 First BBC manager at B.E.M.R.S..

1988 Lady's Mile Transmitter site run un-attended.
MF stand by facilities at Zyyi decommissioned.
Deltics at Zyyi de-commissioned.

1989 Lady's Mile Deltic replaced by 1.2MW Mirlees-Blackstone generator.

20kW HF decommissioned.

1990 Technical shift complement reduced from S.M.E. and 7 MEs to S.M.E. and 4 MEs.

Re-engineered power distribution at Zyyi.

Two Marconi HF B6131 fully automatic transmitters installed and commissioned. BBC designed Automatic Control System installed and commissioned to control the HF transmitters.

1991 ACS extended to control all, MF transmitters. SHF link in service linking Zyyi with Lady's Mile.

1994 Four 100kW Marconi HF transmitters taken out of service.

1994/5 Four Marconi HF B6126 fully automatic transmitters brought into service.

British Eastern Relay Station (B.E.R.S.) Masirah Island, Oman

In 1986 BBC Transmission assumed responsibility for the operation of the British Eastern Relay Station (B.E.R.S.) on the island of Masirah, just off the coast of Oman. Formerly built and operated by the Diplomatic Wireless Service to relay BBC programmes, Masirah Island was the fourth site for this relay following a somewhat chequered history. The original site dating from 1960 was in Somalia, then RAF Aden followed by Perim Island in the Red Sea. The station radiates services on HF and MF to the Middle East and to Asia. The other main occupant of the island is the Royal Omani Air Force, who operate a large air base nearby, formerly an RAF station.

Indian Ocean Relay Station. (I.O.R.S.) Seychelles

Opened in 1988, and situated on the west coast of Mahe, the largest island in the Seychelles group, the station serves an area of east Africa which extends from Somalia and Ethiopia in the north, down to Madagascar and Mozambique in the south. Programmes, relayed from London via an Intelsat 'B' satellite link, are broadcast in English, Swahili and Kinarwanda.

The station is equipped with two Marconi B6131 transmitters pulse width modulated operating at 250kW with Optimod and AM Companding. The aerial installation comprises six four band arrays, and the whole operation is fully automatic.

BBC East Asia Relay Company (B.E.A.R.C.) Hong Kong

In order to provide better coverage of the Far East, BBC Transmission built and operated a site at Tsang Tsui in the New Territories of Hong Kong from 1987 to 1997 through a wholly owned subsidiary called the BBC East Asia Relay Company. The site was established in the knowledge that it would have to close 10 years later as a result of Hong Kong returning to China, but it was regarded as being well worth while in order to build a larger audience in this part of the world and it was a successful enterprise. The site had twelve staff comprising the manager who was a BBC Transmission employee from the UK, two locally recruited staff employed by BEARC and nine staff on contract from HK Telecom International. The site was relatively small, with just two transmitters and four antennas, but it was a model of good efficient design and it was sad that it had to be demolished.

BBC Asia Relay Station (B.A.R.S.) Thailand

In the early 1990s, plans were formed for the construction of a new short wave station in Thailand, principally to improve BBC World Service coverage in the Indian subcontinent. However, when this project was planned in 1993 it had become clear that replacement coverage of China and southern Asia would be needed for Hong Kong following its closure, and this became an equally important objective for the BBC Asia Relay Station.

Site works started in August 1994 for a station with four 250kW transmitters and thirteen antennas, in wetlands close to the city of Nakhon Sawan in central Thailand. The facilities to serve China came into service in 1996, the jubilee year of King Bumiphol of Thailand, and were officially opened by HRH The Duke of Edinburgh during the Queen's royal jubilee visit in October. At this stage, transmissions from Hong Kong were phased out and Thailand took over the role of broadcasting to China. The second pair of transmitters and remaining antennas to serve the Indian subcontinent were put into operation on 1 January 1997 to complete the station. BBC Transmission provided a Station Manager and Assistant Manager from the UK to supervise operations at the station; the other staff being contracted and recruited locally in Thailand.

BBC Asia Relay Station was the last major transmitting station to be constructed and brought into operation under the management of BBC Transmission.

SECTION 4 TELEVISION TRANSMISSION

As early as 1930, Brookmans Park was used to broadcast television with for the first time, simultaneous sound and vision (its second transmitter had already been installed), using the Baird 30 line system. These experimental transmissions took place at night following the close of the radio programmes, and as the Baird system required a bandwidth of only 15kHz, the MF transmitters were perfectly suitable. Interest in television was growing and the Baird system, which was based on mechanical scanning techniques, was soon rivalled by an alternative electronic system designed by a team from EMI. Quite apart from producing excellent picture quality with its 405 lines, this new system proved to be much more flexible in studio operations. In November 1936, a regular 'high definition' television service began broadcasting from Alexandra Palace in north London. Initially shared by the two systems in direct competition (Baird had by that time progressed to 240 lines), they transmitted on alternate weeks, but it took only three months to decide in favour of the electronic scanning system. It is greatly to the credit of that EMI team that their basic scanning system is still universally used to this day.

With the onset of war in 1939, Alexandra Palace was closed down, and television broadcasting had to wait a further seven years before it could be resumed.

In the early stages of the war, when the threat of invasion was at its greatest, the vision transmitter was made ready to jam the communication links of German tank formations. On another occasion a similar scheme was prepared to interrupt German Paratrooper frequencies; fortunately neither of these arrangements had to be used in anger. The sound transmitter was however used to confuse the German 'Y-Gerat' radio navigational system used by their bombers; a very effective system using a series of radio beams. This counter-measure, known by the code name 'Domino', was so completely successful that the German system was withdrawn. In 1944, misleading information about the guidance system used in the German V2 rockets resulted in plans being made to use Alexandra Palace and certain other transmitters to disrupt the system. On the information then available it was believed that the rockets were guided by a radio system capable of being jammed. Before the plans could be put into operation the true details became known and it was clear that jamming in this way was not feasible, and the idea was abandoned.

With the end of the war, it was decided to re-open the television service using the original Alexandra Palace transmitters. The modifications for war-time use were removed and considerable work was necessary to reinstate the equipment. New aerials were erected and the system was ready by early 1946. Following a period of test transmissions for the benefit of dealers, the service was formerly opened by the Postmaster General on the 7 June 1946. The coverage of the station was about 25% of the UK population.

POST WAR EXTENSION OF THE BAND I TELEVISION SERVICE

Plans to extend the television service were made following much discussion regarding the choice of single or double sideband operation. Alexandra Palace radiated double sideband, but such was the available space in Band I that this choice would result in a total of only four channels; single sideband operation however would result in a fifth channel being available.

It was finally agreed that single (vestigial) sideband would be employed at all new stations, and that four main high power stations would be sited in the Midlands, North of England, Central Scotland and South Wales or South West England. It was estimated that this would give a coverage of some 80 % of the UK population. It was further agreed that these stations would be designed to also accommodate VHF/ FM radio services.

The opening of a high power television station was a special event, marquees would be erected, special catering would come from London, and all the local dignities would be invited, with TCPD (Transmitter Capital Projects Department) and the station staff acting as guides for tours of the station. The staff were fully occupied during the day but they were not forgotten by Catering Dept; as when the guests had departed there was always plenty of refreshments reserved for a staff party.

Sutton Coldfield

The first of the new high power Band I television stations was opened in December 1949 at a site 10 miles north of Birmingham, and to a lavish opening ceremony with Sylvia Peters as commentator. Designed to serve about nine million people of the Midlands, the station was to set the pattern for the other three stations that were to follow. A high power 45kW main vision transmitter was backed up (later) with a medium power reserve, and provision was made to add a VHF/FM service at a later date. The transmitting aerials with a power gain of 3dB were supported on a 750 ft stayed mast, and the station radiated on channel 4 (vision 61.75MHz, sound 58.25MHz).

Holme Moss

The second station opened was at Holme Moss, an extremely exposed site over 1,700 ft on top of the Pennine chain. It opened in October 1951, again to a very high profile ceremony introduced by Richard Dimbleby. The site was chosen to serve as large an area as possible of Lancashire and Yorkshire, and brought a further 11 million people within range of television. Technically designed along similar lines to those established at Sutton Coldfield the station was equipped with a 45kW main vision transmitter and a 5kW reserve, the site however was a very different challenge. Remote and exposed, it was subjected to severe weather conditions, at times making normal access impossible. The nearest water was a reservoir 800 ft below, and a pumping station had to be built to provide a supply. To meet local planning regulations, special arrangements had to be made for sewage disposal, resulting in a very costly drain to Holme village some two miles away. Another requirement was dedicated accommodation for staff who would be snowbound during the worst of winter weather. The station is the highest transmitting station in the UK and the 600 ft mast was designed to withstand high wind and ice loading. The aerial system had a power gain of 3dB and the dipoles were equipped with de-icing facilities. The station radiated on channel 2 (vision 51.75MHz, sound 48.25MHz)

Kirk o'Shotts

The third station to open was in Scotland at Harthill, a site 12 miles from Glasgow and 24 miles from Edinburgh. It opened in March 1952 and would serve a further 4 million people. The main vision transmitter was rated at 70kW (run at 50kW) and the main aerial feeder was unusual in as much as its inner conductor was of continuous length and weighted at the bottom; the so-called 'locked-coil winding rope'. This had the advantage of having no joints throughout its length. The aerial system had a power gain of 3dB and radiated on channel 3 (vision 56.75MHz, sound 53.25MHz)

King George VI died in February 1952 and the State Funeral was to be held on the 15th. By this time the installation of the reserve 5kW/1kW transmitters and the aerial system was virtually complete and tested, although the pre-service transmissions for the television trade were not scheduled for a further few weeks. The State Funeral was to be televised, and with Kirk o'Shotts nearing a serviceable condition it was decided it should also carry the transmission, but the in-coming vision signal via the Post Office microwave link from London had not been accepted for service. A special effort was made with the co-operation of Designs Dept. and the P.O. to enable these particular in-coming vision and sound signals to be available on that date.

At this time the permanent station staff were only just being appointed and so were not fully acquainted with the equipment; this being the case the transmissions were undertaken by the TCPD and Marconi engineers. There were two periods of the transmission, one in the morning for the Funeral and then the recording in the evening. The morning transmission commenced at 9 am, which meant a very early and snowy journey from the Edinburgh base to arrive with sufficient time to align the equipment in readiness for the first (and very important) transmission.

Kirk o'Shotts had opened for just one day, and then closed until the Trade Transmissions started a few weeks later. How many viewers there were will never be known, but there could not have been many, as no prior publicity had been given.

Wenvoe

The last of the high power Band I stations was installed at Wenvoe, a site in South Wales about 4 miles from Cardiff and designed to serve some 4 million people in South Wales and the West of England. The technical design followed that of Kirk o'Shotts including the locked-coil rope transmission line main feeder. The station radiated on channel 5 (vision 66.75MHz, sound 63.25 MHz) and was opened on 15 August 1952. It commenced service with only the 5kW vision and the 1kW sound reserve transmitters in operation, the 50kW/12.5kW main transmitters did not take service until the following 20th December.

Previous to the 15th August the weather had been fine and warm, but from early morning on the 15th it started to rain very heavily. The site which was not fully completed with its access paths etc. was turned into a quagmire, and the VIP guests suffered the wind, rain and the mud. It was not until later that it was learnt of the occurrence of the flood disaster at Lynton/Lynmouth which are only just across the Bristol Channel from Wenvoe.

The installation of Wenvoe marked the end of the initial stage of post war expansion, and had resulted in an estimated coverage of 86% of the UK population.

Temporary Low Power Television Stations

The popularity and the demand for television was growing, and this was further stimulated by the announcement that the Coronation of H.M. The Queen in June 1953 would be televised. Financial restrictions, and the short time scale, prevented the commissioning of further permanent stations in the un-served populated areas in time for this important national event.

After the Second World War there became available many items of surplus radio communication equipment, among these were 250W amplitude modulated HF transmitters (RCA Type ET4336). These transmitters covered the short wave frequency bands and were used for general communication purposes. The Director of Engineering,

Mr (later Sir) F.C. McLean, instituted the purchase of about 100 of these transmitters on the premise "that they may come in useful". It is unlikely that at the time he could of realised just how useful they would become, and the variety of roles in which they would be employed.

With the demand by the public to view the Coronation, it was decided that temporary stations were to be installed to cover the North East (Newcastle area) and Northern Ireland (Belfast). As no commercial transmitting equipment was available TCPD was given the task of designing the equipment, and the ex-war surplus RCA transmitters formed the basis of the design.

The design of the modifications for the sound transmitter was relatively the easier of the two problems. The sound modulator was retained in its original form, but all the HF circuitry was removed, and replaced by new coils and capacitors for the higher frequency television band of 45 to 63.25 MHz; different coils being required for each Band I channel. The original HF valves were retained, with the 813 type R.F. final output valve operating at the extreme of its frequency range. This equipment produced an output power of 125W.

The vision transmitter was a more formidable task. The original transmitter was completely dismantled with only the HT components and the transmitter framework being retained, and even the latter had to be extended to accommodate additional components. To achieve the desired peak vision power of 500W, modern vhf valves were used, and the grid modulated R.F. output stage consisted of two QY4-250 tetrode valves operating in push-pull. A television synchronising pulse stabilising amplifier, which was in general use in studio equipment, was modified to provide a picture/sync ratio of 50/50 to modulate the control grids of the output valves. The grid bias for these valves was obtained via a dry battery, and as this battery was being modulated with respect to earth at video frequencies it was mounted in a small container designed to present a low capacity to earth. This was just one of the novel expediencies that had to be taken to complete the design in the short timescale.

Before the project was allowed to proceed, the prototype transmitters had to be approved by the Engineering Directorate. The demonstration took place in the basement of a building in Bolsover Street London, where the equipment had been constructed. Although the equipment had been tested with various generated waveforms, sawtooth, bars etc., the final approval test was with a true picture waveform. To achieve this a complete Outside Broadcast Unit arrived in the narrows of Bolsover St. and a camera channel set up to feed the transmitter. The demonstration was witnessed by the Director of Engineering, who readily gave his seal of approval when he saw on the transmitter output monitor the fine detailed design of the cloth on the jacket he was wearing.

Two sets of equipment were originally produced consisting of two vision and two sound transmitters, monitoring equipment, and sound and vision input amplifiers, this work being carried out by the staff of Equipment Dept. The complete equipment was installed in two self-propelled single-decker type coaches, that had originally housed the pre-war television O.B. units that with the advances in technology were then redundant.

Pontop Pike (Newcastle) was the first to use this temporary equipment as the site and electricity supply were available in preparation for the eventual permanent station. The programme input signals were available from a nearby microwave relay point on the link to the Kirk o'Shotts Station. The aerial system consisted of super-turnstile antennas supplied by the Marconi Company and mounted on 150 ft mast.

The second unit was shipped to Northern Ireland and installed on a site at Glencairn, outside Belfast, as the permanent site at Divis was not then available and the weather conditions at that site would have been too severe for such temporary equipment and the staff. The installation was similar to Pontop Pike with the programme being via a temporary link from Belfast.

The stations had a staff of 8 engineers, 2 per shift, and their domestic facilities were provided in a separate wooden hut. These consisted of cooking and mess facilities and (in their day) the un-enviable Elsan toilet.

The success of these two stations produced pressure and enthusiasm to produce others in time for the Coronation but this was not possible, but eventually three more units were produced.

There were now no more ex-OB vehicles available, so a search was made for an alternative. This took the form of more redundant war-time equipment consisting of four-wheeled trailers that had probably been used to house similar R.F. equipments. These trailers were very high-mounted, similar to the old horse-drawn gypsy caravans, with access via a short run of steps. Naturally the outsides were re-sprayed the then BBC green colour, and embossed with the crest on each side to obliterate their original camouflage.

One of these units did become available just before the Coronation and was sited on the South Downs at Truleigh Hill just behind the town of Shoreham-on-Sea, and provided coverage of the Brighton area. In fact, the coverage was so good that when the planned station at Rowridge on the Isle of Wight eventually came into service, the Brighton residents were not satisfied with a reduced signal, and a separate station for the area was installed at Whitehawk Hill.

The location at Truleigh Hill was chosen for two other reasons besides its coverage potential. Firstly the existence of an adjacent military radar station, with a readily available mains power supply, and secondly, reasonable quality direct reception of the London (Alexandra Palace) transmitter for vision and sound programme feeds. The ground to the North of the site towards London sloped steeply downwards, and advantage of this feature was taken in the choice of receiving aerial, which consisted of four long-wire Beveridge aerials. These were simple to construct and to repair should they suffer damage on such an exposed site. As the sole feed of programme, their maintenance was essential. The aerial system proved very effective and reliable.

With five mobile units available, two ex-OB vans and three caravans, temporary stations were brought into service many months before the permanent installations were commissioned, much to the satisfaction of the viewers. Besides the three stations already mentioned, these temporaries were also used to start the service at North Hessary

Tor, Wigtown (pre-Sandale), Redmoss (pre-Meldrum), Tacolneston and the Isle of Man. The Isle of Man station requires special mention due to the political and technical problems that were encountered.

With the commencement of the service at Brighton, various other authorities with larger populations considered they should also receive a service. For a variety of reasons this was not possible due to suitable sites not being available, no programme input feed, and the effort required to produce another caravan by Coronation time. One of these areas pressing for a service was the Isle of Man.

Now politically, the I.O.M. is an independent province with its own government, the House of Keys, which reports direct to the Home Office. Parts of the East coast of the Island could obtain a fairly usable signal from the Holme Moss transmitter, but these were in the minority and with a population of only 50,000 the island was low on the BBC's priority list. There existed on the Island a very enthusiastic radio dealer who could see the possibilities, and he pressed the Manx Government until he obtained the authority to produce and radiate from a low power booster, so that "the loyal subjects of Her Majesty could witness her Coronation". This arrangement didn't receive the full support of the Home Office, who imposed the condition that the booster should cease after the event and that the BBC would provide the service as soon as was practical. This condition meant that the I.O.M. moved to the top of the priority list and had first call on the next completed caravan.

The Isle of Man is dominated by the 2,000 ft mountain of Snaefell, which is located almost in the centre of the island. This would be the ideal site for the transmitter as all major centres of the population which are in the South, North and West of the island could be served from this one site. There existed on the summit of Snaefell a Ministry of Civil Aviation receiving station, which was one of the main control points for all the trans-Atlantic aircraft traffic. It was naturally a condition on the joint use of the site that no interference should degrade the MCA receiving equipment, as this was essential to the safety of the aircraft.

In November 1953 an ET4336 vision transmitter was installed in the MCA building for interference tests. Attempts were made to screen the transmitter, the mains supply was fitted with filters and RF filters were inserted in the aerial input to the receiving equipment, all without success. The MCA receivers operated at a sensitivity of 1mV, and the well-known 'rusty-bolt' effect can cause spurious radiations of this level. After two weeks of tests the Snaefell site was abandoned, and the decision made to locate a caravan installation just outside the main town of Douglas. The site at Carnane had been used by the RAF during the War, and there existed a mains supply and a 60 ft wooden tower which could accommodate both the transmitting dipoles and the Holme Moss receiving aerials. The target date for the commencement of the service was as soon before Christmas as possible.

The installation went well and the service commenced about a week ahead of Christmas, the weather up till then had been fine and dry and then it started to rain and with the first shower the received vision signal was completely marred by mains-type interference bars. The Carnane site was a large hillock with a clear view to the East over the sea towards Holme Moss, but on the West side of the site ran a 33kV electricity transmission line. Being fairly near to the sea, the insulators of the transmission line were subject to slight sea spray, and therefore a deposit of salt which with the first shower of rain caused spark tracking across the insulators. On investigation it was revealed that this section of transmission line was notorious for this tracking but to eliminate this fault by re-stringing with special insulators could not be justified economically.

Situated down the western slope of Carnane was a farmhouse and after a polite approach it was established that the Holme Moss reception was free of the interference as the farm was screened from the offending transmission line by the slope of the land. A small room was rented in the farmhouse, receiving aerials erected, receivers installed and 400 yards of co-axial cable laid just below the surface across the fields to get the video signal to the transmitters. Appropriate frequency correction was applied to compensate for the loss in this long length of cable. So after two days, interference free transmissions were resumed and this ad-hoc arrangement continued for a number of years until it was superseded by a receiving point on Snaefell and a microwave link down to Carnane.

The saga of the Isle of Man came to a satisfactory conclusion just in time for the 1953 Christmas Festivities.

ALEXANDRA PALACE REPLACEMENT

By 1955 the transmitters at Alexandra Palace were nearing the end of their useful lives, they were some twenty years old and replacement was necessary. The 1952 Stockholm Conference had agreed to a 500kW ERP maximum for the London station, and it was decided to build a completely new station. The site of the old Crystal Palace on Sydenham Hill in South London was chosen, from where it was estimated that in addition to Greater London, coverage of Kent, Surrey and parts of Sussex would be possible. Unlike the other four high power stations, Crystal Palace was not required to carry VHF/FM services as the Wrotham station in Kent provided these. Crystal Palace radiated a vestigial sideband signal in line with all the other post war stations, whereas Alexandra Palace had radiated a double side band signal.

It was the first main station to depart from the established practice of using a high power main transmitter and a medium power reserve, feeding a relatively low gain antenna. The new design utilised two medium power transmitters and a high gain antenna, with each transmitter feeding a separate half of the aerial; the system was two completely separate and identical halves. It was this arrangement that produced what was to become known as the "Penge Effect." Penge is an area close to Crystal Palace, which it was soon discovered suffered from a highly erratic signal, eventually identified as being due to random changes occurring in the parameters of the feeds between the two halves of the transmitting aerial. At that time, the importance of using a diplexer in such an arrangement had not been fully appreciated, and one was hastily fitted!

The complex high gain aerial system required a support structure of considerable mechanical stability, and a substantial 700 ft tower weighing 450 tons was erected. In November 1957, its aerodynamic stability was tested using six reaction rockets mounted at 630 ft. The tower deflection was measured as a thrust of over two tons was imparted to the structure. The result of the test showed an amplitude of the oscillation at the thrust level of some 20 cms either side of the vertical.

Low Power Band I Relay Stations

The first low power Band I television relay station used a BBC-designed valve transposer producing two watts, and it was installed at Folkestone in 1958. The equipment was designed to fit into a metal weathertight cabinet which could be bolted to a concrete plinth, no building was provided so the maintenance engineers worked in the open. Maintenance teams were provided with a set of metal poles and a canvas canopy which could be erected over the cabinet, these were rarely used due to their tendency to get carried away in the slightest breeze!

The last of the Band I 405 line Transmitting Stations was opened at Llanelli in 1970, by which time there were 107 stations carrying the service. Following a phased closing of the Band I network, the service was finally closed in 1984 when the remaining transmitter at Crystal Palace was switched off.

Colour Television

Immediately after the war, Research Department carried out experimental work using various systems until 1953, when the American NTSC System was examined. It was decided that this system offered the best prospect, and work began to adapt it to the UK 405 line standard. Experimental transmissions commenced in October 1955 using the medium power 5kW reserve transmitter at Alexandra Palace, and a low power 500W transmitter at Kingswood Warren. The latter operated on channel 5 and was used in conjunction with a mobile receiving van for local field trials. Operating on this particular channel enabled the tests to be carried out during normal television hours.

The test transmissions from Alexandra Palace were radiated nightly after the close-down of normal programme, selected observers equipped with colour receivers were required to complete questionnaires designed to gather information on colour performance, compatibility and reverse compatibility.

Due to the limited reception area of these lower power transmissions they were soon curtailed and the tests transferred to Crystal Palace where the newly installed transmitters were then in service.

It is interesting to note that there were only a limited number of specially made receivers available to monitor these tests, and being before the universal use of semiconductors the receivers were not small, containing a number of iron-cored components and of course thermionic valves. The screen utilised a 12 inch RCA shadow mask tube and the complete set measured about 3 ft square by 4 ft high and required two men to lift it.

THE INTRODUCTION OF UHF TRANSMISSION

In 1958 it was recommended by the Pilkington Committee that colour television should await the introduction of the proposed 625 line Band IV and V transmissions. In anticipation of the eventual commencement of these transmissions the BBC hired (and eventually purchased) two prototype transmitters that EMI were developing. These transmitters were installed at Crystal Palace, with the objective of assessing the differences in propagation and reception between Band I and the new higher frequencies, and from this information determine the transmitter power and the aerial gain required when eventually the colour service commenced. The opportunity was also taken to evaluate the different colour systems that were being developed.

The transmitters were both of similar design with peak vision power of 10kW and the companion sound equipment set to 2.5kW C.W. i.e. peak output of 10kW at 100% amplitude modulation. The output stage of each transmitter was a high power Klystron with three stage resonators fitted externally. This was the first time that this type of 'tube' had been used in the UK for a broadcast transmitter and a complete new technology and vocabulary had to be learnt. Engineers had to adapt to cathodes being at high negative potential with earthed anodes, cavity resonators, adjustments to body currents, focus coils and collector current all of which are now in common usage but were novel in 1958.

The vision/sound combining unit incorporated the vestigial sideband shaping filter again using cavity resonators with the V.S.B. resonators being temperature stabilised to within 1°C by a heated water system. The aerial system also involved new technology for the engineers with an elliptical waveguide feeding an helical aerial which was mounted on the top structure of the 700 ft Crystal Palace mast.

The complete system produced a peak vision radiated power of 200kW ERP which was comparable with the radiated power of the Band I service thus enabling a direct comparison to be made of the coverage of the two systems.

The test transmissions commenced on 27 March 1958 using the 405 line standard and these were followed on the 5th May by modifying the system to the 625 line standard with FM sound. For the latter the transmitter power was reduced to 2kW.

Then followed an extensive period of tests in which the various proposed colour systems were radiated. First was the 625 line adaptation of the American NTSC standard, then the French proposed SECAM followed by the German PAL system. Various minor modifications to the three standards were proposed and tested to eliminate their defects of colour reproduction. The final decision by the Government in 1966 was that colour should be on 625 lines only, using the PAL system. The majority of the European countries would also adopt the PAL system. The 'battle of the standards' as it became known has been well documented in various technical journals.

It is interesting to note that for the early colour tests use was made of films produced for advertising purposes by industrial companies such as British Petroleum, Shell, BICC etc. as this overcame any payments for copyright. The latter firm, which built the Crystal Palace mast, produced a film called the Phoenix Tower which documented the history of the original Crystal Palace building with its twin towers, the use of the site by Baird for his early experiments with television, the fire that destroyed it in 1936, and finally the resurrection of the site and the erection of the mast. This film was very appropriate for the test transmissions.

Tests were also carried out using an experimental UHF transmitter at Pontop Pike, but in this case the main objective was to study propagation characteristics, and this provided valuable data for the effective service planning of UHF television in the UK.

The Government decided in 1962 that the UHF frequency band should be used to provide four programmes of higher definition 625-line television (BBC1, BBC2, Independent Television and a fourth channel which at that time was unspecified).

In 1963 agreement was reached by the BBC and the ITA (Independent Television Authority) on the responsibility for construction and maintenance of the UHF stations that were to be built and on the way in which the costs should be shared. This arrangement was formalised many years later in the Site Sharing Agreement with ntl[7].

The BBC2 service commenced in monochrome from Crystal Palace in April 1964 by which time the two EMI klystron equipments had been modified to operate in parallel for the vision and two 10kW FM transmitters supplied by Pye had been installed for the sound. The opening had been planned for the 20th April but due to a prolonged and wide spread power failure in West London that blacked out Television Centre, the commencement of the service was delayed until the next day. Later that year transmissions commenced from Sutton Coldfield, and within seven years there were no less than 33

---

[7] ntl is now predominantly a cable TV company, but part of it was formed from the Independent Broadcasting Authority (formerly the ITA).

UHF main stations and 40 relay stations in service, giving a population coverage of about 91%.

The BBC1 service was duplicated on UHF from 1969 and by 1971 the coverage was 87% of the population, with service being provided from 27 main stations and 19 relay stations. In order to avoid the expense of providing separate programme feeds for the 405-line and 625-line transmitters, a BBC-designed standards converter was installed at each main station, which converted from 625 to 405-line. In its day, this was an extremely advanced piece of technology.

The introduction of colour into the BBC2 programme didn't formally occur until December 1967. By 1971 there were 1.5 million colour receivers. This change to colour licences produced a massive increase of revenue for the BBC which, once again, was made possible through expansion of coverage by BBC Transmission.

MAST COLLAPSE

In March 1969, the 1,265 ft mast at the ITA transmitting station at Emley Moor collapsed, causing disruption to the BBC 2 service. A much reduced service was established two days later, but it took 18 months to restore the full power service from a new concrete tower provided by the ITA.

SOUND-IN-SYNCS

Prior to 1970, television sound was distributed using individual 'music circuits' provided by the Post Office. However this was replaced by the world's first integrated television sound system, commonly known as 'Sound-in-Syncs' or SiS. This was developed by the BBC's Research/Design Departments and, when installed at BBC Transmission sites, the result was a large saving in operating expenditure and an improvement in reliability. Basically the system converted sound into digital format and interleaved it with the vision signal so that the combination could be sent along the same vision circuits.

Teletext

Teletext was pioneered by BBC Research Department and the BBC's Ceefax service was introduced into service during the late 1970s. Although theoretically this signal should have passed through the television distribution network and transmitters without any extra work by BBC Transmission, in practice there was a problem as impairments that had negligible effect on the picture had a significant effect on Ceefax. As a result, Ceefax regenerators were installed at transmitting stations and much work was done to improve the alignment of transmitters.

NICAM STEREO SOUND FOR TELEVISION

Around 1980, BBC Research Department pioneered the broadcasting of stereo sound for television, using digital transmission (Analogue stereo television sound was in service in other countries at this time, but the quality was inferior). This system had to cope with the imperfections of propagation to domestic antennas and TV sets, so NICAM728 (a ruggedised version of the NICAM system used for radio distribution) was developed for the purpose and the bitstream was digitally modulated onto a new sound carrier.

Around 1990, after 20 years service, the original Sound-in-Syncs system was replaced by a new design of stereo Sound-in-Syncs, using the ruggedised NICAM system mentioned above. The 'sound' signal is thus carried digitally from studio to listener and it was probably the first digital terrestrial broadcast service in the world.

LOW POWER UHF TV RELAY STATIONS

By 1996, BBC Transmission had 575 UHF TV relay stations producing 2 Watts per service and 285 producing 10 Watts per service. This was the result of a site acquisition and equipment installation programme which started in the late 1960's. At this time all the transmitting stations built to date were comparatively large, high powered and expensive, so a new approach was needed. There was no prospect of the cost per head of population served being as low as it was for the higher power stations, but strenuous efforts were made to minimise the capital cost of the relay stations and minimise the maintenance effort required. At the time, no equipment was available commercially which could offer the required specification, reliability and low cost, so 'transposers' (combination of receiver and transmitter, in simple form) were designed in-house by BBC Designs Department.

The original UHF relay stations opened around 1969 before suitable transistors were available. For this new application parametric upconverters were used, but they were very tricky to adjust and were abandoned for future designs in favour of new transistors that were becoming available. The first fully transistorised UHF transposer was known as the 'Wine Press' due to the way in which its modules were clamped together, but only a few units were made.

The first BBC designed transposer to be used in large quantities (600) was colloquially known as 'Blue Streak', due to its blue colour! Then, in 1982, a new BBC design, colloquially known as 'Silver Streak' was used, bringing the total to about 1,340. By 1992 other, commercially designed, transposers became available.

Costs were also minimised through the use of glass fibre reinforced plastic cubicles to house the equipment, and wooden poles or simple lattice structures to support the antennas. The relay station building programme continued until 1997, with BBC Transmission providing half of the sites but fitting BBC1 and BBC2 equipment at them all. (IBA/ntl did likewise for ITV and Channel 4).

VALVES, KLYSTRONS AND TRANSISTORS

In the early days of UHF television, there was really only one device capable of providing 40kW of output power from a Watt or two of input power (the limit of solid state technology at the time) – the klystron. BBC Transmission used these devices extensively during the sixties, seventies and eighties. During this period the tubes were improved to enhance their electrical efficiency, and BBC Transmission was involved in much development work in this field. Mod-anode tapping, mod-anode pulsing, grid pulsing and grid full-time modulation were all employed for experimental work or programme service. Subsequently BCD (Beam Control Device) pulsing became the norm and all the BBC's later klystron UHF transmitters used this technique, saving some 20% of the electricity bill.

In the seventies and eighties high power tetrode valves were developed for UHF. These offered greater efficiency, ease of tuning, and lower cost, but in general didn't have as long a life as the klystron. They had their place, however, particularly at the 10 to 25kW power range and BBC Transmission operated a number of tetrode transmitters. Some of these were in containers and transportable, to be used if a major station had a serious problem.

In about 1990, high power solid state UHF transmitters started appearing, and BBC Transmission subsequently purchased a number of these, mostly for 10kW output power requirements.

DIGITAL BROADCASTING

In April 1996, Crystal Palace started test transmissions of Digital Terrestrial Television (DTT), using a new internationally agreed specification, marking a new era in television broadcasting.

ILLUSTRATION
PAGES

Picture 1: Lord Puttnam (left) receiving 2LO, the BBC's original transmitter, on behalf of the National Museum of Science and Industry. It was presented by Gavyn Davies (BBC Chairman) and Peter Abery (Crown Castle UK President & Managing Director) on 7th November 2002.

1. R.M. Owen
2. J.M.A. Cameron
3. A.G.D. West (77)
4. H. Bishop
5. P.P. Eckersley(3)
6. H.L. Kirke (77)
7. P.A. Florence(120)
8. V.A.M. Bulow
9. Captain Frost
10. H.H. Thompson
11. A. Cameron
12. H.S. Walker (77)
13. C.H. Colborn(143)
14. A.S. Atkins (78)
15. L. Hotine (108)
16. R.J. Bird
17. C.G. Harding
18. L.A.V. Everitt
19. F.N. Calver (101)
20. R.H. Lyne
21. A.N. Jinman
22. A. Fielder
23. A.C. Shaw
24. H.F. Humphreys(120)
25. A. Birch
26. E. G. Chadder
27. F. M. Dimmock(78)
28. J. Beveridge
29. R. H. Wood
30. L.W. Hayes (77)
31. H.A. Hankey
32. D.A.G. Curd
33. J.K.A. Nicholson
34. Commander Carter
35. C.W. Ingram
36. J.A. Cooper
37. A.B. Howe (77)
38. B.H. Vernon (120)
39. Baynham Honri
40. L. Harvey

Picture 2: BBC Engineering Conference at the Institution of Electrical Engineers, 1926
Page numbers are shown to the right of each person mentioned in the text.

Picture 3: BBC Engineering Conference at the Institution of Electrical Engineers, 1987

Picture 4: "The old gentleman", Daventry G5XX, the World's first high power long wave station, designed for broadcasting 1925

Picture 5: Daventry 5GB the forerunner to the regional scheme, c1927

Picture 6: Sender 1, one of the two original short wave transmitters installed in 1932 at Daventry Empire Station, c1942

*Picture 7: A Technical Assistant (Female) changing a valve at Daventry, c1942
An early example of Equal Opportunities at the BBC!*

Picture 8: Diesels at Daventry, c1960

Picture 9: The imposing façade at the front of Brookmans Park, a Grade II Listed Building, c1970

Picture 10: One of the original twin transmitters at Brookmans Park, with 2LO in the foreground, c1970

Picture 11: Third Programme transmitter at Daventry: combining circuits, c1950

Picture 12: Woofferton HF station, c1980

*Picture 13: Wavechanging a Marconi BD272 HF transmitter, c1980
see section on Post-War HF Reconstruction*

Picture 14: Transmitter hall at Droitwich, c1985

Picture 15: First generation Band II transmitter at Pontop Pike, c1985

Picture 16: Band II combiner

*Picture 17: Band II antennas
(below the TV cylinder) c1990*

Picture 18 (above): 13 Channel PCM and Band II drives

Picture 19 (below): Band II hall at Sutton Coldfield, c1990

*Picture 20: A high power TV transmitter during maintenance, c1970
The klystron amplifier is on the right*

*Picture 21: Norman Shacklady (co-editor)
tuning a 40kW vision klystron at Crystal Palace, c1973*

Picture 22: Martin Ellen (co-editor) demonstrating the newly designed "Silver Streak" TV transposer at a Designs Department exhibition, c1980

Picture 23: A typical site in Northern Scotland, c1990

Picture 24: BBC Transmission's last major transmitting station being opened by HRH Duke of Edinburgh on 30th October 1996 (Sender 703 is on the right below).
The 'Spirit House' (Saan Phra Phum, in Thai) on the left of the main picture shows the mix of Buddhism and Animism that exists throughout Thailand. Every Thai building has to have one, as a place for the spirits of the site to live. Otherwise it is said that the spirits would go to live inside the building and cause trouble. To convince the spirits that they should live in the Spirit House, the Thai people make daily offerings of food, flowers, etc, to make it attractive.

SECTION 5 AUTOMATION

UNATTENDED OPERATION

On 1 December 1947, BBC Transmission opened its first unattended transmitting station. It was at Farnley, four miles south west of Leeds and it broadcast the Third programme at low power on MF. This was the first step towards the present day domestic transmitter network which operates on a completely unattended basis. Further stations followed at Edinburgh (1948), Glasgow (1949) and Newcastle (1950).

The period 1950-70 saw the development of automating the transmitter network and, with considerable foresight, Transmission decided against using remote control in favour of automatic operation. Remote control requires people to make decisions, whereas automatic operation using instrumentation, coupled with sensible logic and monitoring, could lead to a higher degree of reliability. The choice was the right one, and other organisations both in the UK and abroad who opted for the alternative, experienced many problems which the BBC was to avoid.

The first high power (150kW) unattended transmitting station was housed in the original "5XX" building at Daventry and it took over from the Third Programme transmitter at Droitwich in March 1950. It became unattended from January 1952, but a quick response to faults was available from staff at the HF Daventry station about 150 metres away. An unusual feature of this installation was a 2.4 km open wire concentric feeder to a mast at Dodford; this arrangement being necessary to avoid disturbance to the radiation pattern of the HF antennas at Daventry.

By the early 1970's, the trend of minimising costs by establishing unattended transmitting stations had gathered pace and was made all the more necessary by the large number of UHF TV stations required. In order to achieve unattended operation, there were three main requirements: resilient transmission systems, remote monitoring and availability of mobile maintenance staff.

Resilient transmission systems were designed and built in such a way that the service from each transmitter would continue in the event of almost any single fault. According to the nature of the fault, the signal may be radiated at reduced power, but the services were planned in such a way that most listeners and viewers in the service area would still receive a satisfactory signal.

Remote monitoring initially used the tried and tested Telephone Indicator Panel (TIP) using mechanical relays to produce a sequence of dots and dashes. The TIP was only a passive device and relied on routine calls being made from a nearby attended transmitter site to interrogate the state of the remote site.

In 1967 the first of the Automatic Fault Reporters were introduced which could initiate a call to the attended site in the event of a fault occurring. These early devices used a loop of multi-track tape with voice messages recorded on two tracks and telephone dialling pulses on another track, they also incorporated a solid state version of the TIP which gave more detailed equipment status. Problems with the tape drive on these machines often meant they were less reliable than the equipment they were monitoring! Many of the operational difficulties encountered with this and subsequent BBC designed units related to the manual telephone exchanges then in use. Many an unwary telephone operator would attempt to talk to the tape message or not follow the taped instructions – "This is an automatic device on Stanton St John 230, please connect me to Four Oaks 4666".

Monitoring centres

Automatic Fault Reporters (AFRs) using data communications eventually provided the fundamental means of remote monitoring, and these units signalled to the first Monitoring and Information Centre (MIC) at Kirk o'Shotts which opened in 1975. Over the next four years, further MICs were opened at Wenvoe, Sutton Coldfield, Crystal Palace and Holme Moss. Microprocessors became commercially available during this period and the MICs represented the first large scale application of this technology in the BBC.

Data from AFRs enabled the importance of reports to be categorised and displayed on-screen to the MIC operators, who would then take appropriate action. The system registered when there was just one person working alone on site and when the last 'safety call' had been made. If such a call was overdue that fact would at once appear on the MIC screen for checking and if necessary appropriate safety procedures would be initiated.

Arrays of carefully oriented aerials feeding monitoring receivers enabled MIC operators to check the services being radiated by all the stations within range. Some of the medium power stations such as Pontop Pike and North Hessary Tor were designated Monitoring and Collection Points (MCP's) and were usually staffed in the day. In addition to processing data from AFRs, these too were equipped with receivers that were able to monitor stations within range.

The MICs were very successful and remained in operation until 1995 when a central Technical Operations Centre (TOC) at Warwick replaced them all. When the MICs went into service they used leading edge technology, but data communications and computer processing advanced very considerably during their service life, so the TOC was able to meet the demand for far more extensive monitoring at lower cost. Although the TOC is not able to carry out much direct off-air monitoring, it can collect detailed technical quality data from all appropriate transmitters and this arrangement has proved to work well. In the years leading up to privatisation the required transmission service levels became more complex and the TOC was able to meet the demand for detailed performance information.

Mobile Maintenance Teams

Preventative maintenance and fault clearance on the first unattended transmitters was carried out by engineers from nearby studio centres, as it was thought that this could be fitted in with their other duties. It was found, however, that an improvement in the breakdown record of these stations could be achieved using staff specialising in work of this kind. As a result, in January 1951, Transmission's first two mobile maintenance teams were formed, one based at Stagshaw and the other at Moorside Edge. Soon afterwards a third team was formed at Bartley, near Southampton. Each team consisted of two engineers who were issued with an estate car to carry the necessary equipment.

It was arranged that each of the early low power MF 'unattended' stations were assigned a TA (Technical Assistant) who visited the site for an hour a day, five days a week. At other times they were expected to keep a general watch at home on the output of their stations during transmission hours, using a receiver specially modified to sound an alarm if the local transmitter failed. Each station was also provided with a 'telephone indicator panel' to give a coded reply when the station number was dialled.

Many of the 'Technical Assistants In Attendance' were retired members of BBC Transmission staff and, in return for a technically interesting job and some addition to their pensions, they performed a useful service at a time when the development of unattended transmitter operation was going through its initial phase. One of the most difficult aspects for a newly appointed TA in A was to be able to lock the station door, having completed the daily duty, and walk away in the knowledge that no one was left inside! This was quite contrary to all one's trained instinct and experience, and for many it took some getting used to. (Colloquially these TA's in A were known as 'Cabbage Patch Engineers').

By 1960 all new transmitting stations were designed to operate without staff, but with fault and maintenance visits carried out by a mobile team based in the area. The original 3 mobile maintenance teams were replaced by 5 two man teams based at Crystal Palace, Washford, Wenvoe, Holme Moss and Kirk o'Shotts. They were renamed 'Transmitter Maintenance Team' (TMT) and they covered vast geographical areas. It was common practice for the team to leave the base on a Monday morning and not return until Friday afternoon, travelling hundreds of miles on the road and spending nights in hotels or B&B – and it was not unknown to have to spend the night in a transmitter building!

By 1971 there were about 40 'attended' transmitting stations and, in addition to the staff in attendance, there were 13 TMTs each with at least three engineers.

One of the main problems encountered by these teams was a lack of suitable test equipment. It was either simply not available on the commercial market or it was too large, bulky and expensive. As a result BBC Designs Department produced a Comprehensive UHF Test Set which was manufactured by BBC Equipment Department and these units were supplied to all team bases. The equipment was densely packed and somewhat temperamental, but it was a major advance on other equipment available at the time and some units were still in use 20 years later. However as time passed much more equipment became available commercially and teams became well equipped.

The introduction of MICs led to all domestic transmitting stations becoming unattended, but some of the larger stations needed to be re-engineered at considerable expense before they could become completely unattended, and in the case of a few large MF sites this process was not complete until 1991. In 1975 all staff at UK domestic sites became 'mobile' with the UK HF sites following in 1985. Eventually, 28 mobile team bases each covered much smaller geographical areas than the five 1960's teams, but with a dramatic increase in the number of sites.

Increase in efficiency

The large increase in the number of transmitters is illustrated on page 74, together with a line showing the reduction in operations and maintenance staff from 1,150 to less than 600 (including both domestic and World Service).

Mobile Team Transport

The early Teams used 7 cwt commercial vans painted in smart BBC green livery. Portable test gear protection was provided by thick foam rubber sheets on the floor of the van together with loose sheets between the equipment. With the advent of an increasing number of remote TV transmitter sites often with rough access tracks, and the need to carry more test equipment and spares, the 4-wheel-drive Land-Rover soon became the universal team vehicle. The long-

74

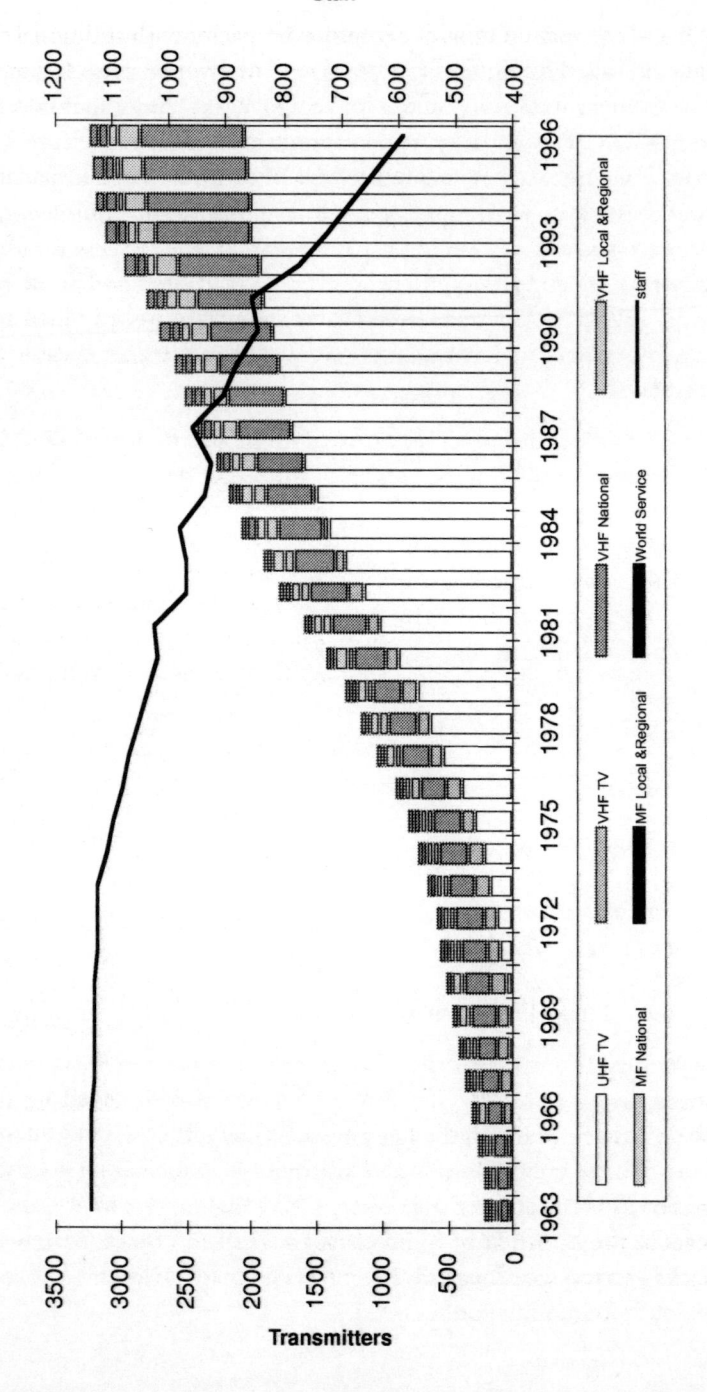

wheel-base version provided improved capacity, with additional shelf racks installed for equipment stowage. The Land-Rovers frequently spent much of their lives fully loaded with test equipment covering the full spectrum of transmission equipment in service, allowing the travelling engineers to tackle all types of maintenance and faults.

As the staff on Teams increased in line with the expansion of unattended transmitting stations, additional vehicles were provided. They included the 1,000cc engined BMC Mini-van, and hatch-back and estate cars such as the 1,800cc Austin Maxi hatchback, the Ford Sierra estate, the Austin Montego estate. These vehicles were very suitable for visits to transmitter sites with surfaced access tracks, and where the carriage of heavy loads was not required. In accordance with BBC vehicle policy to 'Buy British and support UK industry', viability tests were carried out on a number of other UK built vehicles such as the Leyland and Commer 10/15 cwt forward control vans, the 4-wheel-drive Nissan Patrol and Peugeot estate cars over the years. These viability tests generally lasted between 2 weeks and 12 months and vehicles were often moved around the country to allow maintenance teams in different geographical areas to try vehicles over as wide a range of terrain as possible.

As transmitters became more reliable, the need for frequent maintenance reduced. At the same time, test equipment became more compact and the requirement for constantly loaded vehicles diminished, allowing the use of more saloon and estate cars. The 4-wheel-drive Land-Rover was superseded initially by the more suitable and comfortable, but more expensive, Range-Rover and subsequently the Land-Rover Discovery. The department also took advantage of major discount terms available to fleet buyers and standardised on the Peugeot estate and saloon cars as non 4-wheel drive vehicles for all Teams.

Some teams operating in the more remote areas of Scotland used very specialised vehicles for a number of years. A large, tractor wheeled Land-Rover, known locally as 'Goliath' and initially developed as an 'all terrain vehicle' for the Forestry Commission, was used for some years in the North West of Scotland to travel to sites without access tracks - its top speed was 25/30mph on the narrow single track roads which it frequently commanded.

The only tracked vehicle used by the Teams was also used in Scotland, to gain all weather access to a strategically important remote transmitter sited in south west Scotland. The versatility of the engineers in this particular team area was frequently put to the test, when the vehicle tracks were shed on the steep rough boulder strewn route between the purpose built road-side garage and the transmitting station. Subsequently a road-way was built, at very considerable expense, allowing more straightforward 4-wheel-drive access.

The high cost of vehicle re-sprays heralded the end of the very smart standardised BBC Green and subsequently BBC Grey livery on all the Team vehicles, and the loss of the 'BBC' logo and lettering. The vehicle manufacturers' standard range of colours were accepted, with small 'BBC Transmitters' stickers added as the only identity in the front and rear windows. However a small number of Range-Rovers fitted with specialised transmission survey equipment did retain the full BBC livery and logos. These vehicles were used for reception surveys and attendance at exhibitions and shows throughout the country where the BBC image and identity were essential in terms of public relations.

SECTION 6 ASSOCIATED DEPARTMENTS

Like any major enterprise that stays at the forefront in its field of activity, there were many changes in the organisation of BBC Engineering. Most of this book deals with the systems that were managed and operated by Transmitter Department, as it used to be called, but this section gives a glimpse of several departments that were closely associated with Transmitter Department. ('BBC Transmission' was created in 1987 and consisted of Transmitter Department, Communications Department and Transmitter Capital Projects Department.)

The contributors elected to include many names in this section. Relatively few names appear elsewhere in the book, the problem being that a very large number of people worked in Transmission making it unwieldy to include all of the prominent people.

The early days

As early as 1923 a development section under H W Litt had been established, directly responsible to Captain A G D West the Assistant Chief Engineer, which consisted of a number of development engineers plus a mechanic. In February 1924 H L Kirke was appointed Senior Development Engineer and Captain West became Assistant Chief Engineer (Research).

By the end of 1925 the Research and Development sections based in and around Savoy Hill consisted of the following senior personnel:-

A G D West	Assistant Chief Engineer (Research)
H L Kirke	Head of Development Section & Senior Development Engineer
L W Hayes	Assistant to S.D.E (Admin and Finance)
H S Walker	Radio Projects, Workshops and Drawing Office
R C Patrick	Test Room
A B Howe	P.I.E., Radio Receivers, C R Oscilloscopes and A.F. Test Equipment

A S Attkins   Lines and Switching

J A Partridge   Keston Receiving Station

The following year AGD West became Senior Research Engineer, and H L Kirke Senior Development Engineer, both responsible to N Ashbridge who was appointed Assistant Chief Engineer.

In 1927 Research and Development moved to new premises in South London, Avenue House, Clapham. Lines and Switching moved to separate offices in Cecil Chambers near to Savoy Hill.

In 1928 A.S. Atkins resigned and H.B. Rantzen took over as Head of Lines and Switching. In the same year A.G.D. West and both his assistants also resigned.

By the early 1930's separate Departments had evolved comprising:-

> **Station Design and Installation Department** (SDID), (under B.N. MacClarty) based at Gt Portland Street, responsible for transmitting station equipment, diesel engines, generators, batteries and power and lighting in all premises.
>
> **Lines Department,** (under H. B. Rantzen) based at Scotts Hotel Duchess Street, responsible for close liaison with the Post Office, and for equipment associated with line testing, equalisation and repeaters.
>
> **Research Department** (RD), (under H.L. Kirke) based at Nightingale Square, Balham.
>
> **Equipment Department** (ED), (under F.M. Dimmock) based at Avenue House, Clapham, comprising:-
>
> | | |
> |---|---|
> | Administration:- | Central Stores, Transport & Finance |
> | Technical:- | Workshop, Test Room, Drawing Office and the design of various studio and transmitter equipment. |

In 1931 the Designs Section transferred to Equipment Department.

Prior to the outbreak of World War II, it was thought that there would be little demand for new design and installation work. Research Dept was evacuated to Bagley Croft in Oxfordshire, SDID to Droitwich, and Equipment Dept was split between Hampton House, Evesham and the Langham Hotel in London. When the war finally started, emergency work was already underway in Broadcasting House, Wood Norton and other premises, and in fact the requirement for design and installation work expanded considerably throughout the war.

With the end of hostilities, SDID, combined with the design section of ED, and was formed into a new department designated Designs and Installation Department (DID) Later, in 1946, it was renamed Planning and Installation Department (P&ID) with the design aspect moved to a new department called Designs Department under H.B.Rantzen.

The following year Research Department moved to Kingswood Warren and in 1950 Designs Department (under Dr.A.R.A.Rendall) moved to Western House in Great Portland Street.

In 1965 the Planning and Installation Department was split into two separate sections and renamed Studio Planning and Installation Department (SPID) and Transmitter Planning and Installation Department (TPID). Each was to be renamed still further in 1970 and they became Studio Capital Projects Department (SPID) and Transmitter Capital Projects Department (TCPD).

RESEARCH DEPARTMENT

The post war period was an extremely busy time for Research Department. The following notable dates give some idea of the work carried out. The items shown in bold are concerned with transmission - nearly half of them!

1945   **VHF/FM: First transmission tests from Alexandra Palace to determine the range and general possibilities of an ultra shortwave frequency modulated broadcasting service.**
        Type 'D' disk recorder developed and introduced into service.

1946	Television: Proposals made for the setting up of a complete experimental picture channel for the study of fundamental problems.
1947	**Work on scale model cylindrical slot antennas for Wrotham and Sutton Coldfield.**
	Early measurements on the magnetic properties of recording tape.
1948	Kingswood Warren acquired. First Staff move from Bagley Court and Nightingale Square.
	Copenhagen Plan to discuss LF/MF frequency allocation in Europe.
	Wavelength changes in the MF band to be adopted, necessitating many changes of transmitting antennas.
1949	Building of Kingswood Warren B-Block commenced.
	Work commences on producing a smaller, lighter, higher sensitivity commentators microphone, the L2, to replace the L1 (produced by research in 1937). This new design developed commercially by STC and Coles.
	Television: Simple colour channel set up.
1950	**Television: Comparison demonstrations of 405-line and 625-line pictures to CCIR Study Group 11.**
1951	Open Day: Demonstrations of experimental colour television, and high quality sound from magnetic tape being two of the main exhibits.
	Research Department builds and demonstrates the first television standards converter, using a special camera tube and a long persistence CRT picture monitor.
1952	**Stockholm Conference to discuss VHF TV and Radio frequency allocations in Europe.**
	A twin Channel version of the first standards converter used to convert French 819-line pictures to the 405-line UK standard; enabling British viewers to see pictures simultaneously with the French over temporary Paris to London link.
1953	Suppressed-frame telerecording equipment designed; used to record pictures of the Queen's Coronation.
	PGS/1 ribbon-microphone designed and used for recording the Coronation Service. This microphone was selected for commercial production and subsequently marketed by STC as the 4038.
1954	16mm colour film and slide scanner designed and built.
1955	**Wrotham Transmitter opened. First regular VHF/FM service of Home, Light and Third programmes.**

1956	Demonstrations of 405-line NTSC colour television to CCIR Study Group 11 and many other important bodies.
1957	**First experimental 625-line television transmissions at UHF in Band V from Crystal Palace.**
1958	VERA (Vision Electronic Recording Apparatus). Demonstration of Research Department's video tape recorder on 'Panorama' on 14th April. The first video tape recorder ever used by the BBC. Unfortunately, its life was very short, being overtaken by the creation of the Ampex VR100A from the USA.
	First investigations into stereophonic broadcasts (Crosby system). Experimental broadcasts begin using television sound transmitters for the right hand channel and the third programme transmitters for the left hand channel.
1959	Investigations into television picture storage begin.
1960	The first prototype multi-standard converter used to convert to the American standard pictures of Princess Margaret's wedding.
	LS5/1 studio monitoring loudspeaker put into service.
1961	A-Block extension completed – Acoustics Section moves in from Nightingale Square.
	Stockholm Conference on VHF/UHF planning. Detailed proposals for frequency allocations in Bands I, II, III. IV and V submitted by Research Department to the Conference via the Post Office.
1962	Pilkington Committee on Broadcasting issues its report on the future of television broadcasting in the UK.
	First transatlantic colour television link by satellite from Goonhilly Down to Andover, Maine, using Research Department slide scanner, 16th June.
	UHF monochrome and colour television field trials from Crystal Palace to determine, among other things, the problems involved in transmitting more than one programme from the same site using the 625-line standard.
	Experimental transmissions of the Zenith-GE stereophonic system on a single VHF channel from the Wrotham transmitter.
1963	First proposals for electronic field-store standards converter made and patents filed.
1964	Line-store standards converter (625 to 405-lines) installed at Television Centre.
	First studies into digital techniques for television.
1965	**Sound-in-Syncs, a method of transmitting audio signals in the television signal line synchronising pulse period, first assessed.**

	Experimental PAL colour transmissions from Crystal Palace.
1966	Colour pictures of the General Election relayed from Television Centre to the USA via the Early Bird satellite.
1967	**BBC 2 transmits first regular colour television service in Europe beginning 2nd December.**
	Investigations into optical spatial filtering techniques in motion picture film printing.
1968	Royal Television Society Geoffrey Parr Award to C.B.B. Wood and his team for inventing TARIF -an electronic colour correction system for colour film.
	Field-store standards converter made its operational debut, converting 525 / 60 NTSC pictures from Mexico City Olympic Games via satellite to 625 / 50 PAL at Television Centre.
	Linear matrices, which improve colour analysis, fitted to operational colour television cameras in studio TC7 at Television Centre.
1969	Queen's Award for Field Store Standards Converter (with Designs Department).
1970	Digital line-store standards converter work commences.
	First attempts at automatic colour balancing of television cameras.
	Investigations into colour optical telerecording begin.
1971	Research Department gives world's first public demonstration of digital recording of stereo audio signals.
	Early experiments on digital video recording.
1972	**Teletext experiments begin; BBC announces proposed new service called CEEFAX.**
	Quadraphonic recordings made at the 50th Anniversary Promenade Concert at the Royal Albert Hall.
1973	Sub-Nyquist sampling technique for composite PAL television signals invented.
1974	**Queen's Award for Sound-in-Syncs (with Designs Department).**
	Regional Administrative Broadcasting Conference (First Session) in Geneva, to re-plan the LF & MF bands throughout Europe, Africa, Asia and Australasia. Research Department provides considerable input via CCIR and EBU working parties. World coastline and country boundary databank compiled.
	Agreement of Unified Data Standard for teletext in the UK.
	Quadraphony demonstrated at IEE.

Research Department demonstrates world's first *digital* television recorder at the International Broadcasting Convention, Brighton.

1975 Successful transmission of digital television signals over 120 Mbit/s PO link between Guildford and Portsmouth.

1978 **LF & MF national frequency plans resulting from the Regional Administrative Broadcasting Conference 1974/5 implemented.**

'Teletrak' special effects equipment used for World Cup football.

Research Department demonstrates first broadcast quality 34 Mbit/s PAL digital television pictures at the International Broadcasting Convention, Brighton.

First digital stereophonic sound broadcast experiments from Pontop Pike (in Band I).

Demonstrations of VHF radio data reception (later to be known as RDS) given on 'Tomorrow's World'.

Director of Engineering's Presidential Address to the IEE and at the International Broadcasting Convention, Brighton.

1979 **World Administrative Radio Conference 'WARC 79', Geneva, held to review international agreements on radio frequency spectrum allocation until the end of the century.**

First 60 Mbit/s digital television sound transmissions made via Orbital Test Satellite.

1980 Research Department's graphics computer 'ERIC' demonstrated and licensed for manufacture by Logica as 'Flair'.

1981 Digital television picture stills store, to enable 'grabbed' pictures to be recorded, under development in co-operation with Rank Cintel who dubbed it 'Slide File'.

Mixed polarisation introduced into main London VHF FM transmitter (Wrotham) as part of the re-engineering scheme to improve stereo reception on portables and in cars.

Optical fibre link equipment built to study serial digital communications.

1982 Research Department, Designs Department and Communications Department co-operate in establishing an experimental digital optical fibre link (at 280 Mbit/s) between Television Centre and Lime Grove. Semiconductor laser transmitting equipment built at Research Department in 1981 was used for the tests.

1983 Queen's Award for teletext (with IBA).

1984 The world's first YUV component-coded signals transmitted over a 140 Mbit/s link (London to Birmingham) first used to send PAL coded signals in 1983.

Amplitude Modulation Companding (AMC) tests from the Mangotsfield Radio Bristol transmitter. AMC is a method of reducing the mains power requirement of transmitters and thus making them more economical to run

Video watermarking, a method of electronically labelling television pictures, devised.

First 'all digital' transmission of stereo sound from Crystal Palace using the Research Department proposals of last year for a digital subcarrier. This system later becomes known as NICAM 728.

Research Department's film dirt detection and concealment equipment installed at Television Centre.

1985 405-line television transmissions, first launched in 1936, come to an end.

LF Radio Teleswitching service commences in April. This enables the Electricity Supply Industry to remotely control radio teleswitches in homes, offices and factories in order to optimise power distribution at peak demand times.

1986 HDTV picture store and high line-rate picture monitor demonstrated at the International Broadcasting Convention, Brighton.

1987 Queen's Award for LF Radio Teleswitching (with the Electricity Supply Industry).

World Administrative Radio Conference 'WARC 87', Geneva. Research Department provides support to the World Service in analysing International Frequency Registration Board plans for high frequency broadcasting.

'Art File', the Rank Cintel version of Research Department's add-on graphics system for Slide File, introduced into service.

The Department's digital audio editor demonstrated.

1988 12 GHz radio-camera antenna developed with Television Outside Broadcasts for the Seoul Olympic Games proves highly successful and assists with the first public demonstration of an advanced digital sound broadcasting technique under the auspices of the EBU.

BBC RDS service publicly launched at the Earls Court Radio Show.

Digital audio editing equipment on trial at Broadcasting House.

Acoustic Transmission Suite, for the testing of studio partition and acoustic treatment, completed.

1989 Experimental steerable flat-plate antenna demonstrated receiving new DBS television broadcasts.

Helitrak (automatic helicopter-tracking radio-camera link) successfully demonstrated during the Boat Race.

1990 **Tests of Digital Audio Broadcasting for fixed, mobile and portable reception from Crystal Palace and Kenley. Associated evaluation of various bit-rate reduction codecs.**

Installation of the first digital audio routeing system in Broadcasting House, London (with Design Group and Network Radio).

1991 **Demonstration of Digital Audio Broadcasting (DAB) to the press and other selected parties. DAB compared with the FM service on board a specially adapted coach in Birmingham.**

The NICAM 728 television stereo service was officially launched on BBC 2 during the summer.

The Eureka Project 625 VADIS (Video-Audio Interactive System) commenced, with 12 European partners, to develop world standard digital compression algorithms for Phase 2 of the Motion Picture Experts Group (MPEG).

1992 **Queen's Award for NICAM 728 television stereo system.**

World Administrative Radio Conference 'WARC 92', Torremelinos. Particular attention given to provision of two new frequency bands for HDTV and DAB transmissions.

DAB single-frequency network tests carried out at Kingswood.

Low power digital terrestrial television transmission tests carried out from Crystal Palace.

Tests with switched-horn radio camera carried out at Wembley stadium by Television Outside Broadcasts. Consequently, improvements were incorporated. Commercial exploitation was then sought.

1993 **DAB network of four transmitters set up in the London area and demonstrated to the trade. Government made a frequency band available for possible future DAB broadcasting.**

High power (10kW) field trial of digital terrestrial television from Crystal Palace transmitter. HDTV signal used 34 Mbit/s data rate with 5-channel sound. Good results obtained, even in areas where reception of standard PAL was very poor.

DRACULA system (for unobtrusively providing audio dynamic range compression) now under development.

Com3[8] -Composite Compatible Component system, developed at Kingswood for upgrading PAL / NTSC studios to component quality at minimum cost, now being commercially marketed.

---

[8] This is a registered trademark of Snell & Wilcox Ltd.

1994 Following restructuring with Development Group and the closure of Avenue House, re-named Research and Development Department (R&D).

R&D Service Planning Section at the forefront of planning the DAB broadcasting service, to commence in September 1995. An initial 27-station transmitter construction plan established.

Construction of prototype hardware for constant luminance coding commenced, following the promise shown by simulation work.

Eureka 147 phase II was completed, with the provision of the DAB specification to ETSI and written user guidelines, giving the system protocols. R&D had provided chairmen for four key committees responsible for the DAB standards.

BBC formally announces launch of DAB.

R&D won the International Broadcast & Television Buyer Award for "the most innovative transmission solution" for its work on the high power London DAB Experiment.

1995 **The new Digital Radio service started in September 1995. The system was implemented using technology and support provided by R&D.**

Tests of satellite Digital Radio by R&D using the Mexican Solidaridad satellite were a great success. R&D was pipped at the post for a world first by the Australians who won by a matter of days using their OPTUS satellite.

Demonstrations were given of the new fibre-optic studio routing system developed as part of the COBRA project. It was the first Wavelength and Time Division Multiplexing system used for this purpose.

A new 2D system for Virtual Production was demonstrated for the first time.

The new dynamic range control system for audio broadcasting was demonstrated for the first time.

The Montreux demonstrations of digital television (based on work in RACE dTTb and HDSAT projects) gave the DVB standardisation process a major boost.

The VALIDATE project was set up to test and assess the new DVB standard as it evolves.

The CEPT held a DAB Planning Meeting to allocate spectrum for new digital audio services. A significant contribution was made by the R&D team who provided and operated the computer planning facility for the UK delegation.

The BBC, ITC and ntl commenced preparing a joint plan for digital television broadcasting in the UK.

1996 R&D was transferred from BBC Resources to the Policy and Planning Directorate.

A Digital Television Pilot was set up. This was the first fully compliant test of the new DVB transmission standard.

An end-to-end pilot of a digital transmission chain, using the new 16:9 format, was assembled as part of the Trooping of the Colour broadcasts. These demonstrated the issues involved in linking programmes through a complete production chain from an Outside Broadcast through to two transmitters.

A new multimedia system was demonstrated for Digital Radio.

IBC awards received for work on Virtual Production and techniques for 'mix-minus', a system which removes unwanted audio commentary from a received off-air cue signal.

An Emmy award was received for work carried out in the 1980's on the error feedback system for reducing unwanted quantisation effects in limited accuracy digital signal processing.

1997 BBC Invents the Mole — a tool which minimises distortion in digital signals which are subject to repeated coding and decoding.

First demonstration of *Trumatte* at IBC '97. This is a retro-reflective screen invented at R&D which replaces the traditional blue screen in Virtual Production Studios. At the same time, a new method of measuring the position of the camera in a studio, now called *Free-d*, was demonstrated.

The CEPT Planning Meeting at Chester provides the ground rules for co-ordination of digital terrestrial television services. R&D provided specialists who took on key roles at the meeting.

BBC Web services start. R&D provides the hardware and network communications to support the service, as well as technical guidance on the emerging features of streaming audio, video and push technologies.

1998 Queen's Award to Industry received for R&D's work in motion compensated standards conversion (joint award with Snell & Wilcox).

BBC launches digital satellite television service on 22nd June. R&D provides the system design authority and makes a major contribution to the commissioning of the new studio play out centre.

BBC R&D collaborated with LSI-Logic to produce a new receiver chip set for Digital Terrestrial Television.

Sunday 15 November saw the public launch of digital terrestrial television in the UK. BBC R&D were a key part in the team which delivered the technical infrastructure for this service. [*The system design, engineering, project management, operation and maintenance was provided for the BBC and ONdigital by Crown Castle International (ex BBC Transmission), following hard fought competitive tender.*]

Designs Department

The post war era provided considerable challenges for all the specialist departments and not least for Designs Department. The first priority was the design of audio and video test and measuring equipment which could be used to check the performance of the expanding network of permanent and temporary sound and vision circuits (provided mainly by the Post Office). A portable variable audio-frequency oscillator (PTSlO) had been designed by S.N. Watson and a complete set of audio measuring apparatus was produced by Special Projects Section under F.A. Peachey. This Section also produced Automatic Monitors applicable to short and long audio circuits and staff could then be released from the unrewarding and tedious task of continuously monitoring programmes.

TV Transmission Section under S.N. Watson designed a multi-purpose Test Waveform Generator (TVTG/l) and a Waveform Monitor Type B; meanwhile S.H. Padel developed equipment for the precise measurement of 'Group-delay' - one of several transmission parameters directly associated with picture quality.

The expansion of the Band I TV transmitter network required the use of high-quality vestigial-sideband receivers for both 'rebroadcast' purposes and for measuring transmitter performance. Transmission Section under S.H. Padel undertook this work and J. Shelley designed well-screened multipurpose receivers (TV/REC3 & 3a) to meet these needs. Over 100 of these were manufactured but by 1956 the design was becoming obsolescent and so J. Shelley and J.W. O'Clarey produced a new receiver (TV/REC4) with a watertight masthead mounted pre-amplifier and a delay-corrected intermediate-frequency amplifier. The performance of this receiver was close to the theoretical optimum for a positive modulation vestigial-sideband system.

Meanwhile S.H. Padel and D.C. Savage designed a large range of variable (Bode type) video equalisers and variable group-delay correctors which, when used together, provided an extremely powerful means of improving the overall performance of most types of vision link including international connections.

In 1952 Dr. N.W.Lewis of the P.O. Research Branch proposed the use of video waveform testing to replace the conventional steady-state amplitude and group-delay measurements.

This was an interesting suggestion and TV Transmission Section and P.O. engineers joined in a prolonged series of tests to establish the relationship between waveform response and picture impairment. After many months the 'Pulse and Bar' method of testing was established together with limits for the departure of the waveforms from the original for various lengths of circuit.

The nationwide expansion of 405-line and subsequently 625-line PAL colour services raised many questions about the end-to-end 'Waveform' performance of the networks as well as that of individual links. The setting and maintenance of standards had to be agreed between the BBC and the P.O. and this work was undertaken by S.H. Padel and D.C. Savage. In addition, standards for long satellite and terrestrial connections had to be established and J. Shelley and D.C. Savage represented the BBC on the ITU and EBU International Committees. Engineers in Measurements section under L.E. Weaver (who later wrote the definitive book on the subject) became expert in television measuring techniques. A complete range of test and measuring equipment for colour TV was produced as well as Insertion Test Signal generators and numerous TV filters.

As the hours of broadcasting increased the time available for maintaining link and transmitter performance decreased and 'in-service' measurements became essential for routine purposes. Monitoring and Control Section under J. Shelley developed apparatus for measuring Insertion Test Signals automatically, and this information was used to generate alarms when pre-set limits were exceeded. An automatic equaliser using the Insertion Test Signal was also designed and used to correct automatically the video signal level and waveform response over the distribution networks.

Whenever video signals are transmitted over circuits having imperfect low-frequency performance, stabilisation (clamping) of the video signal is necessary. Although 'clamps' had been in use for many years,

D.C. Savage designed various new and more efficient types of 'Stabilising amplifier' which overcame the problems associated with earlier equipment. He also developed systems for sending two TV signals simultaneously over a single coaxial cable. The introduction of TV transmissions in the UHF band required the development of a high-quality receiver which could function as either a rebroadcast receiver or a transmitter demodulator. This work was carried out in Transmission Section by J.W. O'Clarey, D.A. Carter and S.W. Collier.

J.E. Holder produced the Sound-in-Sync system while J.O'Clarey's Section engineered various NICAM high-quality digital sound-transmission systems.

The Radio-frequency Section under G.G. Johnstone designed a versatile range of FM and TV transposers (the most notable being the 'Blue Streak' and 'Silver Streak' series) to serve small areas of population which could not receive satisfactory signals from the main transmitter. This work was also accompanied by the development of a self-contained comprehensive radio-frequency test equipment for use either at a base station or by a mobile maintenance team.

By 1973 it had become evident that most transmitters could be designed for fully automatic operation thus releasing staff for other duties. It was proposed that supervision of the overall network would require a small number of Monitoring and Control Centres located at strategic points in the distribution network (the high-power transmitters). D.A. Carter and others in Monitoring and Control Section, in close co-operation with Transmitter Department and Transmitter Capital Projects undertook the design work associated with receiving, processing and displaying all the necessary information on the state of all the transmitters within a designated area. The first Centre was opened at Kirk o'Shotts in 1975 and this was followed by 4 further Centres.

Monitoring & Control Section also produced the World Service HF Transmitter Control System for the automatic switching of transmitters, aerial arrays and programme sources.

Equipment Department

Many TV transposers, computer control systems and items of test gear used by BBC Transmission came from Equipment Department. The department also served the rest of the BBC and more information, including several amusing reminiscences appears in Section 7 of this book: "Sound Studio and Control Room engineering, 1929-1971 by L G Smith".

Communications Department

BBC Transmission can trace its responsibility for BBC networks back as far as March 1923, when the first experiments were carried out to feed programmes over long distances to transmitters (London to Birmingham). In September of that same year, an outside broadcast from Liverpool was carried simultaneously by all the main stations then in service. It caused a considerable stir, being described at the time as a "Milestone in radio development," and "an achievement unsurpassed by any other country." The occasion was an address given by Sir Ernest Rutherford to a meeting of the British Association in the Philharmonic Hall. The broadcast was carried to the transmitters on Post Office open wire lines with no attempt at equalisation, but was successfully received throughout the country. The use of overhead open wire lines with no equalisation between studios and transmitting stations was at this time normal practice, and the subsequent performance was very inadequate. In order to improve the situation, the BBC's Lines Department engineers carried out considerable work in the design of suitable equalisers and amplifiers which, by 1927, were in use with Post Office 'land lines'. This resulted in the first permanent SB line network providing Simultaneous Broadcasts from MF transmitters throughout the regions. Long range communication by cable was well established, e.g. the Eastern Telegraph Co. (later Cable and Wireless) global networks, but they only conveyed telegraph traffic. High quality audio was far more difficult and the SB network was a major achievement. The contribution of BBC engineers in this branch of communications was paramount.

In 1937 Lines Department was involved with the early transmission of television signals over the EMI balanced-pair cable between Alexandra Palace and Broadcasting House, from where it could be extended to cover strategic points in central London. To extend these facilities, a team of Lines Engineers including S.N. Watson, T. Worswick and S.H. Padel under the guidance of. Dr. Rendall, developed equipment for sending television signals over telephone cables. This was very successful and post-war opened up many more possibilities for Outside Broadcasts from the central London area.

Lines Department eventually became Communications Department and by the 1980's was responsible for broadcast, telephone and data circuits throughout the BBC, including procurement, engineering and operations. Communications engineers dealt with the provision of PABXs, data switches (decades before the Internet!) and broadcast circuit switching. Probably the most well known operational areas were the Switching Centre and ATA (Audio and Telecommunications Area) in London's Broadcasting House.

More information, including several amusing reminiscences appears in Section 7 of this book: "Life in Lines Department, 1944-1979 by Geoff Martin".

Engineering Training Department

The high standard of BBC engineering is, to a large extent, a result of the training provided at Wood Norton, the BBC's home of Engineering Training near Evesham. Every BBC Transmission engineer benefited from this training and there are many happy memories of time spent at Wood Norton.

Unfortunately this book does not have a contribution from Engineering Training, but it is to be hoped that one day its history will be recorded and published.

Transmitter Capital Projects Department

When BBC Transmission was created in 1987, TCPD formed a major part and it continued to bring together all the contributions from the other BBC departments and outside industry in order to create the transmission systems that are outlined in this book.

The BBC's Charter required it to "construct or acquire and establish and install" transmitting stations for the transmission of its programmes for general reception both at home and overseas. Those words describe the work of Transmitter Capital Projects Department (TCPD) as it became known as a consequence of the McKinsey management studies of 1968. That was a re-naming of Transmitter Planning and Installation Department (TPID), once the Transmitting Section of Planning and Installation Department (P&ID), which was the descendant of the pre-war Station Design and Installation Department.

Research Department's Service Planning Section specified the optimum location and broadcast characteristics for new transmitting stations, based on BBC requirements and interference constraints. TCPD then co-ordinated the work needed to create new transmitter services. Obtaining a transmitter site was a delicate operation carried out by Transmitter Department's Site Acquisition Section. Transmitter Department had staff all over the UK with valuable local knowledge and this often helped the site finders to reach a successful outcome when dealing with local land owners, estate agents & planning authorities. The optimum site could not always be obtained, but a well established process ensured that the chosen site did meet the requirements of Service Planning Section.

The Transmitter buildings, based on TCPD's requirements, were designed in detail by Architectural and Civil Engineering Department (previously called Building Department) who contracted and supervised the work of erection. In conjunction with TCPD's Antenna[9] Unit they also specified and supervised the erection of masts.

Britain pioneered many aspects of broadcasting, helped by BBC needs for the development of new designs. BBC orders for equipment to TCPD specifications were placed after competitive tender from several firms, and this often enabled British industry to develop new products which could be sold overseas. If the BBC needed special equipment that TCPD could not persuade industry to produce, then Designs Department often produced a design which industry or Equipment

---

[9] A decision was made in 1987 to use the term "antenna" instead of "aerial"

Department could make. A BBC design sometimes led industry to seek a licence to make the equipment for sale at home and overseas.

TCPD engineers could discuss knowledgeably the BBC's requirements with industry's development and design departments. Their known integrity for respecting technical and commercial confidentiality enabled frank discussions when it seemed to a manufacturer that the BBC asked the impossible. Certainly in the pioneering days BBC needs pushed at the frontiers of known techniques, (e.g. TV transmission needed new developments for higher power operations, and various station operational modes, as yet untried, required investigation).

TCPD prepared specifications for transmitter, antenna, power and associated systems, then placed orders after competitive tenders from competent manufacturers. Subject to ensuring value for money, TCPD spread its orders to avoid dependency on one firm and seldom ordered all its known requirements at one time. This spread of reasonably sized orders, which usually included installation of the equipment on site, suited both the BBC and the manufacturers. The manufacturers retained capacity to make and install systems for other customers, while pressure on BBC cash flow and on its engineering resources was eased.

For both manufacturers and the BBC there was another advantage of ordering stage by stage. Pioneering at the edge of technical boundaries sometimes resulted in unforeseeable problems and these were best resolved when there were not too many units to modify. Negotiations between manufacturers and TCPD as to the solutions were much eased when the manufacturer expected to remain in business and hoped for more orders.

When the sealed tenders were opened the quotations could contain clauses proposing modifications to the BBC Specification requirements, offering as the specification suggested, an alternative solution to a particular clause or an alternative rate of delivery of spares. TCPD assessed the acceptability of these and, in the comparison of tenders, could adjust the total cost to the BBC. Then, save for minor orders, the approval of the Director of Engineering, (DE), would be sought. Very large orders required further approval by the Director General's Board of Management.

Having established suppliers of the transmitters and other major equipment such as antenna combining units, TCPD confirmed the details. Every site differed and often different equipment combinations meant building variations. For the larger isolated hill top relay stations access roads and water storage could be needed as well as sewage systems.

Once the building and mast was sufficiently completed, with power available, then TCPD arranged for the equipment to be delivered, normally by the manufacturers concerned. Except at the smallest relay sites, a telephone line (underground within the mast falling radius) was essential for use by installation and then by maintenance engineers.

Transmitters, combining units, test dummy loads and transmitting antennas were usually installed by the manufacturers, while TCPD installed any BBC Designs Department equipment and receiving antennas etc. The manufacturers were then required to demonstrate to TCPD compliance with the BBC specification. All test results and the settings to achieve them were logged for TCPD to include in the Acceptance of Plant documents which were both TCPD's receipt and the future maintenance staff's yardstick.

TCPD was responsible to the Director of Engineering for the technical capabilities of transmitting stations. When a station was ready to operate the TCPD installation engineer would explain and demonstrate the equipment to a Transmitter Department engineer, often from Head Office, who noted the test results and checked that the installation was safe to operate.

TCPD's work encompassed nearly all of the systems covered in this book and the approach outlined above applied, in general, to most of them. Apart from differences due to project size, the main variation was a greater reliance on suppliers to carry out complex multi-discipline projects once the relevant technologies became mature.

SECTION 7 REMINISCENCES

A selection of reminiscences from staff for whom typically a career in Transmission was more than just a 'job':-

Growing up with Broadcasting	Alan Herbert
The Phantom Winch Winder	Bill Skelton
A Visit to Stagshaw	Peter Pearson
MF Stations	Derek Hearn
The War Reporting Unit 1944/1945	E C P Metcalfe
The "Singing Arc"	Bob Crawford
Installing Kirk o'Shotts and the "Ladies Stocking Factory"	
	Dennis Surridge
Sound Studio and Control Room engineering, 1929-71	L G Smith
A Scottish Threat to the Coronation Broadcast	Dai Thomas
Life in Lines Department, 1944-1979	Geoff Martin
Atlantic Relay Station & the Falklands War	Norman Shacklady
Crystal Palace and "The Rockets"	Ian Blanthorn
It all began with "What's My Line"	Tim Burrell
Sender 3 and "The Apiezion Q"	Dick Skyrme
New Blood and Ideas were needed	John Packman
Snowtracs, DE's muddy shoes and Wind Sites	Roy Dalrymple
Bagpipes, Grallaching and Goliath	Syd Garrioch
The "Quality Street Gang"	Jim McPherson
Crossed lines, Power, Christmas trees, Spiders & Diesels	
	Peter Condron
Life on a Maintenance Team and in TCPD	Roy Sharp
Rigging Services: a brief history and some memories	Clive Hosken
Daventry Remembered	Norman Tomlin
Spanner in the Rigging	Rex Boys
Fareham and the Electricity Board	Dick Stibbons
Starting with the BBC in 1941	Don Bowman
Finishing with the BBC in 1997	Martin Ellen

Growing up with Broadcasting, R. A. Herbert MA, MIEE

I was seven years old when I sat on the running board of my uncle's Wolseley, in its garage, and heard from 2LO, through a single earpiece, voices, music, and the footsteps of Uncle Rex (the Director of Programmes) coming down a passage. My mother and aunt were more impressed than I was, for when I had heard my grandmother on the telephone, I had been able to reply to her. I did not understand that thousands of other people could hear these things at the same time. It was 1922 or perhaps 1923.

My cousin, ten years older than I, had been constructing wireless receivers before the BBC began, and he continued to do so throughout the Twenties. Having more pocket money than I ever got, he was able to produce a series of broadcast sets with every development of components, valves, and loudspeakers. In a far more modest style I followed his example from 1928, and became an avid reader of "Wireless World" from about 1930.

In 1925 my cousin built a one-valve receiver for my mother, and on this we received 2LO, 5XX, 5GB from 1927 and Croydon Airport traffic on 900 metres. We had a set of Igronic plug-in coils from 25 to 500 turns marked "What are the Wild Waves saying?" When the BBC was off the air we could hear Radio Paris, Eiffel Tower, Hilversum, and other stations. A wooden pole supported our aerial, and I used to water the earth tube in dry weather. The pole, like thousands of others, lasted about ten years, after which time more sensitive receivers rendered them unnecessary.

When the twin transmissions from Brookmans Park began, we could not separate them. I tried the then fashionable advice to "shorten the aerial", but it did not work, so I studied and experimented with the input circuit, with much better results. This taught me not only a little technology, but also not to believe everything that people tell you.

In 1932 I heard on the National Programme the Opening of the BBC Empire Service. Amateurs of the RSGB had put out programmes on short waves from a station at Caterham in 1927, and BBC programmes were broadcast on 25 metres from G5SW at Marconi's, Chelmsford, which I had occasionally heard on a home-made receiver.

Stuart Hibberd announced:- "GSG, for Greeting", and "GSF, for Fading". What a way to introduce your new Service! Why advertise this unfortunate feature of shortwave transmission? I am glad to say that within a few weeks (or months) it was changed to "F for Fortune". It may be remembered that the Empire Service began with eight frequencies only – GSA to GSH.

Later, more and more frequencies came into use, the call-sign letters having splendid far-flung Empire words, and when the "GS" series was completed, we had "GR" "GV" and "GW". But this was far in the future in 1932. The widening bandwidths were to have implications on the performance of the transmitting aerials, as will be told.

In 1936 I joined the BBC as a 'Student Apprentice', with seven others, of whom two were Indians. We were sent in pairs to work for a month or two at Studio Centres, Transmitting Stations and numerous Departments. As to "Transmission" I went with my partner, Bob Tanner, to Brookmans Park, Washford, Wychbold (Droitwich), Daventry and Alexandra Palace.

I was very fortunate to be sent to Daventry in April 1937, when there was great activity to get Senders 3, 4, 5 and 6 and numerous new Aerial Arrays ready for the Coronation in May. The original ST&C Senders 1 and 2 were carrying on in their 1932 Building.

Sender 3 in the old 5GB building was a combination of parts of 5GB and G5SW. It had been put together after the 50kW Midland Regional at Wychbold had begun service in 1935, superseding 5GB. In 1937 a new Output stage, a Class B Linear Amplifier of twin demountable Valves, was being installed to increase the output power to some 60kW. This stage had inductance coils allowing continuous coverage of the whole shortwave band. Mr C W Skinner was in charge of this. The whole set-up of Sender 3 was magnificently Heath Robinsonian. I liked the Emergency Stop feature. A string attached to a knife switch ran the length of the room, and it was only necessary to grab this to close down the whole thing.

The new 50kW ST&C Senders 4 and 5 were in the large new building. These had Class B high power modulation, and circuits for four wavebands set up on turntables for quick wave-changing. Also their own crystal and variable-frequency drives. (Sender 3 was driven by oscillators belonging to Senders 1 and 2). These senders had their full share of "teething troubles." Sender 6, Marconi 100kW, was not ready. Instead, they installed temporarily a well-tried 20kW set, and used one valve of the four-valve Class A Series Modulator (with Floating Carrier) which would serve the big one when it was ready. This necessitated a 22kV supply from the mercury-arc rectifier. Later, in 1938/39, drives from S4 and 5 and other new ones were collected together in a 'Drive Room'.

Mr E W Hayes, newly appointed Aerial S.M.E., took me up with him to inspect newly built "H" mast. I believe that this mast is the only survivor. This is most suitable, as not only he and I, but other people who worked on the Daventry aerials, had surnames or Christian names beginning with H, including rigger Horace Hancock, with both.

My second visit to Daventry came in the spring of 1938 when Bob and I were attached to the Design and Installation Department. This time it was to help build a new intermediate amplifier for Sender 3, to replace archaic parts from G5SW. This had a Philips water-cooled pentode valve. Bob and I sawed, filed, and drilled, but the thing was still unfinished at the end of our time, partly because our Supervisor, Laurie O'Neill, kept returning from London with a new set of instructions and ideas from above, cancelling work that had already been done. However, it did eventually go into service.

At this time the new Sender 6 was being tested. It was eventually restricted to 70kW, I think on account of limitations of the aerial and feeder system. The big building was being extended to double its original size in order to accommodate Senders 8, 9, 10 and 11. (Later called the 'East Hall')

At Alexandra Palace I had been allowed to be useful, by 'going solo' on the Sound Transmitter, and so relieving AP staff. This was good training for the bigger Senders at Daventry, to which I was to return. At the end of the course, Bob opted to go to 'The Palace', and I to Daventry, where I became a Maintenance Engineer Class 2 Grade E, with two years' seniority (£265 per year) in September 1938. I began in the Control Room, situated between Sender 4 and the General Office. Arabic and South American Portuguese and Spanish programmes had begun, and the day was divided into separate Transmissions, between which all Senders closed down for re-selection of frequencies and aerials. Hence the word 'Senders' to avoid confusion. The time of Transmission 1, to the Antipodes, varied throughout the year, and there was a long gap before or after it. Several times no Announcer could be found, and I remember the news being read in a very strange voice one morning. Robert Dougall tells about such occasions in 'In and Out of the Box' and while he was 'Alone with the Empire' in BH, one of us was often alone with the Control Room mouse, which came out regularly in the small hours to share our crumbs.

At Christmas everyone at Daventry received a packet of tea from a listener in India, and of coffee from one in East Africa. This was very pleasing.

On 3 September 1939 I was at home on leave. I was 24. I had been told from Head Office that if war came I should no longer be required. But I received a telegram (from 'Jock' Cunningham, who was running the rotas) to return at the end of my leave. Several of my contemporaries, Maintenance Engineers and Junior Maintenance Engineers, had disappeared, having been asked (or told?) to volunteer for Radar, etc. Many strangers appeared on our shifts, including a large contingent from Alexandra Palace, among them W C Pafford, who issued a long series of magnificent cartoons throughout 1940. The Winter of 1939/40 was very severe, and we skated on the canal reservoir. Freezing fog caused colossal build up of ice on everything and all the aerials suffered; some were almost completely destroyed. Cylinders of ice several inches thick formed on the wires. The ARP people were upset by the firework displays. The riggers and aerial engineers kept some sort of service going. I was indoors throughout. When it thawed, huge spears of ice fell from the masts. Steel helmets were of little use, but no direct hits were scored.

We had heard rumours of a new station to be built, and eventually found out where it was to be. When the Arctic conditions were over I visited Bridport, hired a bicycle, and took it for a long walk up the hills to Rampisham Down. The Clerk of Works showed me a huge hole and many enormous ammonites, and masts A and B had begun to sprout from their bases. I asked EiC Frank Calver that I should go there and did, in November, with several others including Mr Calver.

Marconi returned to install Senders 10 and 11. I and others helped with the testing a little I think. ST&C came too, to install Sender 7 in the space opposite Sender 6. This had four channels, of which two could be used at a time (7A and 7B).

We all joined the Local Defence Volunteers. S.M.E. Nigel Wilkins was the first C.O. We drilled with broomsticks on the school playground and patrolled Borough Hill with American 0.300 rifles, for which I remember no ammunition.

With the war, the Overseas programme became more continuous and the title 'Empire' was dropped. With increasing numbers of Senders the pattern of aerial switching changed. Selections at the gantry became fewer at one time, but more frequent, and had to be done with adjacent switches on power. It was a good plan to carry some dry rag under your coat in case hooks were dropped and found rather too lively to pick up. A second switch man was employed, separating 'the Gantry' from 'the Field' though of course they would help one another when necessary.

The practice of driving two or more Senders on the same frequency had begun before the war. We used to enjoy hearing the announcers on the South American transmissions instructing listeners North or South of the Amazon to "tune to the other transmitter on GSB." No advice was given for anyone on an island or raft in the river.

At Rampisham things were well advanced in the building, though rain water was collecting in buckets and tins. The aerials had been built by Marconi, the feeders by Callenders Cables, and the junction was to be made by the Station Staff. "Jock" Cunningham was S.M.E. Aerials and EW Hayes A/EiC. At Daventry all "matching" had been done by "Tails", and all the switches at the arrays were on quarter-wave tails, so the lines under the arrays were a quarter wave high. (40 feet on 49 metres, 25 feet on 31). At Rampisham all lines were at ten feet, and hook-and-eye and direct short-circuit switches were used, to avoid high-altitude work and do away with all tails, which are a nuisance and a danger.

Zinc plates had been supplied, to be bolted to the lines to add capacitance, like a short open circuit tail. On the shortest waves, they worked all right, but on 25 and 31 metres, where greater capacitances were required, they became impracticable, and it would have been worse on 41 and 49. On copper wires they would not do either, for electro-chemical reasons, but they did not survive long enough for this to show, for they were all blown away by a storm, which wrote off weeks of work.

I think it was S.M.E. J L Bliss, from Alexandra Palace, who saw that the addition of wire "loops" which effectively turned two-wire line into four, would do the same thing. It was he who did some maths and produced curves from which the sizes and positions of loops could be predicted. When I arrived, in November, there were two "Matching Teams" out in the fields trying to make up lost time. We took turns at operating the Bridge, and humping the trestles and ladders about, to fit the loops. The riggers were kept busy replacing lines which fell, owing to faulty insulator end caps. Insulators on lines and aerials were identical, but only those on the lines failed. Every replacement one was tested by lifting a 900 lb block of concrete, with a shock load administered by Senior Rigger Fred Reynolds beating the rope tackle with a stick. After passing this test they might still give way at any moment. We tried weighing the end caps, but some had one big blow-hole and others many little ones, so you could not tell a bad one by its weight. (editors note: This was still a problem in the 1980's !)

The main Feeders had four wires, and Bliss' Loops were attached to the bottom pair, with no thought of bonding the ends to the top wires. Sometimes this worked, though not very predictable. Sometimes it had remarkable results which made no sense. The afternoons got shorter and darker, and urgency for Marconis to start testing arose. In despair, somebody tried pinching top and bottom wires together, which sometimes had the desired effect. Somehow the arrays were all made to accept power. I and the others from Daventry went indoors to teach the uninitiated to run the Senders.

16 February 1941 was the official opening day, with continuous rain, and two (I think) of the four trunk feeders (from Senders to Switching Tower) fell onto the flat roof, setting the coating on fire. (All these roofs were subsequently covered with concrete) The insulators at the windows were replaced by two in parallel so that this should not happen again. I was not on duty on this day.

The four-wire feeders were supposed to take more power than the two-wire ones at Daventry, so that 100kW could be used, but they gave spectacular pyrotechnic displays, arcs feet long sometimes appearing. A good many lines burned through and fell, often setting fire to the grass. On seeing an arc between top and bottom wires, 'Jock' said "I don't understand it, but I know how to stop it." By means of a pair of brass spacers.

Mr Hayes told me to go out and work with Jock and his men, find out what was happening, and stop it. (I was still Maintenance Engineer Class 2 Grade E). The weather was dreadful. I rigged up a quarter-scale four-wire line in 18 SWG wire inside the Riggers' hut, and took Bridge measurements at many frequencies with different arrangements of side spacers. The clear and simple result was that an un-damped resonance occurred when the spacers were half a wavelength (or multiple) apart, and with "loops" or the equivalent on the bottom wires this was accentuated. On the main runs the spacers were at about 40 ft intervals ($\lambda 2$ on 25 metres) and near the arrays and Switching Tower there were other lengths sensitive to various wave bands. I went out with the riggers and we moved dozens of pairs of spacers to better positions. At Daventry in 1943 I found that the Air Ministry "Boffins" on the Gee System had fitted damping resistors between top and bottom wires of their lines. We had avoided trouble, but they had cured it, so long as the resistors remained intact. (I saw a good many that had not.)

There was a little icing. Some of the arrays sagged and lifted their balance weights. On Arrays 315 (13m) and 314 (16m) the bottom elements lay across the driving lines short-circuiting them. Messrs. Hayes and Cunningham took one look, and the bottom elements were amputated without compunction. These arrays were of form 4/6/0.3, i.e. 4 elements wide, 6 elements high, lowest element 0.3λ above ground. Spacing 0.5λ, so the lowest elements were only a few feet above the lines, even on paper, before they came down. The reason for the 4/6/0.3 type was, I think, the result of a test at Daventry with Arrays 29 and 30 between A and B Towers, one 4/4/1 and the other 4/6/0.3 both on 31 metres. Apparently the extra 50% of weight and complication had produced a fraction of a decibel gain in India or somewhere. Thus was the 4/5/0.8 array born, which proliferated at Skelton. At Woofferton, if I remember right, they reverted to 4/4/1. (As nature intended?)

One morning we heard a regular swishing noise from the North end of the site. The halyard of Array 303 between Mast H and the twin poles M, which ran up direct to the masthead from an anchor near the base, was gyrating like a skipping rope 320 feet long, chafing a mast stay. Everything was covered in ice. Fred and I climbed the ice-covered ladder to the first stay point 100 feet up, and sat down on the ice-covered steel plates, belting ourselves securely to the ice-covered structure. We pulled a big shackle up the halyard and, like "playing" a fish, gradually absorbed the kinetic energy, which turned to heat in our arms and bodies. When the wire became inert, we tied it in to the mast, and stood up. Two puddles were gently steaming. "Cor lumme Mr 'Erbert" said Fred, "and my old woman says I got a cold arse!" When we got down, the ground crew asked what we had laughed about. The shackle remained in place for about 25 years. I have it now. It is 1.1/8 inches in diameter and there is a notch 3/8 inch deep worn in it.

I investigated the problem of "Pinch Matching" on the four-wire lines. The answer was simple enough. It is the inverse of the "Bliss" Loops. I wrote it up, showing how to compute it and the Loops from the "Circle Diagram", which preceded the "Smith Chart." We cleared all the loops off the four-wire lines and re-matched them with "Pinches". Years later HV Sims at Wood Norton used to teach the Students:- " ..... That was due to Mr R A H, and for it he received a Suggestions Grant of £5.5.0 ..... pause ..... less Income Tax." He told me that this was always greeted with loud applause. (I can find no record of this income tax)

I could not believe that our fixed tune reflectors could be effective over the whole band widths of the frequencies then in use. Maintenance Engineer Class 2 Grade E, J R Sandison, formerly of Alexandra Palace, who had "double Banked" with me at Daventry, and later became SME Aerials at Skelton, joined our section for a while. On 9 September 1941 "Sandy" and I organised a little test to check the tuning of the reflector of 25 metre Array 307 (4/5/0.8). I had built a simple receiver, with one valve, and a milliammeter borrowed from the stores. With a Sender on reduced power, we moved the tuning short-circuits along their lines and observed the signals behind the array. These short-circuits were normally fixed at a nominal $3/4\lambda$ at mid-frequency from the lowest elements. We found that the minima were very sharp. On 12.04 MHz (GRV) the distance was 57 feet, or 0.70λ, and on 11.82 (GSN) 65 feet or 0.79λ.

Unknown to us, Mr H Page of Research Department was planning a series of test measurements on our arrays using a balloon-borne receiver. He was interested in the size, shape, and strength of the main beam. When he was given our results, he included reflector tuning into the test programme, which was carried out in April and May 1942.

In 1941 we put up three temporary arrays, for which we erected an 80 ft pole, and filed out bolt holes to take big shackle pins at the tops of Masts C, K, and J. Later, new masts P and Q were built to accommodate these arrays properly. "Sandy" was replaced by Gerald Grover, who also took part in this work.

Also in 1941, Technical Assistants (Female) began to appear. Until then, transmitting stations had male staff only, in every department, including Office and Catering. A memorable memorandum from the Engineering Establishment Officer allowed them to wear trousers "of a sober hue." The meaning of this was never precisely defined, so far as I know, nor was any procedure instituted to grant official approval. The girls made a cheerful and colourful addition to our lives throughout the 'Forties. Early in 1942, a large bunch of TA's of both sexes arrived at Rampisham. Rigger Tom Cleall (of Somerset) advised me:- "You do want to go and talk to some of they maidens." But I had no need of his advice. Seven girls stayed at Rampisham and ran the Control Room and Drive Room. With many other couples throughout the Corporation, Eileen and I are profoundly grateful to the Management for thus bringing us together. We met in the romantic atmosphere of the station van in West Street, Bridport; "The Tumbril," as Jack Shallcross called it. We were married in 1943.

Mr Page's performance tests ran from 13 April to 9 May. A balloon with lorry-mounted winch, and crew of three or four, came from Cardington. A bedding site for it was chosen, and it was inflated with hydrogen from a trailer load of cylinders. Putting it to bed each night provided first class entertainment and exercise for as many people as could be mustered. It was covered with a net, weighed down with sandbags, and anchored with screw pickets and anything heavy that we could find. Some of the test sites were inaccessible, owing to trees. We had some excitement getting the balloon under telephone wires at Kingcombe Cross (on A356, at the Eastern end of the Station) as the winch could not pull it low enough. Sandbags and human ballast were used; several of us travelled by air into the hedge. The receiver hung from the winch rope, and a thin steel wire led from it down to a hand winch mounted on insulators. This little wire was connected to the earthed main wire through a series of quickly interchangeable meters (milli and micro-ammeters). I had the honour of sitting here and recording the measurements as the balloon rose to, or descended from, 2,500 feet; every 100 feet being announced by the driver by banging on the door with a hammer (Air Ministry property).

The tests required much organisation involving nearly everyone, as time was limited to when a Sender could be spared, between service transmissions. When the balloon was up the array could be reversed or slewed, or have the reflector tuning altered, but the frequency could be changed only when it was down, as the receiver had to be re-tuned. When near the ground, the balloon behaved wildly in the lightest wind, so this was no easy matter.

Gerald had a theodolite under the array, so that he could record the actual direction of the balloon, and Pat Priestman was beside me, with a protractor and plumb line, trying to estimate its direction from there. At the end of each run, Gerald announced "Balloon up and Steady", or "Down" (and Unsteady). This was telephoned to Jock in the building, where he could supervise the Sender, a sound safety precaution. When all was ready for a run, the Sender was powered, and pips of tone radiated, at which I signalled the driver to start, up or down. One of the Balloon crew worked the little winch.

We had to be ready at any time to haul down if so required by the Royal Air Force. In this case, steady tone was to be radiated. We never had to do this, but on one day all flying was forbidden. We had no other communication with the station. We were out in the sun with nothing to do for much of the time. Poor Mr Page had little fun. He sat all day in a dark corner, digesting the previous day's results; but eventually, after the war, he received a Gold Medal after reading a paper before the IEE.

Following the tests all the arrays were eventually rebuilt, or new ones built, with two wires in each element, to improve the band widths. At Rampisham, provision was made for three adjustments of reflector tuning on each array. With only four Senders to cater for, using these did not impose excessive work load on the aerial switchers, but at the other stations it was never done.

I suggested that it was time I was promoted to Class 1, Grade D. The Superintendent Engineer, Mr Hotine, told me that they were going to have an examination for this, which I should await. I said that I was ready then, so he called up Mr A N Thomas by morse key and buzzer (!) and they asked me questions. The first one, about a D.C. generator, scared me, for I had forgotten all about such things, but I recovered in time. I was promoted to Grade D and posted to Daventry to be a Supervisor, or Assistant to the Shift SME, a post unique to Daventry.

At Daventry I renewed my acquaintance with Senders 6 - 11, and learned a bit more about S1, 2, 3, 4, 5, and 5XX ("Daventry 5"). Also S7 and AM1, the Air Ministry Marconi "Q" set, at 5XX, which had carried "Weather London" when I was in the Control Room in 1938. It is not for me to write about any of these, but I hope that somebody has, for they were all of interest.

As Supervisor, I was in charge of the "Tally Board" and the issuing of "clears for power" in conjunction with the aerial switchers. The tally board had two rows of hooks. On the top row hung square wooden tallies painted S1, S2, etc. On the bottom one, discs painted with the array numbers. When an array was switched to a Sender and clear for power, top and bottom hooks were occupied. When work was in hand, the relevant tallies were removed by an aerial switcher or rigger, so you could see at a glance the state of affairs.

On the back of Array 10 Tally (I think) were inscribed the letters "BD". I was told that this stood for "Baldy's Downfall." Apparently the unfortunate "Baldy" had given the "Clear" but forgotten the "Bif." (Not the first time anyone had done this). The Sender was powered into an open circuit and blew up some insulators, so that the line fell from the tallest pole in the gantry across several other lines, bringing off several senders. I was glad I was not on duty on that occasion.

On our rota were three full SMEs and three "supervisors;" the seventh man was A D Maltman, who did equal numbers of duties in each seat. The usual comings and goings, leave, sickness, etc., soon resulted in me occupying the S.M.E.s chair from time to time. Our office was a box ten feet square built between Senders 6 and 7. One night George Vokes leaned back in his spring-loaded rotating chair, and the cast iron spring housing broke. George fell backwards and a projectile escaped through a window and sailed right over Sender 6 to fall on the floor. It was a mercy that nobody was hurt.

The LDV had been transformed into the 10th Northants Home Guard. We had had no Home Guard at Rampisham, I do not know why not. I was promptly conscripted. My colleagues of 1940 had become Corporals and Sergeants. Captain F J Cooper was now in charge. Before the war he had been in charge of the Tannoy Van which accompanied the Daily Mirror Eight girls on the seaside beaches, assisted by Gerald Grover, with whom I had had many adventures at Rampisham which cannot be reported here. Fred Cooper went to Germany as Recording Engineer with Richard Dimbleby.

In the Autumn, Aerial S.M.E. Hilary Wright was sent into hospital and EiC Douglas Birkinshaw put me into his place. Hilary's Assistant was Hugh Sims, who had been at Daventry since 1940 or 1939. (Two names to remember when contemplating "H" mast). The first thing we did was to have the right angles at the corners of the paths filled in with concrete, so that aerial switching cyclists could go round without stopping. Hugh said that he had long wanted to do this. I said "Why ever had it not been done before?"

In 1939, 5XX had been resuscitated and put on the Home Service on a medium wave. A lop-sided T aerial was hung from a 500 ft mast to "G" mast, 150 feet. A little ATH was built, and a coaxial feeder laid. Some very small-gauge wires were buried to form the earth. In 1941 it changed to long wave, European Service. The aerial was lengthened to reach "H" mast, and some 12 gauge wires put under this new position.

In 1943 the ground was always warm and dry, till it steamed whenever it rained. On investigative excavation a notch was burned in the spade of Dave Ellerman, accompanied, I have no doubt, by a burst of

European Programme. Digging was then restricted to the hour's break every afternoon. Only the 12 gauge wires could be found.

Every bit of scrap copper wire of any gauge that could be collected was joined end to end and wound onto a big drum, to the great improvement of the tidy appearance of the Station. I should think that nearly a mile of wire was buried, in hand dug trenches. An old piece of copper bus-bar was drilled like a Meccano plate and fitted with numerous brass bolts. Hilary and Hugh had constructed a device based appropriately on a "vintage" Sullivan wavemeter, with which to measure the 200kHz impedance. To cut the story short, one night the complete earth system was joined together, and Hugh and I re-matched the aerial to the coaxial line (75 ohms, I think). The transmitter was retuned, and the aerial current was found to have been doubled, as was the rectified current in Mr Birkinshaw's receiver at Staverton, and the ground remained wet.

For Short Wave people to meddle with medium or long waves was sacrilege, for a Head Office department was very jealous about this activity. Mr J B Webb was sent, with "black boxes" (more likely grey?) to correct our homework. We showed him a little RC network to simulate the impedance, "9 - j14 ohms." After diligent knob twiddling he pronounced the official figures "8.9 - j14.2". He moved the tap on the matching coil a full half inch and honour was satisfied.

One morning Mr Birkinshaw rang to ask if we could slew Array 40 to a new bearing. I thought at first that this would mean just moving the slew taps, but it meant moving the 100 ft pole which, with "C" mast, supported this Array.

"You can do that, can't you?" he asked. Of course we could. The Daventry riggers had erected many such poles, and Senior Rigger Charlie Sterrett had been doing it when I was a child. I had helped with one at Rampisham, and I knew that Hugh would check everything, and make sure that we had all that was needed. All I had to do was to make quite sure that we put it up in the right place, and that nobody was hurt. And so it was done.

Finally a Home Guard exercise. One Sunday morning the Company were trying a strange weapon, the "Sykes Spigot Mortar", with sand filled practice bombs. A faulty Bowden cable caused a hang up, and all the motor-cyclists and mechanical experts crowded round with advice. Private Herbert took a few strategic paces to the flank. Away went the bomb, striking a steel pole with a satisfactory BOING, and severing one wire of the line to Array 14. Captain Cooper did not hesitate. "Sergeant Sterrett, Corporal Sims, Private Herbert" he ordered. "Revert to civilian duty and put it up again"!

My time with Hugh was one of the best periods of my career. Our abilities were complementary, and we really enjoyed our work. Many years later, in the Wood Norton Club, Hugh told my son Giles: "If your father and I had been one person, we would have been unbeatable!"

In the Spring, Hilary returned from hospital, and I was sent to Skelton to be S.M.E. i/c Shift.

Sometimes the Police told us of escaped German POW's. We never saw any, but we saw gangs of Italians clearing ditches on the bus route. The aerial switchers were envious of their fine wellington boots, their own communal ones being usually leaky or split. They used to remove their socks and wrap their feet in rags before setting out.

In 1946, Sandy returned to his job, but Head Office wanted him to go back to Alexandra Palace. I was told by Mr Wheeler, Senior Engineer, Transmitters, that I was to go to Woofferton as A/EiC to Mr Laurence Ivin. Mr Bowden, formerly S.M.E. and then AEiC at Rampisham, who had become EiC (or perhaps Acting EiC) refused flatly to let us both go. After some delay it was decided that Sandy should stay for a while, and I must go. Jock Cunningham arrived from Rampisham and took over the aerials from Sandy. I asked Mr Wheeler what Mr Ivin thought about his new Assistant, and he said "we haven't told him yet". On my first day at Woofferton Mr Ivin explained that he liked his staff to run the station "in parallel all nice and easy. *But sometimes we have to work in series and I am in front!"*

At Woofferton early in 1946 only four Senders were working. The RF parts of all six (I think) RCA 50kW sets had been commandeered and removed by the Royal Air Force at the time of the V2 Rockets. Senders 83, 84, 85 and 86 had been restored, but not 81 or 82. Sender 81 was being rebuilt by P&ID and the station staff, with British valves and continuously variable inductances like those of Sender 3, and it soon went into service. After that, enough parts were found or improvised for Mr Ivin and station staff to do a private venture, to restore Sender 82 to something resembling its original state, which was successfully done; whereupon he embarrassed Head Office by demanding a programme schedule for this "non-existent" Sender; and to everyone's credit this was done and the administrative problems overcome.

In 1946 I had been sent to Woofferton with no option, but by 1950 a new system was in force; all jobs were to be advertised, and candidates must apply. The telephone rang, and Mr C J Strother of the Engineering Establishment Office asked:- "Why have you not put in for Droitwich, Herbert? You had better do so." or words to that effect. And that is why at the end of 1950 I found myself at Wychbold, on the long and medium waves, like a fish out of water.

Television interference at Wychbold took the form of splashes of Light Programme, and flashing on the picture, during gusty winds. We looked at the long wave aerial and the masts.

From the A38 main road you can see that the backstays of the two 700 ft masts are not in line with each other, or with the Aerial. I have no idea why not. I went up the North mast with Rigger-Labourer Teddy Sutton. At the top, the aerial halyard goes over a big pulley, and then over a little roller supported between two channel irons, not pointing directly at the other mast; so that the halyard very nearly, or just, touched the end of one. Every time it did we could see a tiny spark, and crashing noises on a VHF receiver were reported to us by visual signals from the ground. We could cause them to start or stop by quite gently pushing on the halyard. So we fixed a piece of wood between, and a copper wire to bond the halyard to the nearest bolt that we could undo. This would have to be removed when the aerial was to be lowered. I don't think it happened on the South mast, but we treated that too.

Every Monday night the old 50kW Regional Transmitter was tested and given a run, in readiness for emergency. The service was carried on the 150kW ex-longwave set. It was time for the big tank of distilled water in the crypt to be cleaned out, a fearful job which took several days, so old "5GB" was put on instead, and the tank opened up. After that the telephone lines were continually busy. We tried to improvise filters or wave-traps at the transmitter and in the Aerial Termination House, and listeners at Tatsfield, Droitwich, and, I think, Bromsgrove, all reported differently on their effectiveness. Presumably there was radiation other than from the aerial mast, so that we were just pushing the resultant about.

The horse having bolted, the stable door was overhauled; or rather, the "D" unit was completely rebuilt, with much bending of copper tubes, in the form of a low-pass filter, which did the trick. But it was not long before the whole transmitter was scrapped. Why had nobody ever complained during the Monday night tests?

I was out of place at Wychbold, so in 1956 I went on a Secondment to Nigeria, at the other end of BBC Transmission. The first voice I heard from home was that of John Arlott at a cricket match, and somehow the whole business seemed to be very much worthwhile; though I am not a cricket fan. Reception in the daytime on 13 metres was excellent; and on 11, when it was used, even better. I do not remember which Senders or aerials were on. Rampisham and Daventry respectively I suspect.

In 1958 I became attached to Hugh Sims' Section at Wood Norton as a supernumerary. I helped the students with practical work, and had a go at lecturing. I helped Peter Green with a demonstration of distortion on FM, due to reflections from Bredon Hill; and made my first acquaintance with the Wayne-Kerr B801 Bridge, which was later to play a big part in my work. With this we tried unsuccessfully to prove that the impedance of a vertical $\lambda/4$ unipole over a conducting plane is 36 ohms; crouching under a steel table. We ought to have investigated why it didn't come right.

Hugh had a wonderful selection of miniature aerial demonstrations using UHF. A little HR/4/4/1 array with a row of five receiving dipoles with lamps, suspended a few yards ahead of it, was used to demonstrate slewing. These lamps had become very dim. I overhauled the little Sender, fitting some new valves, and modifying the output coupling. I tuned the reflector for maximum forward radiation, and the lamps lit brighter than ever.

A proper post was found for me in Duncan MacEwen's Section, to teach Sound and Vision Technical Operators. As I knew next to nothing about studios and television, I was sent to Birmingham and to Lime Grove to learn. I learned something, but scarcely enough to teach from. The best thing I did was to accompany Studio Managers on trips to Daventry. We were always welcomed by EiC Harry Masters, who made them a little speech. I would take them out to the Gantry and show them how the voltage increased from zero up a short-circuited "Tail", by drawing tiny sparks off it with a pencil point, growing larger as it went up the tail, till it caught fire. Then with a piece of unburnt coke between the lugs of a switching pole, I would draw several inches of arc off the line itself, so that we could hear the programme, with excellent quality and volume.

On a visit to Bush House with other Lecturers in 1960, we bumped into Eddie Beaumont, who had been S.M.E. at Rampisham in 1940. He took us into his office and showed grandiose plans for 250 and 500kW transmissions. I felt more at home here, and as a result got myself talked into joining Planning and Installation Department.

On our visits to Daventry I had observed the Aerials and I could see precious little sign of progress in any details of design or construction since the 1940's. Evidently the External Services purse had remained firmly shut. Now however, it was to be opened, and new developments embarked on. There was speculation as to how 250kW could be conveyed to the arrays, but nobody seemed to be wondering what would happen to them if this was achieved.

At Rampisham in 1941 Fred Reynolds had driven six nails into the bench and wound a piece of 12 gauge wire round them to form the first "sausage feeder" spacer. Short pieces of six-wire (on each leg) "sausage" were used for tension frame jumpers and the like, and longer lengths were produced to make a neater job of the lines from Senders to window insulators.

Somebody said "has anyone ever seen a flashover on sausage feeder?" The answer was "no." So one solution of the problem had perhaps been found already. Miles of sausage were erected at Daventry and Woofferton, but it is intractable stuff, not convenient for repairs or alterations. Later it was found that four-wire 6 SWG line would usually do (provided that there were no resonant lengths-see my remarks on Rampisham 1941 – A photograph from Skelton in "Ariel" in June 1984 shows that this could still happen more than forty years on.)

I was given the job of developing 250kW Dual Band Arrays, for which a list and time-table were drawn up. It was apparently thought that this would be quite easy, and that radiating elements of two 16 SWG wires fan-wise could be used in a 4/4 array, resulting in lighter head loads on the masts. I cannot tell the whole story here, but I spent many months at Daventry in 1961 and into 1962, with the backing of Mr H Page, (he of the balloon) on Array 34 (4/4 17/21 MHz), which was not successful, but on which we began to learn useful things. We then turned to a simpler Array of 2/2 form, at Rampisham. It is a good idea to try walking before you run. This resulted eventually in a workable (but by no means perfect) set of designs in three sizes, (15/17, 9/11 and 6/7 MHz) but the elements had to have three, four, and six 12 gauge wires in each fan arm so that they were monstrously heavy and wind resistant. Another go at a 4/4 array (No 8 at Daventry, 15/17 MHz) in 1963 was marginally successful, with two 12 gauge wires in each fan arm, but it would never have been a successful prototype. It *did* work at 250kW after a lot of bother. Mr Brady from the USA (VOA?) looked at it and said "Boy, what an Antenna!"

Even more ambitious was Array 308 at Rampisham, (4/4 for 9/11 MHz) which (expectedly) fell even further short of requirements, and I was still working on it when Dual-Band development was ordered to be stopped, in 1965.

The trouble was not the dual-band feature,(I invented a method for Dual Frequency Matching in 1961) but the widths of individual bands, the widest being 2.5% on 31 metres. Our target, for the whole width of each band, was a Standing Wave Ratio (on the main feeder) of 1.2; for the new Senders were designed for SWR up to 1.4, and the feeder systems, when properly terminated, did little better than 1.2. (This included the new power-operated selector switches, with which I had absolutely nothing to do).

In the worst condition, therefore, 1.2 x 1.2 = 1.44, but hopefully this would not often be met, and a little attenuation on the line would help reduce the SWR at the Sender. To the disapproval of my superiors, I spent some time trying to investigate the accuracy of B801 bridge measurements on "balanced loads" with bifilar chokes; which is another story. Allowing for errors up to 10%, it seemed to me, meant that a genuine 1.2 SWR could only be assured by achieving a measured 1.1 approximately, but a superior official suggested that this would allow us to tolerate 1.3. Like Frank Whittle in a similar circumstance I was too stupid to understand this.

Until this time, aerial matching had been done at mid-frequency only, with no attention to the band edges. On the old single-band arrays, with their thin elements, the spread of admittances over the longer wave bands had to be measured to be believed. I measured a number of old arrays at Rampisham and at Daventry. It was well known to the aerial S.M.E.s that very bad loads were often encountered on the longer waves. It was often helpful to adjust reflector tuning in order to get a better load impedance. If length of elements doubled to double the wavelength, then "Fatness" must also be doubled to achieve the same percentage bandwidth. This had never been done.

As to the tuning of the reflectors, on the 2/2 dual band arrays we were helped by some unbelievably good luck in that line lengths were found which nearly achieved correct mid-band tune on both bands. But I found that the reflector tuning was much too sharp for good front-to-back ratios over the whole bands. Tuned reflectors are only good for single frequencies (as was the case when the Empire Service began).

To cut another long story short, I had many arguments with my superiors, and I was finally eased gently out of the Corporation in 1970; but before I went, I wrote a memo to the Director of Engineering, pointing out what was wrong, but that I did not know how to put it right.

It was interesting to watch, from over the fence, aerial developments at Rampisham throughout the 'Eighties. For months the forest of new towers carried no arrays at all; and I occasionally met people in the streets who told me things like that there were more Senders operational than Aerials. In 1984 an article in "Ariel" told us of a competition between arrays designed by the BBC and those by the Americans, TCI. I only ever saw one BBC type, and it disappeared after the gale of 1987. All are now by TCI or Marconi, I think.

THE PHANTOM WINCH WINDER, BILL SKELTON

I was fortunate to move to a village near Withernsea at a time when the BBC was recruiting replacements for the staff being called up. I applied and was granted an interview with the EiC – H.W. Baker and he had the power to employ (and presumably fire) staff, because I was taken on as a Youth in Training without further question apart from a report from my headmaster. Several other lads joined at about the same time.

For the first few months we didn't see much of OSE5 as we were sent back to school under the care of the so called On Station Instructor. As the school room we used was in a private house in Withersea and OSE5 was near Ottringham – 6 miles away, the only 'on station' we saw was a half day visit, once a week when we collected our pay of £1-7-6 (£1-37$^1/_2$) plus oddments.

The weekly visit gave us a chance to familiarise ourselves with the station and the staff and we were given various tasks to do, which usually meant getting dirty, wet or cold, or all three. Back in class, we were taught the theory of radio and electricity and all in all were happy in our lot.

When this period ended, we were split up by being put on the station rota. It was an eighteen day rota with five evening shifts (17.30-23.30), five days (09.30-17.30), day off till 23.30, five nights (23.30-09.30) and two days off. Each rota position had an Engineer and a Technical Assistant and we Youths-in-Training were distributed on the rota to look, learn and perform menial and messy tasks. Some of the T.As who were on a rota position without a YiT felt very overworked.

I made all the usual errors that all new boys did: I took home the ATH key which had a 6 inch loop of heavy-gauge feeder wire as key ring and a big chunk of lead as a key fob. I'd vaguely wondered why this was but it wasn't till I got home after a night shift on GS duties and found it in my pocket that I realised what the weight was for and why I'd had a list to port as I cycled home. Several times I carelessly put a spanner down on a lead-acid battery shorting several cells and spattered the place with molten metal and of course, once when allowed near the bays put a plug in the wrong jack and cut the programme.

At OSE5, we had the *Phantom Winch-winder*. On still moonlight nights, the sound of an aerial winch being ratcheted could be heard coming from the direction of the long wave antenna area. This dipole was suspended between four 500ft masts and was hauled up to near the same height as the masts.

At the base of each mast was a manual winch needing two men to work it, an operation that was only performed in daylight and required the AEiC to stand on the roof of the ATH in the centre of things, armed with a megaphone to try and keep the four teams in sync. As some of the strong-arm brigade thought it was a race, the umpire was essential.

Anyway, one still and moonlight night, the clacking noise was reported again and the S.M.E. decided to settle once and for all, what was going on: so he gave his orders and set off with that part of the shift not tied to duty positions. He, leading the way and followed by half a dozen engineers and technical assistants the team set off – in Indian file and strict order of seniority.

The sound seemed to be coming from differing places as they advanced and as it got louder one or two of those near the front were glad to give up their 'droit-de-signeur' to drop towards the rear of the party from where they found reasons to return to the transmitter buildings. When those remaining reached the site, they could see in the bright moonlight that the winches were all snug in their tarpaulin covers and the sound seemed to be coming from above. The S.M.E. declared that the noise was coming from "a loose corona ring on the aerial" and the group returned to the canteen for a round of toast: the S.M.E. no doubt to his office to record his findings in the S.M.E.'s log.

The explanation was accepted and the sound was heard from time to time without further action. Months later the aerial was lowered, scrapped and replaced with a new design and lo – the sound continued to be heard on bright, still nights.

A VISIT TO STAGSHAW, PETER PEARSON

Leaving school, aged 16, at the end of 1938, my ambition was to join the BBC, however, my original application was returned, saying that the minimum age of entry was 21, and if I was still interested, when I attained that age, I should re-apply.

I obtained a job with a local photographic firm, as a tea-boy, and learnt the skills of window dressing, washing floors, and eventually, using cameras, including 16mm. ciné, and processing. When the war started, in 1939, the retail photographic trade slumped, but the C.O.I. (Central Office of Information), engaged small firms to provide mobile cinemas in order to show a series of propaganda films to various sections of the community. In the winter of 1940/41 I was travelling around, in a Morris 16 car, with cinema equipment, and I had to visit Stagshaw for some shows to the troops who were guarding the BBC site.

Having erected the equipment I had a problem with pick-up of the radio programmes on the sound section of the projector. The officer in charge asked the BBC for help, and I then learnt, from the engineer sorting the problem, that due to wartime staffing, the BBC had lowered the entry age to 18.

Within a matter of days, having consulted the owner of 'Dawson Home Movies Ltd.', who was anxious to reduce his staffing, I wrote out another application, and was rewarded with an interview, in Manchester Piccadilly Studios, with the EIC Basil Vernon, which took place on 17 June 1941. As a result of that interview I received a letter, signed by P.A. Florence, E.E.O., offering me a post as Junior Maintenance Engineer, on the unestablished staff.

Anticipating the princely sum of £2. 10. 0d., plus 2/6d. Cost of Living Bonus, per week, I duly reported, for Training, to the instructor, Douglas Hamilton-Schaschke, at Maida Vale Studios. Douglas eventually became an EiC, and retired from that post, at Rampisham, in April 1963. This course was somewhat historic because it was the first one to have members of the female sex in the Engineering Division. Until the War, the Engineering Division had been a male-dominated preserve. A highlight for me, was that during a visit to the Course by the Senior Superintendent Engineer (S.S.E.), R.T.B. Wynn, he gave me his BBC lapel badge, which I still have today some 55 years later. Because this was the first engineering course to include females, the Press were invited. Several photographs were taken but the nearest I got was to have my notebook and pencil reproduced, my male colleague Jimmy Neal and myself being moved out of our front row seats to allow a couple of girls from the second row to occupy our positions for the benefit of the photograph. Looking at the photograph today, one wonders what the attitude of Health & Safety officials would be to having terminals on a mains transformer exposed as they were on the power supply for the model transmitter.

Following the training in London, I spent another 4 weeks at Daventry before being posted to Droitwich, under the watchful eye of EiC H.F. Humphreys, as a fully-fledged Junior Maintenance Engineer. One outstanding memory, from those wartime days at Droitwich, was the operation of the pair of 200kW transmitters in the 'New' building. The high power of some 400kW was used to transmit slow-Morse, in an attempt to transmit British propaganda into the heart of Germany which could be received literally on a piece of coal and a cat's-whisker. These transmissions played havoc with any rusty joints on the station security fence and barbed wire, which initially created some alarm amongst the residents in the village of Wychbold where Droitwich station is situated. The rusty joints acting as diodes and the subsequent arcing caused the Morse to be heard throughout the village. A couple of years later saw the opening of O.S.E.5 at Ottringham, with the intention of running 4 x 200kW transmitters in parallel. I think that they only managed about 600kW, but it still became the most powerful transmitter in the world. It was whilst I was at Droitwich that I learned about the dangers attached to RF burns. My first visit alone to read the meters in the ATH produced a burn on my finger because I switched on the lights, using my finger to operate the metal toggle switch. I had not been told that the earthing wand should be used to prevent such accidents. It taught me that an 'earthed' appliance did not offer sufficient protection in areas of such high levels of RF radiation.

Although BBC posts were a reserved occupation, at that time, it was evident that there was no guarantee that they would remain so, therefore along with several colleagues I volunteered for service in the Army, where I served from November 1942 until March 1947, mostly as a Corporal Instructor, attached to the Royal Artillery School of Electric Lighting. I was actually a member of R.E.M.E., having been transferred from the R.A.O.C., when R.E.M.E. was formed in 1943.

On demobilisation I returned to the BBC, as a Technical Assistant Grade 3, on the unestablished staff at O.S.E.3 Rampisham, in Dorset. The outstanding memory, of that period, was when one of the 14 masts, supporting the curtain arrays, collapsed due to the heavy ice-loading which was present during the big freeze of '47.

In February 1948, my application for a transfer to Moorside Edge, was accepted, and I moved there as a TA2, under the EiCship of

C.H.J.Wheeler, a kindly disposed gentleman who suffered from rather poor eyesight. One anecdote concerning C.H.J. was when he was carrying a bag from the kitchen to his office, he thanked the cook for "Bones for his dog," but could not see that the bag was dribbling sugar grains along the floor. (Sugar was still rationed at that time). During my stay, at Moorside, I became a member of the established staff, this was in 1949.

When Holme Moss was being built, in the late 49/50's period, along with my colleagues, I had an ambition to transfer to Television. A number of us from Moorside Edge were invited to London, to be interviewed by the man who was to be the EiC, Charles Buckle. Unfortunately, I was not to be one of the chosen few. Donald Hinchliffe, L.F. Allen (Fred), Joe Eastwood, and Will Harper were selected, and early in 1951 the engineering staff went to Evesham on a Television conversion course, and then to Holme Moss with all the excitement of the equipment installation and eventual opening, on the 12th October.

Along the line someone must have had second thoughts, my guiding star was shining, and I was offered a post at Holme Moss. Having missed the Holme Moss Television conversion course I had to attend the next one, designed for Kirk o'Shotts staff, which took place in the October that Holme Moss came on air. On this course I met, and shared a room, with 'Tommy' Douglas, who eventually transferred from Ko'S to become EiC Sutton Coldfield. I joined Holme Moss, some three months after it opened, in December 1951, as a TA1.

Over the years I progressed to a Grade C engineer, then OP4, 5 & 6, which became 2S6P, in a grading shuffle, and I remained there, for some 31 happy years, until I retired on the 6 December 1982, my 60th birthday.

There are many memories, and anecdotes, associated with those 30 odd years, ranging from the hazardous journeys through heavy snowdrifts to get to work, right up to the social activities of the Club. In the early years the Press made much of our isolation. In truth, the isolation was as much for staff benefit as the BBC. Having struggled for several hours to climb up the hill, it was preferable to stay put for a few days, until relieved by other staff, and then have a few days at home. One problem, however, was fresh produce, such as milk, eggs, and bread. Charles Buckle arranged with a local farmer to provide milk in a large metal can, with two handles, rather than separate bottles. The eggs were in cardboard boxes, tied up with string, and the people carrying these through the snow would produce a cross and a circle whenever they stopped for a rest. This inspired some of the staff, who were mostly mischievous young men, to print messages in the snow, which are mostly unprintable here.

An incident, involving Charles Buckle was his enthusiasm for cricket. With long breaks in transmission, it became the practice for the male members of staff to play cricket on the forecourt. When C.B. went in to bat he took delight in swiping the ball, as far as he could. The bat belonged to him, and all was well until he eventually knocked a ball through the control room window, breaking the glass. That was his signal to take his bat home and ban the playing of cricket on the site.

A novel pastime was developed by some of the young engineers, which, with hindsight, was a rather dangerous practice. The steep hillside at Holme Moss was littered with dry-stone walls, in various states of disrepair, and the game of 'Drosser Rolling' evolved. This consisted of rolling large stones down the hillside, towards the reservoir some 1,000ft below. There were no reported incidents of any sheep, or even people, being hit with one of these missiles, but that was due to luck rather than management. Other pastimes, in winter at any rate, was to go sledging.

The Club purchased a sledge for this purpose and many a lunch hour was spent in this way. All these activities came to an end as transmission times extended, from the original morning Trade transmission, with a break until teatime, and yet another gap before the evening programme began.

Even in those early days we had our share of security scares. Not least of which came from a group called the 'Welsh Nationalists', who objected to the lack of Welsh language programmes transmitted from

Holme Moss. During the early hours of the night, when the nightwatchman, plus one engineer, called Harry Taylor, were on site, a group of Welsh Nationalists broke a window into the Control Room, entered the building and caused damage to several pieces of equipment. Harry effected a citizen's arrest on one of these characters and held him until the local police arrived. The man was later charged with the offence, and was reported as being defiant, in court, and even threatened further similar actions. On the occasion of threats, and during programmes of national interest, such as the Coronation broadcast, we had local police presence in the control room. During this period there was a series of programmes, introduced by Richard Dimbleby, produced by Derek Burrell-Davies, called 'Other People's Jobs'. One of these featured Holme Moss and called 'Top O't Moss'. The programme, as was normal, went out live, and involved switching on the control desk to provide it to the network. My duty was on the control desk, and several of us, including Charles Buckle, Donald Hinchliffe, Will Harper, 'Fred' Allen, Frank Dobson (Rigger), and Mary Searson (Cook), were interviewed by Richard.

One of the aspects of those early days of television was the transmission every morning, of the Demonstration Film, with segments of Test Card thrown in. Mainly for the benefit of dealers, the film attracted an audience of enthusiasts, and the section which dealt with the building of Holme Moss, to the music of Mendelssohn's Scottish symphony, together with the commentary about nothing to stop the winds from the Urals reaching the site, the post office cable bringing the signal North by weaving through the silk mills of Macclesfield, is etched in my memory. The Dem. Film originated in London, but to enable the release of the links, it was necessary for Holme Moss to originate test signals, from time to time. These consisted of a caption scanner, for the Test Card, and special music tapes played on a Ferrograph tape recorder. In addition we had the facilities to originate our own apology captions, and sound apologies. These were personalised and included Holme Moss on the caption, and in words. Some of the discs were in Welsh, presumably to placate the Welsh Nationalists. Another ritual, in the early days, concerned broadcasts of national interest, such as The Queen's Christmas Day Broadcast.

On these occasions it was considered necessary for the Engineer-in-Charge to be present at the station, so depending on his mood at the time, staff could look forward to an extra treat in the form of a drink of sherry or even Christmas cake, brought in by the EiC.

1956 saw the building of an extension to house the FM transmitters, and Holme Moss was now able to utilise the cylindrical section of the 750 ft mast, with its slot aerials. Together with PCM distribution we were able to provide a much better quality radio service than had been possible in the past. Progress continued, over the years, with the introduction of 625 lines television, Sound-in-Syncs audio distribution. UHF Transmitters co-located with the I.T.A. at Emley Moor, with its 1,265ft. tubular mast. Transmitters that would operate automatically, without staff in attendance, and things were looking good, as Colour Television became a reality.

Emley Moor was the responsibility of Holme Moss staff, and in the early part of 1969, the I.T.A. were branching into UHF, with a new building to house the transmitters. Staff from Holme Moss would share the maintenance duties for the BBC transmitters at Emley. It was a cold winter, with much ice forming on the stays of the mast, causing quite noticeable sagging. Joe Eastwood and myself were carrying out maintenance one Wednesday, and the ice on my car windscreen, at lunchtime was almost quarter inch thick. The following day, the builders handed over the new building to the I.T.A., and just cleared the site, when shortly after 17.00 hrs. on 19th March 1969 the 1,265ft mast collapsed. The BBC engineer who had just started duty was Frank Orme, who, on being asked on the telephone from the Holme Moss duty S.M.E. Johnny Wilson, who had started his first shift as an acting S.M.E., what was happening, is reputed to have said "The mast has fallen down," Johnny then said "What, all of it?", and Frank replied, "I will go outside and have a look." On his return he replied that only about twenty feet was still standing. Frank's main concern, however, was that he had just washed his shirt and was drying it in the warm air from the transmitters. Now that they had closed down how could he dry his shirt?

The collapse of the 1,265ft mast became the subject of legal proceedings when the I.B.A. sought out someone to blame. It was not until 1977 that the outcome of the case, in front of High Court Judge, Mr Justice O'Connor, was published. The judge said "There was no evidence from any witness or instrument as to the state or behaviour of the mast at the time of its collapse." Will Harper, and myself, were both called as witnesses for the I.B.A., to this case at the Law Courts, in London. Will because of his experiences with ice-loading effects, both at Holme Moss and Emley Moor, together with his first-hand knowledge having climbed both masts on numerous occasions. I was asked to give evidence about the unusual movement of the Emley Moor mast, since it came into operation. I had complained to Engineering Information Department about my home reception being affected by varying signal strengths, causing slow oscillating chrominance changes and of a reflected (ghosting) signal. This was confirmed by field strength measurements, and I was told that my house was in a v.r.p. minima, and the variations indicated a slow oscillation, and twisting of the mast in certain low wind-strength conditions. These slow oscillations continued throughout the existence of the tubular mast, and the I.B.A. thought it would be useful evidence to support their case. Although we all knew of the movement of the stays, and twisting of the mast, the weather conditions at the time of the collapse included very poor visibility, and the judge decided that no-one was able to actually see what was happening at the crucial moment. The court hearing lasted fifty-three days. E.M.I. Electronics Ltd., and British Insulated Callenders Construction were judged liable to pay damages to the Independent Broadcasting Authority. The damages to be assessed at a later date by a High Court Official Referee. The judge also went on to say that air pressures and asymmetric ice loading at 1,027 feet caused the mast to break. The cost of the action so far in 1977, was unofficially estimated at £250,000.

The duties at Holme Moss changed considerably, with the introduction of UHF and the subsequent multitude of relay stations. We had to become used to working around the country, usually as teams of two engineers, equipped with test equipment, and Range Rovers. I, personally, spent many happy hours with my colleague

Maurice Lovelock, later to resign in favour of a job with a Cable company, in Canada. Relay Stations brought their own problems, several being sited on farmland. At Saddleworth, on one occasion, I was driving to the site, with the Range Rover window open, when I was suddenly showered with foul-smelling liquid from the farmer's vehicle which was spreading slurry. Another time, at Ladder Hill, the BBC paid for a firm to empty the cess-pit. We were in attendance, and the site owner told the firm that he could use the slurry, so all that happened was they pumped the contents of the pit straight on to his land, and got paid again. Stories about these farmers abound. At Keighley, the farmer was quite an accomplished yodeller and used to treat us to ad-hoc performances. Once at Keighley, one Saturday, my colleague, who had better remain anonymous because he is still employed in a senior post, was a model aeroplane fan. He decided that when we finished at Keighley we would go to Rochdale and visit his flying club. This was not strictly in the line of duty, but he was quite nonplussed when the S.M.E. at Holme Moss called us on the radio, thinking we were still at Keighley, to ask us to go to Shipley, just a few miles away from Keighley. We did rush up the motorway, but the round trip was probably nearer 90 miles than 20.

The original base, for Holme Moss was to be Holmfirth, but when it was realised that a large proportion of Holme Moss staff was formed by people from Moorside Edge, and moving house would involve the Corporation in many allowances, the Base was changed to Huddersfield, and the BBC Bus then operated from the Town Centre. The 12 mile journey, taking approximately half-an-hour, was repeated several times a day, with shift transport at weekends and late night being taken over by a taxi firm in Holmfirth, called Baddeley Brothers. These Taxis were of somewhat questionable vintage, and one of these had a differential which attacked people in the centre of the back seat with a series of painful knocks on the bum. Joe Eastwood was renowned for his quips, and he christened this particular car as 'Baddeleys Pile Driver'.

There are many more memories associated with Holme Moss, not the least interesting being the Open Days. Hundreds of cars, thousands of people, and much swelling of the Club funds because wives and families manned refreshment stalls, selling snacks, sweets, minerals and ice-cream. A never to be repeated experience, I suspect, but memorable ones to boot. If you have never faced the problem of temporary chemical toilets overflowing into a water-catchment area, then your experience as a transmitter engineer has not been completed. To end on an Open Day note, on 24 June 1961, Holme Moss was visited by a film crew for an item in the evening news. We all sat, expectantly in the Control Room, that night, to see ourselves, on the 'telly', but, as Joe Eastwood says in the commentary to his 8mm. film of the event, "such minor personalities as Kruschev and Kennedy, were featured, but of the IMPORTANT event of the day, not a mention". Our BBC News film was never shown.

Some unique facts & figures about Holme Moss.

At some 1,720 feet above sea level, Holme Moss, when it opened, was the highest Television Transmitting Station in the UK, and is probably still the highest transmitting station.

The original site spanned the County Boundary between Yorkshire and Cheshire. In order to simplify administration, the border was changed, to enable the site to become wholly Yorkshire.

Being situated in a Drinking Water catchment area, special precautions had to be taken to prevent any oil leakage from the Diesel Alternator fuel tanks spilling onto the land. Concrete base and retaining walls being provided.

Septic Tanks were not acceptable, so a private sewer had to be built to carry the waste some 2 miles downhill, in order to join the existing sewer at Holme Village.

Water, for use on the station, is pumped uphill, for almost 1,000 feet, from Yateholme Reservoir. A private pumping station was built near the reservoir and there is a water treatment plant at the station. Large bitumen-lined storage tanks are situated just below roof level.

The station is served by two BT telephone exchanges. One at Holmfirth is connected by overhead line, up the hillside from Holme

Village. In 1951, this was a manual exchange, and the PBX board, at Holme Moss, used plugs and cords, plus a magneto ringer. The other telephone line, ran underground, from the exchange at Mottram in Cheshire, and this had dial facilities from the start. B.T., or the G.P.O., as it was then, took special precautions to prevent 'Local' calls from one exchange being plugged through to numbers on the other exchange, and thus depriving them of possible 'Trunk Call' revenue.

An electricity substation, with Yorkshire Electric switchgear occupies part of the building, fed by 2 x 11kV feeders following different routes to minimise the risk of complete supply failure. During power shortage periods in the 60's. & 70's, the Electricity Board could 'Blackout' local villages yet maintain the supplies for the station.

The original underground signal cables were lead-covered and carried the vision signals on coaxial 3/8" diameter cables; TV sound, and later radio programmes, were on copper screened pairs. Because there is no real Earth on the site, the lead sheath of these cables provided an efficient lightning conductor during thunderstorms, and this caused many failures in the early days. The technology of the day required that the cables had to have repeater stations every six miles, all the way south to Birmingham. Up until the Sutton Coldfield station, vision signals distributed by the Post Office, had consisted of copper coaxial cables of 1/2" diameter. With the advent of Holme Moss, coaxial cables of only 3/8" were used. There were six of these 'tubes' in the system from Birmingham to Mottram (12 miles from Holme Moss), and then just two tubes from there. One tube carried the incoming vision signal, and the other was used to convey outside broadcasts, received on portable microwave links into Holme Moss to be sent to Manchester, and beyond, for inclusion in the network.

Where the Post Office cables entered the building was a room next to the Control Room, which housed the Post Office terminal equipment. This room, for several years, was manned by a P.O. engineer during transmission hours. Arthur Stafford was the senior man, and he and his colleague Geoff Bingham, became an integral part of the Holme Moss team. Geoff even helped me with the organisation of some of the BBC (Holme Moss) Club social activities. Geoff was probably instrumental in me becoming involved with the running of the Annual Christmas Parties, for the children and families of staff.

The standard vision test signal, used by both the BBC and Post Office, was a 'Pulse & Bar'. This signal did not have frame syncs so was not locked, and use of this caused great consternation once the network was extended North to Kirk o'Shotts. Whenever a P & B was on the return circuit south, it used to cause travelling bars to appear on the main distribution. This interference was easily recognised and on many occasions the operator manning the control desk at Holme Moss would have to report the problem to the G.P.O., and request them to remove it.

In common with most BBC premises, Holme Moss was equipped with its own Master Clock and slave loops. One of Will Harper's duties was to maintain this system. It was a common sight to see him with his collection of 'Pennies' and small pieces of metal, adding or removing from the top of the pendulum bob to correct timekeeping. The pendulum of the Master Clock was made from a metal called 'Invar', used because, unlike most other metals, it has a negligible coefficient of expansion. Now in the late 90's, Invar has again come into prominence in the TV industry, as it is being used for shadow-mask material in the latest versions of colour c.r.ts. Once again its limited expansion is used to prevent 'Doming', which affects the convergence efficiency with conventional tubes. Until recently, only Panasonic used Invar tubes, but now Nokia have started to use them.

Personalities

Having solicited several retired colleagues, for their anecdotes, I only received feedback from Dave Taylor, Joe Eastwood, and Derek Lawton. Dave recalls that when he was a T.A. at Washford, one of the S.M.Es. there, Charles Gladwell, had actually worked at 2LO, which was housed on the top floor of Selfridges store, in Oxford Street. This led me to recall that one of the original staff at Holme Moss, Ken Archer by name, had been at Alexandra Palace prior to joining Holme Moss. Further to this, when I was at Rampisham in 1947, one of the S.M.E.s. was Mark Savage, who had been a cameraman at AP in the pre-war

1930's. transmissions. When I joined Holme Moss I was amazed to see Mark every morning on the Demonstration Film, for it is he who is the cameraman featured in the AP sequence 'A mighty Maid, of Magic Mystery.' Another colleague, Will Harper, now in his 91st. year, is something of a legend in his own right. Employed as the Electrical Maintenance Engineer, since before Holme Moss opened, Will was a leading light in the Holme Moss team. His skills as an engineer proved invaluable. Working with lathe and raw materials he created many of the spare parts required by the transmitters. Sophisticated ball contacts, for the high power RF circuits, were such an example, and he saved the Corporation huge sums of money by manufacturing these 'in-house.' His fame soon spread and transmitter department heads in London soon expanded his output to cover many other transmitting stations. Will was also the man who was responsible for maintaining, and replacing bulbs on the navigation warning lights on the 750 ft mast. Even as he approached retirement age he could still climb masts quicker than many people much younger. At the time of the Emley Moor Mast collapse, in 1969, he was able to climb the 300 ft temporary replacement mast quicker than any of the P.I.D. engineers from London. In recognition of his services to the BBC, and his years of office for the BBC (Holme Moss) Club, Will was awarded the B.E.M. (British Empire Medal), on his retirement in 1972. The medal was presented to him at Admiralty House, by the Posts & Telecommunications Minister, Christopher Chattaway, in the presence of the then Chairman of the BBC, Sir Charles Hill. This was a very proud moment, for Will and his wife Marjorie, who, incidentally was one of the few wartime Technical Assistants F (female), and who met Will when they were both stationed at Moorside Edge. The day was also a memorable one for myself and my wife Joy, who accompanied them to the presentation, as well as all the celebrations arranged by the Director of Engineering, James Redmond, which included the use of his own staff car.

Joe Eastwood joined the staff, at Moorside Edge, before the War. His recollections come from wartime, when, like most 'high risk' installations, Transmitting Stations were provided with military guards. The original group of soldiers at Moorside Edge, were typical of those stalwarts of the 'Home Guard' as portrayed in 'Dad's Army.' Joe says that whenever he watches that programme, he is reminded of the similarity of the Officer, to Capt. Mainwaring, his N.C.O. to Wilson, the straw-filled palliases on the gallery overlooking the Transmitter Hall, where the troops slept, and the fact that whilst guarding the site with rifles and fixed bayonets, one soldier sneaking behind the building for a crafty fag, allowed his bayonet to get too close to the open-wire feeder, drawing a singing arc in doing so, and frightening himself to death. Joe was also a member of the BBC Home Guard, and remembers well that the only member of staff with any military experience was one of the cleaners, Jack Howe, who had been a soldier in the 1914 War. Jack took great delight in drilling his squad who were actually armed with broom handles instead of rifles. Anyone behaving badly was threatened with being put on a charge, by Jack, although his authority did not extend beyond Home Guard duties.

Eric Senior and Will Leonard were one of the original Transmitter Maintenance Teams, based at Moorside Edge, but transferred later to be based at Holme Moss. I recall Eric's frustration during a visit to the Keighley relay station, and finding it on fire. He called the fire brigade and whilst waiting outside the building heard the sirens approaching, then driving straight past the site and disappearing in the distance towards another transmitting station on the moors. Eventually the brigade returned but the equipment had suffered considerable damage in the meantime.

MF Stations, Derek Hearn

Transmitter Department staff realised that modern air-cooled valves could make a simpler and smaller transmitter which would be easier to maintain compared with the Regional MF transmitters that had been built in the 1930s. The original transmitters had sufficient spares to make another transmitter using modern air cooled valves and as the station staff were not all fully employed on operational duties every day, they built a transmitter in an empty machine room. This could keep the transmission going while the old water-cooled transmitter was being replaced by modern transmitters. The high voltage oil cooled modulation transformers caused a problem because the designer had long retired, the drawings had not survived and they were a difficult art to design and test. The transmitter manufacturers were not interested in making any more but a spare was found; the oil cleaned out, the "fur" on the insulation brushed off, and fresh oil poured in. A new transmitter made from spares was built and presented for TCPD's "acceptance tests." It was a remarkable achievement. Praise was due to the Transmitter Department engineer whose enthusiasm had inspired staff from many stations to locate the spares and then to build the transmitter. When finance allowed, industry was asked to tender for the replacements for the original "Regional" transmitters and Marconi's successfully provided a modern Doherty transmitter design.

Plymouth station, opened in 1924 at Seymour Road, had its sound studio & MF transmitter in the same building and a T aerial in the garden. When it became a TV studio, the studio was screened with chicken wire netting but great care was still needed to ensure that the MF signal did not get visibly onto the video signal sent to the TV transmitters. When Studio Capital Projects Department was planning to modernise the TV facilities they submitted a plan which included completely encasing the studio building in copper, with a roof top transmitter and aerial. The Deputy Director of Engineering, once a Transmitter designer and then Head of Transmitter Unit, intervened and a TCPD MF group leader was sent to Plymouth to investigate. It transpired that it was a 1kW RCA transmitter in which all of the vulcanised rubber wiring had perished and the Plymouth engineer rightly refused to touch it. The TCPD engineer reported that it would not be possible to move the transmitter and expect it to work. As its valves were of pre-War design he advised building a new modern transmitter station, away from the studio, and this was agreed. However, local planning approval halted this until TCPD got *evidence* that an aerial wire would not garrotte a local fancier's pigeons!

The work of bringing 20 MF Local Radio transmitters into service in a short time scale needed all the resources of TCPD's small MF Group, greatly helped by Transmitter Department staff. All the planned MF transmitters came on the air at 06:30 on 2 September 1972 as planned, save one 5 minutes late (never admitted!). Shortly before the service was due to start, the Leicester MF transmitter reported "Failed and no spares" to TCPD control at Daventry where centralised spares were located. Leicester's 'Speedy' had a Lotus Elan car and the motorway. He came, collected the spares, returned to the transmitter, got the carrier back on and then went to the studio. Programme started but not on Leicester MF - the line to the transmitter U-links were still out! But not for long.

THE WAR REPORTING UNIT 1944/1945, E C P METCALFE

As far as the transmitters were concerned, MCO was the first one on the beaches and this was a 250-watt transmitter mounted in a three-ton truck (MC was the series of call signs assigned to each transmitter). Later, on 28th July 1944, a 5 kW HF transmitter - the first MCP - was taken in at Mulberry in crates and was erected at Creully, near Bayeux. I don't remember this transmitter ever having gone on the air and as events moved rather fast, a second high power transmitter - the 7.5kW mobile MCN - was sent over on D Day plus 87 (1st September 1944). The Creullly transmitter was then re-crated and sent down to Paris to be used until a french transmitter there could be re-built after destruction by the departing Germans.

The MCN transmitter which I took over at Droitwich was very poorly arranged from the operational point of view, as the people who had designed the layout had little knowledge of the operational requirements in the field. To start with, the receiver was on one side of the cab and the transmitter controls were on the other. As it was necessary to switch the transmitter off completely before you could receive and it was necessary to switch off the receiver before transmitting, this was a far from convenient arrangement. So one of the first things we had to do was to modify the station to a 'press-to-talk' system, which meant a fair amount of rearrangement of the cab in itself. The towing vehicles provided were three-ton trucks one of which carried the diesel generator set. Our first sample of trouble was at Evesham prior to leaving for the embarkation port. All the trucks had been arranged in convoy on concrete ramps and I don't think we had gone more than twenty yards when the driver managed to put the first trailer over the edge! This meant we had to call on R.E.M.E. to haul the trailer back with a Scammel and this delayed our start by some two hours. Having got away from Evesham, the very first stiff hill we reached beat the three-tonner towing the transmitter trailer. We had to supplement it with one of the Utility trucks and that happened on every single hill right the way down to Portsmouth and on to Fareham where we eventually embarked on an L.S.T.

Having got the trucks disembarked in Normandy, we learned that the main fighting was taking place around Lisieux and Caen, and it was decided that we should go forward with the 2nd Army. We managed to drag the trailer along as far as Lisieux where we had a flat tyre. There were no spares available and E L Lycett and P H Walker went on in front to try and find some spares. Unfortunately they took all our rations with them so we had to spend three days by the side of the road with our 'iron rations' and nothing else! I managed to find some R.E.M.E. people who were engaged on clearing the road verges of mines and we went back to their Mess where we had our first real meal for three days. We didn't see Lycett and Walker again until they caught up with us in Brussels, as they went on to Paris for the liberation, leaving instructions for us to meet them in Rheims at a Hotel which we later found had been bombed out of existence three years earlier!

While we were in a little village called Villers Bocage, near Caen, we were shown several radio sets which had been built locally to instructions that had been given 'over the air' from Droitwich in the European Services. I remember that quite a few caustic remarks had been passed at Droitwich at the time concerning the futility of putting out such instructions but they seemed nevertheless to have been a great success, as quite a number of these sets had been made. In fact the chap who showed us his receiver in this village said: "Thank you, BBC. You were the only help we had for four years".

We had a great deal of trouble getting the trailer on the road again and in the end received help from Montgomery's H.Q. from where a Scammel was sent with instructions to assist us. They got us going but on the first hill they stripped the clutch of one of the three tonners. As a result the Scammel had to tow us all the way to Brussels! Having got into Brussels on liberation Day (September 5th 1944) we ran into difficulties with the Army Signals people. The first thing they said when they found that we proposed to operate a 7.5kW shortwave broadcast transmitter was: "Take the thing away because it will black out all Army communications in North-West Europe! In spite of many discussions and arguments with them they refused to relent and still held to the view that we should pack up and go home. After high level pressure was applied however they eventually agreed that we could go to a site at Gevissy, just outside Brussels - it used to be the site of the old Brussels frequency checking station, I think - and they said that we could go on the air from there but must close down as soon as they found we were interfering with Army Signals in any way. We set the station up at Gevissy and after we had been working MCM (Broad-casting House) for about three days, we went back and asked for their verdict on inter-ference. They said: "We're waiting for you to come on the air!" So when we told them we'd been transmitting for several days there were some rather red faces about! I think most of the chaps we were dealing with were in civilian life servicemen at radio shops and the like. After further high level pressure was put on by London – I believe to Montgomery himself – we got much better treatment all round.

It was planned that we should use a rhombic aerial and we were supplied with four 110 ft. sectional masts. To erect these required a large area of clear ground and the operation took a considerable time - about two days. In the meantime the Front had usually moved on and this meant for example in the Scheldt-clearing operation that correspondents had to drive anything up to 60 miles with their despatches to the transmitter, and then 60 miles back to the front again. The only alternative was to send one of the Recording trucks back with discs. So at this time we gave urgent thought to making MCN much more mobile. It was then decided to move us up to Eindhoven, despite the fact that we would then be only about 10 miles behind the front line. In fact, on two occasions when the enemy counter-attacked they got within 5 or 6 miles of us before being pushed back, and we were cut off for a while with Chester Wilmott having to drive through the lines to get back to Brussels!

While we were at Eindhoven, MCO which had been moving up along the coast with the Canadians, finally joined us. MCO was now pretty well out of range of the Ramsgate receiving station, but we used MCO as a mobile 'front line' transmitter by picking up his signals and relaying them direct to London through MCN. This technique was particularly useful during the Walcheren operation and also for the drives north into Holland.

We decided that the rhombic aerial was a major contributing factor to our regrettable lack of mobility, and what was really wanted was something we could erect very rapidly, allowing us to keep up with the Army Signals H.Q. We were lucky enough to pick up a couple of German 70 ft. hydraulically operated telescopic masts, and we re-designed the aerial system with directors and reflectors for our 7 MHz channel. We had managed to obtain this frequency from the Services, although they seemed very loathe to relinquish it as they hadn't used it since D Day. We were now able to work direct back to London using these masts which we were able to dismantle in about 45 minutes and erect in about an hour. This made us very considerably more mobile than before. The only remaining problem was the endless mechanical trouble we were having with the three-tonners. Luckily the Army managed to get R.E.M.E. to allocate to us two Matador trucks complete with their drivers. This made the job very much easier - these vehicles were designed for towing heavy guns about - and in one of them we installed the diesel generator set and the other one we converted to carry our spares and serve as a work-shop. We were thus able to build a complex consisting of two transmitter trailers, the studio truck and the workshop, making a complete unit roofed over with canvas and making everything snug and weatherproof.

The Front was moving pretty quickly by now, so we evolved a technique of having MCO go on ahead to the next site and set up, whilst we would remain on the air until they were operational. We would then join them. We were able to do this overnight, and from then on we were able to keep up with the Army Signals H.Q. at all times.

While we were at Eindhoven, the Paris transmitter (the first MCP) had been handed over to the French. The crew went back to the U.K. and came out with another mobile transmitter - a duplicate of MCN but to operate under the MCP call sign. Unfortunately in spite of all our comments and suggestions concerning the unsuitability of the initial layout, the new MCP arrived with all the well-known faults on it! So it had to be taken to Brussels and made more mobile. This was completed in time for it to take part in the coverage of the Ardennes offensive, and from then on this transmitter went forward with EAGLE TAC to Cologne, and from Cologne with the Americans through to Berlin where it remained until its last assignment came up - the Nuremburg Trials. It was finally handed over to the British Forces Network.

MCO and MCN continued their leap-frogging progress behind the front line and, at the time of the crossing of the Rhine, we were only 10 miles away as the bombers and gliders went in. Wynford Vaughan Thomas went in with the Green Howards immediately following the bombing attack, and MCO went over the next day on the first pontoon bridge to be erected. They established contact with us and we relayed their despatches directly on to London. As soon as they were ready to go forward again, we dismantled our MCN station and went over the Rhine on a bailey bridge near Wesel. While at Soltau, on the way to Luneburg, I went up to Hamburg and there found that the Army Signals had no one to operate the Hamburg transmitters. As it was wanted for an important broadcast that night we took over the job of operating it. Whilst at Luneburg, we took one of the Correspondents to Flensburg which had been the O.K.W. H.Q. to get interviews with the high-ups who had just surrendered, and on the way back we were stopped at a little village by a couple of German civilians, who said in very good English that they wished to surrender a transmitter to us. When we came to look at this equipment we found that it was the German equivalent of a War Reporting Unit detachment. It had apparently been in use on the Eastern Front, but the crew, realising that all was over, had driven back, collected their wives and families and had moved out to this village near Kiel. They then waited until they could find somebody to whom they could surrender! They handed two complete transmitters over to us and also tape recorders and studio equipment mounted in Volkswagen saloon cars, together with a collection of still and cine cameras and a complete dark-room. In all, there were about twenty vehicles.

After the signing of the Instrument of Surrender on 4th May 1945, we spent a short time clearing up the station and then returned to London. The transmitter was taken back to Droitwich and eventually it went to Engineering Training Department where it became a training transmitter.

During our journeys with the MCN through North-West Europe there were many instances of our vehicles getting bogged down with the subsequent difficulties in extracting them. While at Luneburg, the Army Press transmitter was out of action on several occasions - sometimes for two or three days at a time - and on these occasions a Censor was sent to read over the Pressmen's despatches to the general Press in the U.K. using MCN as the communication link.

While at Eindhoven, I remember that Bill Downs of C.B.S. suggested that we should try and work New York direct. This was found to be quite possible and as a result we evolved a system whereby time checks were fed back from New York through MCM (Broadcasting

House) to MCN. By working exclusively on time cues, Bill Downs was able to go straight into the American Networks. Most of the other American Correspondents followed his lead contributing direct to the Stateside broadcasting networks on time cues. They were all rather amazed at this because their own transmitters - the JESQ Group of Type 399 transmitters - were unable to work the States, let alone work on time cues! We also did two spots each week direct to Australia through Tatsfield. This was for Chester Wilmott to go into the A.B.S. system. These broadcasts usually took place about 5 a.m. and some of the American contributions also took place in the early hours. At this time therefore we were giving almost a 24-hour service!

Finally, some dates of MCN events:

Landed in Normandy	1 September 1944
Brussels	from 4 September 1944
Eindhoven	from 5 October 1944
Straelen	from 15 March 1945
Crossed the Rhine	23 March 1945
Ibbenburen	from 6 April 1945
Sulingen	from 14 April 1945
Soltau	from 26 April 1945
Luneburg	from 30 April 1945

The "Singing Arc", Bob Crawford

The story of the "Singing arc" I have heard repeated frequently in various forms, but the original occurred at Westerglen one summer's evening in 1938.

In those days, on medium waves, before the number of insulators on aerials and mast stays were greatly increased, it was a fairly common experience for an arc to develop across an insulator. Once started, the transmitter power maintained the arc – no lightning protection equipment then- until the transmitters were run off and then re-powered. Meanwhile, out in the field, due to the non-linear characteristics of the arc, demodulation took place and the programme bellowed out at enormous volume – much to the surprise of many a farmer.

On the occasion in question, for some extraordinary reason the G.S. engineer on duty, Andy Scougall, whose duty it was to visit the feeder huts out in the field every two hours, had never heard of the singing arc effect. Late on this very dark and thundery evening Andy collected his torch and bunch of keys and set out into the field. Suddenly there was a great flash of lightning, a deafening crash of thunder, over went the aerial insulators and a sepulchre voice roared something about "amen" followed by a rather full volume singing of a choir of angels. Andy did not hesitate. Away went the bunch of keys and the torch and he raced back to the building in which he collapsed into a chair in the transmitter hall. We told him of the singing arc effect and explained that there had been a religious service on at the time of the arc. We asked him why he had run into the building if he thought it was the end of the world? Did he think that the transmitter hall would be saved? Andy replied that he felt that if he had to go then would like to go along with someone else.

INSTALLING KIRK O'SHOTTS - AND "THE LADIES STOCKING FACTORY", DENNIS SURRIDGE

The Kirk o'Shotts site is situated almost halfway between Glasgow and Edinburgh, with (then) no reasonably accessible or attractive town nearby. The initial Building Dept. architects and TCPD installation engineers decided that Edinburgh should be their base, this was in no small way influenced by the presence on the west side of Edinburgh of the Clarendon Hotel. The building and installation of equipment took place during the winter of 1951/52 which was not the ideal time for working in incomplete buildings especially in Scotland. The installation team stayed at the Clarendon Hotel and the project definitely benefited from the care and comfort (to the inner man) given by the hotel staff. On returning in the evening, regardless of the time, there was always a hot meal awaiting and everyone was sent off in the mornings with a breakfast of at least two eggs and this was during the period of food rationing. The Hotel is well remembered with appreciation by all of the installation engineers of 1951/52.

At the site there were no facilities for a mid-day meal. At some HP TV sites the building contractors had a small canteen but not at Ko'S. Until the station canteen was available an arrangement was made with a local factory, a distance of about 6 miles, that use could be made of their canteen after their staff's lunch hour. The factory manufactured ladies stockings and employed about 200 girls. There were usually about 6 engineers who would arrive just at the end of the girls lunch break as, for courtesy, they did not want to prolong the catering staff's working hours. The daily arrival of 6 or so fairly young strange men walking past 200 girls set off many female whistles and suggestive remarks, but it was all taken with good humour and the hot mid-day meal was appreciated.

SOUND STUDIO AND CONTROL ROOM ENGINEERING, 1929-1971, L G SMITH

The text below offers an insight into the very early days of Equipment Department and acts as a reminder that studio engineering also had its challenges. It is based on a talk given by L G Smith at a RELIC (retired BBC engineer) lunch on 21.4.99.

"I joined the BBC direct from secondary school as a tracer in Equipment Dept Drawing Office in 1929. During the whole of my career my work was associated with the design, planning, installation and testing of Sound Studio and Control Room equipment through many changes and transfers of department names- ED, SDID, DID, PID, SPID. I retired in 1971 but worked part-time until 1974 on 'Special Duties' attached to DE's office.

In the early days at Savoy Hill, equipment such as amplifiers were provided by Marconi or Western Electric. They were huge units in mahogany boxes about 6' x 4' x 2'.

Programmes were routed to transmitters by the shortest available route over the S.B. (Simultaneous Broadcast) Network. Thus a Programme originating in Birmingham would be routed northwards via Manchester, Leeds, Newcastle and Edinburgh for the Northern Transmitters and southwards via London and Bristol for the Regional Transmitters at Brookmans Park and Washford. Continuity Suite working was not introduced until 1940.

Many programmes originated in the Regions for Regional Broadcasting but Big Ben and the main news broadcasts originated in London and would be fed via all regional control rooms to the transmitters.

Thus switching of lines was carried out in all control rooms via plugs and jacks following standard GPO practice and needed accurate timing and monitoring to ensure that all lines were 'over to London' for Big Ben and the News for instance.

There never seemed to be any difficulty in this switching throughout the 1930's and I cannot understand why so many video programmes I try to record have missed beginnings and endings due to early starts and overruns.

Since there was a close relationship between BBC/GPO engineers, a Lines Section of BBC Engineers at Savoy Hill under a Mr. Atkins was responsible for the rebuilding of Manchester Control Room, a main switching centre, to replace the plug and jack switching facilities with Strowger 2 motion selectors. The equipment, including amplifiers was rack mounted, finished in a GPO grey/green paint and operated from GPO type mahogany switchboards.

Although this type of switching was acceptable for automatic telephone working, the clicks and unreliability were unacceptable for BBC purposes, although it still remained in service until the mid 30's.

Following this failure a small Designs Section was formed as part of Equipment Department to design the switching equipment and associated amplifiers for Broadcasting House.

This Section consisted of 'Uncle Colborn' and Mr J Locke as engineers, with two draughtsmen all accommodated in one room at Avenue House.

The first results of this Section were the rebuild of Edinburgh Control Room using relays with platinum/gold/silver contacts for programme switching with the old mahogany desks replaced by the now familiar BBC grey finished rack mounted equipment and metal desks.

It was at this time 1929 that I joined as a junior tracer.

Equipment Department was located with Research Department in Avenue House, 87 Kings Avenue, Clapham, a former residence of the Governor of Brixton Prison which was within 50 yards of Avenue House.

A small workshop and a stores had been built in the forecourt of the house and a garage held the transport fleet of about 8 vehicles with a hand operated petrol pump from which one could get petrol for the equivalent I think of $12^{1}/_{2}$ pence a gallon.

The Head of Equipment Department was F.M. Dimmock, father of Sports and OB Dimmock. The only ladies on the staff were Mrs. Lewis who brought round the tea at 1 old penny a cup, and a part-time cook. These two provided two sittings of lunch in what used to be the lodge of the Governor's House. All secretaries, typists and the switchboard operators were male – one of the switchboard operators Holmes in later years became Head of Research Department drawing office at Kingswood Warren.

We worked till 6 and every other Saturday until 1 o'clock. There were no proper salary grading systems, no overtime, extra duty pay or leave in lieu, everyone worked to do a good job and particularly in setting control room equipment to work, many evening and all night sessions would be worked to clear faults without thought of time off.

There were moans. A cost of living allowance had been paid to staff working in London at Savoy Hill and within 10 miles of Savoy Hill to cover the many premises in Central London. When the Headquarters moved from Savoy Hill to Broadcasting House, Avenue House was outside this 10 miles radius and the allowance was ceased.

In the economic depression of the early 30's a meeting was called by Sir John Reith of all BBC staff in the Concert Hall of BH to consider a contribution by deduction from pay, to open a centre for the unemployed in Gateshead. E.D. staff including workshop staff came up from Avenue House and a representative from the Ministry of Labour sat on the platform with Sir John to say his piece. After hearing all about the project, suddenly one of the workshop staff got up and said – "Before collecting for the unemployed in Gateshead, what about the workshop staff at Avenue House. I have been working for the BBC for 5 years and only get 6d. an hour" or words to that effect. He was followed by about half a dozen others.

Sir John immediately adjourned the meeting, called for any other complaints, took the names of the workshop staff and arranged to see them all in his office the next morning, before continuing the meeting. As a result many had their wages doubled and all had rises of some sort. Their wages had been the responsibility of Mr. Dimmock and many wondered how he survived the matter.

In those days we all had a Christmas bonus equal to a week's pay notified in a letter from Sir John. Although a strict teetotaller, instant dismissal at the first hint of a divorce etc. as I understood it, he was highly esteemed by all staff. Everyone had the right of direct access to Sir John if occasion demanded. An engraving head and shoulders of him was inserted in one issue of 'Ariel' and this found its way on to many office walls and framed on to some desks. I don't see this happening with one of the present D.G.

It is difficult to appreciate that in the late 1920's and early 30's virtually no commercial equipment was available to satisfy the standards required by the BBC. Components such as transformers, resistors, volume controls etc. were therefore designed and made by E.D. Resistors were made by turning slots in 1" diameter ebonite rod and winding these with resistance wire. Six such resistors about 4" long connected to a 24 way stud switch also made in E.D. formed a main volume control.

All components were tested before being incorporated into amplifiers and other apparatus which were built on 3/16" steel panels for rack mounting. Terminal blocks for these units were of 3/16" ebonite having each soldering tag fixed with a nut and bolt. Wiring inside the units was carried out in 16swg bare tinned copper wire covered in red sleeving with all the wire running straight with right angled bends.

As E.D. expanded to provide for the installations in Broadcasting House followed by the re-equipment of the Regional Premises, an asbestos bungalow was built in the garden of Avenue House. Designs Section occupied a long room across the end of the bungalow, the drawing office expanded to six and two new engineers from ST & C skilled in relay circuit design and cableform design assisted 'Uncle Colborn'.

There were lighter moments, of course. The head draughtsman Alan Holden lived very near Avenue House and as there was plenty of garden available, he started a little allotment outside the drawing office window which he cultivated in the evenings. He proudly announced one day that he had planted some runner beans, so in his absence we dug up these beans and planted instead some giant sunflower seeds which we encouraged Alan to water every evening. When these were about 3" high they looked very similar to runner bean plants and Alan duly erected an array of bean sticks. At 9" high we persuaded him he had to tie them first clockwise and when they still would not curl round, to try anticlockwise round each bean stick. Alan was not a very knowledgeable gardener and it was not until the sunflowers were about 2ft. high that Alan realised what was going on. We did, however, enjoy a great variety of birds eating the sunflower seeds.

Drawings at that time were drawn in Indian ink on tracing linen, circuits had resistors drawn as about a dozen zigzags all lines at the correct angle, and transformers needed about 20 semicircles joined with straight lines to represent the coils. All lettering was hand done – no stencils or stick-on labels for circuit components.

Tracings then had to be taken to a firm in Kingsway for industrial prints to be made which were in the form of white lines on a bright blue paper – hence the term 'blue print' used nowadays in the context of plans for any new National Health proposals or whatever. Later these reproductions became dye line prints – brown lines on white paper much easier to mark up or revise.

Having learnt something about E.D. Test Room activities by coming in on my Saturday mornings off duty, I began working there part time and then full time as the work load increased with the equipment requirements for Broadcasting House and later the Regional Control Rooms. Although it was a long time before I was officially designated an engineer from being a drawing office tracer.

The Test Room was located in what was the old dining room of the Governor's House and judged by today's safety standards was a lethal place to work. There were two test positions for rack mounted equipment consisting of bay frameworks with terminal blocks of brass pillar terminals which carried 300V HT, 6V LT and GB voltages, all fully live and it was advisable to keep one hand in your pocket when connecting wires to these. The main 300V HT came from accumulators kept under a bench fed through open knife switches.

Amplifiers were tested for frequency response by switching a thermocouple from input to output to measure tone from the bay-mounted variable oscillator to a fixed oscillator mounted as far away as possible high up on the far side of the room. Most of the time was taken up by tapping the glass of the thermocouple meter to get as high a reading as possible.

We still enjoyed a few lighter moments, particularly at the expense of one engineer 'Auntie Kidd' ex Research Department whose responsibility in Test Room was the testing of microphones. He used a large coffin shaped box which had the microphone under test at one end and a loudspeaker at the opposite end into which tone was fed. The box was very heavily sound proofed and the lid fitted with a very large number of screws requiring removal for access. A headphone jack was provided to check that the loudspeaker was working. Time after time the diaphragms were removed from Auntie's headphones giving him the onerous task of removing the screws and lead to check the loudspeaker. He never seemed to learn.

Broadcasting House came into service in May 1932. The studios were contained within a tower built of blue engineering brick with very few doorways or other openings. This tower was surrounded by corridors and offices constructed as normal over a steel girder framework with no girder connection to the studios thus those were well insulated from outside acoustic interference and were further insulated vertically by quiet areas such as libraries and storage areas.

The existence of the blue brick tower which is 4ft. thick in the basement areas appears to have been overlooked in recent times as a request for a 6" x 6" cable hole through this at the time of BH's extension work was dismissed as "no problem, a few days' work". I seem to remember work still going on several weeks later to make this hole.

A fact not generally known about BH is that it has an artesian well which provides an excellent programme earth.

The Director of Administration at that time was Mr Ralph Wade who was of the opinion that the whole of the BBC revolved around him and his department. Engineers were but glorified plumbers who should be confined to the basement and the eighth floor. He supervised the six page boys who sat in the entrance hall to run errands and he stood about in black jacket and pin striped trousers wearing a monocle. One day he sent a new monocle to a small workshop attached to the eighth floor control room to have it drilled for its black ribbon. As he did not specify where it was to be drilled it was returned to him with a single hole in the middle of the glass - not a person popular in the Engineering Division.

Re-equipment of the Regional Control Rooms proceeded after BH, and I was very involved in this work. Newcastle, where the BBC occupied what had previously been a maternity lying-in hospital was another building where the thick granite walls caused problems, this time for the GPO, in routing cables into the new Control Room. Cardiff was done in June 1934 where the BBC was located in an old house in Park Place, followed by Glasgow where the studios and Control used an old house in Blytonswood Square.

The procedure was for an engineer from E.D. to go to site with a mechanic and three or four wiremen from E.D. workshops to the new Control Room. Full installation information, cable runs, interlay wiring connection sheets were available and having seen the 10-20 bays erected and desks positioned the engineer would leave the wiremen to carry on with the work paying visits every few weeks as required.

The chargehand wireman, one Freddie Mott, was an elderly man, very unobtrusive but a superb wireman. Every wire to a jackfield etc. carefully curled to exactly the same curve with a button hook, inter-bay cables laced, covered with insulating tape and finally finished with yellow empire cloth tape and never, ever, a wrong connection or dry joint. All wiring was carried out in lead covered 1 pr/10. No multi core cables were used for programme wiring in studios or control rooms until 1940.

It was thought that Freddie Mott should write progress reports to confirm the need for an engineer's visit, but his first report caused some amusement when received at E.D. - it read 'Dear Mr Dimmock, the boys' colds are much better. F. Mott'.

The testing and setting to work of those control rooms with their relay switching systems was an intensive period of extra hours of work. Very little was known of the causes and cures of clicks and crosstalk or of the principles of earthing and shielding from interference. All was the subject of much discussion and experiment since the BBC requirements were much more stringent than those of the GPO for their automatic telephone exchanges, and it is thanks to the insistence on these high standards that the BBC enjoyed such a high reputation at that time amongst the broadcasting authorities of the world.

There were no small diodes and such-like to incorporate in the wiring and no electrolytic condensers. The standard anti-click device was a 2µf condenser (about 2" x 2" x 1") in a tin case in series with a 600 ohm works wound resistance across the coil of a relay and finding space and mechanical mounting for these or the 25µF condenser about 6" x 3" x 8" was always a problem.

Like the test room, 300V HT was fed through open knife switches and open terminal blocks. Each individual unit supply was routed via a small glass fuse, one of 24 similar fuses closely spaced and completely uncovered. Removing or replacing a fuse required very careful holding of the glass between thumb and forefinger without touching the end caps. Sometime later I believe insulated pliers were made available for this but I never saw any.

Both Research and Equipment Departments expanded and outgrew existing accommodation. Research Department moved first to Nightingale Lane and then to Nightingale Square in Clapham, whilst an extra building was built on the Avenue House site. This was mainly a single-storey block which housed test room, battery charging rooms, and additional stores areas with a second storey at one end of the building for Designs Section engineers and the drawing office.

The test room had several small rooms for microphone and loudspeaker testing and the drawing office had nice large windows for the draughtsmen. The only minor faults in the design were the omission of any stairs to get to the second storey of the building and some problems with a patent parquet floor in the test room. The stairs were fortunately able to be fitted in before final completion although unfortunately they were not wide enough to take the drawing office plan chests. The test room floor was more serious and its fault came to light after we moved in. Every time anyone touched a 300V terminal a shock was received and this was traced to the floor made of wooden blocks set in a 'muckite' of sawdust which had a resistance of only a few thousand ohms. This fault was got over by providing each engineer with a rubber mat to stand on when connecting up H.T. terminals.

Outside the front door of Avenue House there stood statues of two beasties. Lion like creatures about 4ft. high. These were originally painted all over cream but over the years were just dirty white, until after the extension was built when the house was repainted by Bill Picket. He was a notable character from Building Dept. with a real Sergeant Major type waxed and pointed moustache, who was so taken with the beasties that I think he spent more time on them than on the house. He finished them in a dark chocolate colour with teeth and claws in gleaming white and tongue in red. He managed to produce a most wicked look in their eyes. So much so that one instinctively glanced over one's shoulder when going in the door in case of attack from the rear. When Avenue House moved to Chiswick the beasties were moved there and put inside the entrance hall, and I now understand that they are in residence at Kingswood Warren.

A SCOTTISH THREAT TO THE CORONATION BROADCAST, DAI THOMAS

A few days before the Coronation in 1953, a Scottish organisation threatened to put a stop to the broadcasting of the ceremony in Scotland. The obvious target for achieving this was to interfere with the PO TV distribution chain from London to Kirk o'Shotts at some vulnerable point and the PO link station at Pontop Pike was considered to be highly likely.

A meeting was arranged between Scotland Yard and Transmitter Dept represented by Edward Bonong of Head Office, Sid Goodyear EiC Stagshaw, and myself representing Peter Brett EiC Pontop Pike who was on leave. It was held at Police HQ Durham I seem to remember.

The outcome was that for some days prior to and including Coronation day, the whole area of the hillside surrounding the prefabricated hut containing the temporary transmitters mounted in a caravan was heavily policed, special identity cards issued to the staff and dire warnings expressed of the possible consequences of failing to follow police instructions. The whole issue was taken exceedingly seriously. However the attack failed to materialise and the broadcast went ahead without incident.

LIFE IN LINES DEPARTMENT, 1944-1979, GEOFF MARTIN

As the war progressed BBC Engineering took on a number of women and girls, and a larger number of young men who would be "called up" in due course. In 1944, at the age of 16 I wrote enquiring if there were any vacancies and following an interview received a letter, which I still have, offering me "a post as Youth on the staff in Lines Department at a weekly wage of £1.7.6 (£1.37^1/$_2$p) plus 8/6d (42^1/$_2$ p) Cost of Living Bonus". If I accepted I was "to report to the Head of Lines Department at Broadcasting House on 3 April 1944", which I did.

Lines Department and Esther's father

On arrival I didn't see the Head, H B Rantzen, whose young daughter Esther was to become very well-known, but was sent to one of his assistants for a short briefing on the department and its responsibilities. These were the provision and maintenance of the links carrying programmes between Studio Centres, and to Transmitters, as well as those for Outside Broadcasts and inter-office communication. All these were carried on what were then called 'land-lines', rented from the Post Office (now British Telecom).

The lines fault log

Maintenance of the country-wide networks of hundreds of lines was important, as a fault could seriously affect broadcasting, although there were some reserve arrangements. After the briefing I was sat at a telephone to take reports of faults and then pass them on to the appropriate engineers who would report back when the fault had been cleared. The details had to be entered in a Fault Log and I was instructed to take this to HLD each afternoon at 3 o'clock. It was explained that HLD was the abbreviation for Head of Lines Dept. thus I was introduced to the BBC's world of titles and abbreviations. I got the impression that HLD was held in awe and the initials were another way of spelling GOD. He was certainly tall, and of quite striking appearance, but although we didn't meet for some time I found him to be most courteous to a raw youth of sixteen. On the first afternoon I took the Log to his office with some trepidation, which proved to be justified for I met my first formidable secretary. Rantzen had, like a number of other engineers in Lines Dept., come from one of the telephone cable companies and had brought his secretary with him. Whereas he was over six feet tall, she was about four foot eight, but I felt that it would have taken one of Hitler's Panzer Divisions to get past her. She took the Log into his office and after what seemed hours came out and sent me on my way. Thus began a daily routine.

Programme lines and equalisation

The lines rented from the Post Office to carry programmes were basically telephone circuits not designed to carry the wide frequency range (bandwidth) required for broadcasting quality, especially music. That is why specialist engineers, like Harry Rantzen, had been recruited by the Corporation to carry out pioneering work to 'condition' circuits so that wherever a programme originated, or however far it travelled around a network, it would be heard by the listener just as it left the studio. The problem isn't just that as a signal passes down a line it gets fainter, but that the higher the frequency the greater the attenuation, or loss.

The solution was to measure the loss over the required frequency range and then build a passive network of resistors, capacitors and inductances to introduce further losses in a mirror-image fashion. The overall loss would then be the same at all frequencies and an amplifier could raise the signal back to the required level. For fairly obvious reasons the process was called equalisation, and the network an 'equaliser'. These were custom-built for permanently rented circuits as no two were the same. With some types of lines it was found that the frequency/attenuation characteristic changed during the year and it was regularly necessary to alter the equalisation. This was due to temperature variations affecting the underground cables so Temperature Correction Units (TCUs) were designed to modify the Equalisers. The Met. Office was paid to report ground temperatures at several depths around the country throughout the year and these were used to calculate when it was necessary to alter the settings of the TCUs.

Outside Broadcasts

Variable equalisers were designed to be used on circuits for Outside Broadcasts. These were many and varied during and after the War, "Worker's Playtime" from factories, Church services, organ music from cinemas, football commentaries, etc. At one time there were four hundred permanently rented lines from regularly used OB points in the London area alone. These terminated in the OB Gallery of the old Control Room in the basement of BH. mostly in pairs, that is 'music' and 'control'. At the OB point they were always left connected together 'A' leg to 'A' leg, and 'B' to 'B'. As they were all unamplified this allowed Control Room engineers to carry out DC tests round the loop, for insulation, loop resistance and A/B balance using a 'Bridge Megger'.

Temporary circuits were ordered from other OB points and if these were long, and therefore amplified, they were routed from a special PO exchange near St Pauls referred to as 'London Trunks'. In view of the limited number of this type of line, and hence the much greater costs involved, they were only rented for short periods. This was usually one hour for testing several days before the OB, then the actual time required for the broadcast, with half an hour beforehand for setting up the equalisation, adjusting amplification and carrying out programme quality tests. For the pre-OB tests we would visit the venue with a portable telephone, oscillator, 'Megger', a case of hand tools, wire, a field-book and equaliser masks. The 'Megger' was used for DC tests (as above), back to the first PO Repeater (amplifier) Station, and the book was for logging test results and drawing the resulting music line frequency characteristic. The masks were transparent sheets on which were drawn the inverse characteristics of the different equaliser settings and the task was to match one with the graph. Sometimes this was not possible and two equalisers were required in tandem. When equalisation had been successfully carried out two further tests were made, measurement of the signal-to-noise separation, and harmonic distortion. Details of equalisation requirements etc. were passed to the Control Room so that the appropriate settings could be used for the actual broadcast. At some locations such as cathedrals, race-courses and greyhound tracks the PO also provided microphone leads. These too had to be 'Meggered' and I remember finding myself in such diverse places as high up in the Hare Control Box in a Greyhound Stadium and in the Clock Chamber behind the face of Big Ben.

For some remote locations the PO was unable to provide satisfactory lines and allowed us to install portable equalising and amplifying equipment in their Telephone Exchanges en-route. In this case we would have to return after the test for the broadcast and I once spent a week in a tiny Post Office building, miles from anywhere, during a Labour Party Conference at Margate.

The earliest type, known as an ERU, (Equaliser Repeater Unit) was built like the proverbial battleship. It had two units inside a teak box, measuring about 50cm square by 22 deep and must have weighed at least 25kg. Although mains-operated it was, of course, accompanied by a set of lead-acid batteries and a large HT dry battery. The unit was not dubbed P(Portable)ERU and lugging this lot up several flights of stairs in a Telephone Exchange was no mean feat. The available equalisation and amplification was fairly limited but the equipment which succeeded it, the PER/5 (Portable Equaliser Repeater Type 5) had a large range of equalisation, higher gain amplifiers, built-in metering and, above all, came in three aluminium cases which were designed to be stacked. Separate LT and HT batteries were still taken in case of mains failure but the former were no longer the lead-acid type, but sealed units, type WF. They were actually designed for sale to farmers for low voltage electrified wire fences, to restrain animals, hence WF.

The blacked out broadcast

I wasn't personally involved, but was listening to a Church Service one evening when suddenly the Vicar stopped speaking and all that could be heard was coughing which went on for several minutes until the Continuity Studio announcer apologised and played some music. I met the OB engineer a few days later and he told me that the lights had fused in the Church but he was in the Crypt with his equipment and had no idea what the problem was because the lights there were OK. He left the microphone faded up, and the red light on, so the Vicar didn't know what to do.

Split band equipment and the Michelmores

All our equipment was unique, having been specially designed for the purpose, none more so than the 'Split-Band' system. This was developed because the bandwidth of some telephone circuits was too narrow and couldn't be equalised to broadcasting quality. At the originating end the programme was fed into equipment which split it into two bands, hence the name, of lower and higher frequencies. The lower were sent down one line and the higher frequencies were translated into low frequencies and sent on a second line. At the far end the process was reversed to restore the original programme and I liked to think of this as making a silk purse out of two sow's ears! It wasn't often required but in due course it was used every Sunday between Hamburg and London for "Two-way Family Favourites". The programme was introduced by Jean Metcalfe in London, and Cliff Michelmore in Hamburg, and their subsequent marriage was a result of their weekly "on-air" date. Without our split-band equipment it wouldn't have been possible!

My time as a recording operator

After my return from National Service in 1948 I was transferred to Recording Dept. for a time. There were three main recording centres in London, one in Broadcasting House for the domestic services, another nearby in 200 Oxford Street for the General Overseas English language programmes and a third in Bush House for the European Service and other foreign languages. Initially I worked in Oxford St. and then at Bush House. This was before the introduction of modern tape-recording and we used 'Presto' equipment supplied by America under the Lease-Lend Program.

Recordings were made on cellulose coated aluminium discs in which the groove was cut by a sapphire needle. Short recordings of about $3^{1}/_{2}$ minutes were made at 78 rpm on 12 inch discs, but larger discs, running at 33 rpm, could be used for about 14 minutes. The latter were used to record complete programmes with a short overlap from each disc to the next. We also played back these 'on-air' and the skill was to get both discs in synchronisation before switching over. The 78 rpm recordings were used for short inserts into programmes, or items which were to be edited such as sports commentaries, and were handled by non-engineering Recorded Programme Assistants who were adept at juggling with discs revolving at twice the speed.

Tony Benn and the fire

A recording channel had two turntables side-by-side so that continuous recording was possible as mentioned. Two operators were employed, one to set up the next disc while the other concentrated on the actual recording. As the sapphire cut the groove a fine ribbon of cellulose, called swarf, came off and this had to be continually swept off with a soft brush. Being highly inflammable it was then dropped into a red pedal-bin (swarf-bin) which a BBC Fireman would empty daily. During one Wimbledon fortnight a North American Service Producer, well known as a pipe smoker, was in the recording channel and absentmindedly put his foot on the pedal and tapped his pipe into the bin. The resulting fire burnt out the wiring and the equipment was out of action for several days. Some time after this the pipe smoker, Anthony Wedgwood Benn, simplified his name and went into politics.

Back to lines

After a couple of years I returned to Lines Dept. where I remained for some 26 years before taking early retirement. The department was then organised into a number of sections, each responsible for a different aspect of work that is:

- SB (Simultaneous Broadcasts): the network of permanent audio circuits for Radio and Television.
- OB (Outside Broadcasts): temporary audio circuits, for Radio and Television.
- TV (Television): permanent and temporary (OB) video circuits.
- Telecommunications: inter-office speech (inter-PBX) and Teleprinter systems.
- Telephones & Finance: provision of office telephone systems and the administration of finance involved in renting circuits.

For a time I worked in the Telecommunications Section which provided the Corporation's inter-office speech and teleprinter facilities. The inter-PBX circuits linking the BH Switchboard to the Regional offices were obtained by exploiting music-quality lines which had a bandwidth of about 8kHz. BBC designed Carrier Systems broke this down into three narrow channels of about 2.4kHz, which were adequate for telephony, and later, when some 10kHz lines became available, four channels were possible. In addition very narrow channels were filtered out for telegraphy and were used for the extensive BBC Teleprinter Network. This terminated in the Teleprinter Room in The Langham where we had a workshop employing about five mechanics maintaining the machines. Our colleagues in the Regions could carry out first-line maintenance, but machines were sent back to London for major faults and overhauls.

In due course the Department had to provide networks of superior lines to match the high quality of transmission which the new VHF FM allowed, and later came stereo, for which 'matched pairs' of circuits were required.

Years later, as the Corporation expanded we ceased to be a Specialist Department and were reorganised by being split into 'Operations' and 'Planning'. The latter was still arranged in sections, similar to the old arrangement, but was mainly concerned with planning and setting up the permanent networks, whereas the operational staff were involved with the day to day running of networks and systems, including the Television Switching Centre in Broadcasting House. The OB circuit testing group was hived off to Television OBs and moved to Kendal Avenue. Operations also included the Circuit Allocation Unit (CAU) which was responsible for ordering temporary sound and vision circuits, and allocating these, and the permanent circuits, as required to meet programme requirements.

The return of television

Years before this, Television, which had started pre-war in black and white, had returned. Television pictures required about three hundred times the bandwidth of music, so transmission over ordinary lines was only possible for a few hundred yards. So when EMI designed the Television system they incorporated line transmission based on a new kind of balanced pair cable. The Post Office installed this in a huge loop round London with connecting points at, or near, many places such as Olympia, Earls Court, Buckingham Palace etc. The loop started, and finished at Broadcasting House where it terminated in a Switching Centre equipped with test equipment and video equalisers, rather more complex than their audio counterparts. This allowed the Television OB Units to send pictures back to Broadcasting House, from where they were sent on a similar cable to Alexandra Palace which housed the Television Studios and Transmitter serving the London Area. The Switching Centre engineers could also remotely operate switches along the balanced pair and a special team of PO engineers could provide short extensions over telephone cables so that Television OBs were possible from most parts of Central and West London. TV OB Engineers could also send pictures by radio but originally the PO only waived their monopoly, and allowed this, when they were unable to provide a line.

In due course television spread across the country as transmitters and Regional Studios were built, and the links provided to connect them together. These links were still rented from the Post Office and the first was established to Birmingham from Museum Telephone Exchange, where the BT Tower now stands, near BH. Thereafter most were provided by co-axial cable systems with channels in both directions ('Distribution' from London, to feed programmes to Transmitters, and 'Contribution' in the reverse direction). It therefore became possible for Regions to generate programmes for the Network and for OBs to be arranged from many parts of the country. Switching Centres were therefore established in the Regional Centres to handle the growing complexity of sources and destinations.

With the growth of public telephone traffic, and the introduction of Subscriber Trunk Dialling, the Post Office had to expand its network and this was done by routing thousands of voice circuits over links which were like television channels. Spare links, (dubbed Protection

Channels) were arranged in order to cope with breakdowns and we were able to rent these if the BBC network was fully booked.

The Coronation

The BBC pulled out all the stops for the 1953 Coronation and this was credited with the phenomenal growth in Television licences which subsequently allowed the Corporation to expand. Interest was not confined to the UK as there was a strong demand from abroad which the BBC met by providing large numbers of commentary positions for foreign radio and TV Broadcasters along the processional route. All this was grist to the mill for Lines Dept. which had to order, test and equalise hundreds of lines. A special Microwave link was also required from London to Dover, to carry pictures to the Continent, and as all BBC equipment was engaged this was set up by a contractor. The handover point in London was on the roof of Senate House, London University, in Bloomsbury which was linked to the Switching Centre by a direct cable. It was there that I spent Coronation day, some 150 feet above London, and although quite a distance from the thousands thronging the streets, the cheering could be heard across the rooftops.

The Archbishop's lost pictures

At this time there were no Video Recorders, so programmes were recorded from the screen onto film, and from time to time viewers are still shown extracts of the Coronation telerecording which was made at Alexandra Palace. The Archbishop of Canterbury had expressed a wish to see this so a few days after the event he came to Broadcasting House with a number of other notabilities and senior BBC staff. The recording was played back from AP but not transmitted, just sent down the cable to BH Switching Centre and we routed it to the Council Chamber where everyone was gathered. Shortly after the start I received a phone call from a Post Office engineer to say that he had to test the Outside Broadcast Balanced Pair cable by intercepting it just outside Broadcasting House. I impressed on him the need for care as there were two cables, the OB loop, and the link to Alexandra Palace, and on no account was the latter to be touched. Murphy's law prevailed and shortly afterwards we lost the picture. I dashed outside and found two men with an open man-hole cover on the pavement, oblivious of the consternation they had caused. Happily all was restored within 20 minutes but it brought home how fragile the broadcasting chain was.

Grade One broadcasts

As the majority of broadcasts were live, the most important ones were dubbed 'Grade 1' and involved special precautions. Lines were duplicated, as were microphones etc., and certain OBs came into this category. The Lord Mayor's Dinner was one, for during the Cold War the Prime Minister always took the opportunity to speak on foreign policy.

Other events which were considered important were live transmissions of the Glyndebourne Operas, which were broadcast by Radio 3. I had to go there a couple of hours before each broadcast, carry out a test to London, and then remain to the end of the evening. As a result I now have an abiding love of Mozart's music.

The most prestigious occasion was the Royal Christmas Message broadcast live from Sandringham. For this the lines were not only triplicated but the PO ensured that they were routed through different telephone exchanges, or at least in different cables. The speech always drew enormous audiences and in due course it was televised, still live, not recorded as it is today.

With the coming of commercial television the broadcast was made available to the ITV companies but most viewers watched the BBC's transmission and for a number of years it was immediately followed by a live OB of Billy Smart's Circus, which had an enormous following. This too was made a Grade 1 broadcast to ensure that nothing went wrong and the captive audience was retained. As a result on occasions I, or my colleagues, sometimes found ourselves spending Christmas Day in a remote Telephone Exchange with only a Post Office engineer for company.

Another major event was Churchill's funeral in 1965 and plans for this had been drawn up many years beforehand. These were dubbed 'Standard Ceremonial Procedure', and typically within the BBC as 'SCP'. Extensive Radio and Television plans were made to cover the processions, Cathedral Service, carriage of the coffin on a barge along the Thames etc. By now the old Balanced Pair cable had been replaced, and not only had the Post Office installed additional cables but Television OB Engineering was able to provide many of its own radio links to carry pictures.

Because of Churchill's failing health, plans were discussed with our PO contacts, and orders placed for lines from all the required locations, years before the event. Occasionally meetings took place to update the requirements and at one of these a BBC man referred to Standard Ceremonial Procedure only to be met with blank faces on the PO side. He explained that this was SCP, only to be told that as far as they were concerned SCP meant 'Special Circuit Provision' which in this context amounted to the same thing.

Titles and initials

The use of initials was widespread and everyone knew that an S M E was a Senior Maintenance Engineer, or an S Tel E was a Senior Television Engineer. However there were hidden dangers in the practice and when Television spread to the Regions it was promulgated that the senior radio engineer would henceforth be called the Regional Studio Engineer, abbreviated to R S E. This was hastily withdrawn the next day when it was realised that his deputy, the Assistant Regional Studio Engineer, would be an A R S E.

Expansion and developments

Developments seemed to came thick and fast, the acquisition of the old film studios at Lime Grove, expansion into the Regions where we had departmental colleagues doing similar work, the building of Television Centre and more regional Television Studios, plus closer links with the Continent for Eurovision and of course, the establishment of BBC2. Technical developments allowed programme makers to think up more interesting ideas and programmes like

'Grandstand' and 'Sportsnight' made greater demands on the Networks, Switching Centres and the Circuit Allocation Unit. Princess Margaret's wedding aroused huge interest in the States and the three American networks sent video recording equipment and operators over. The gear was very large, although basic by today's standards, and was installed in temporary wooden huts at Heathrow. I was sent there on the day to ensure that the American programme feeds from Broadcasting House were OK. When the recordings were finished a van took them straight onto the runway where an RAF Vulcan Bomber was ready for take-off with its urgent cargo. The pictures were seen on the American and Canadian news bulletins the same evening and this was considered a marvellous achievement. This was before the advent of satellites and it seemed inconceivable that one day live pictures would be transmitted round the world. Before this another method was sometimes used to send important items across the Atlantic. The pictures were filmed off a television screen and then sent one frame at a time by facsimile over a telephone circuit. At the far end the individual frames were reassembled to produce a rather crude film. Of course it took a long time to send even a short item, but in the absence of any other method it was sometimes worthwhile.

Another method was once used by a US Network for a series involving four contributors in different countries. A film camera team was sent to the home of everyone taking part and all were connected by international speech circuits, with a feedback of the others plus the chairman, the veteran American broadcaster Ed Murrow. Our responsibility was to be present at the British end and equalise the circuit, routed via BH, so that the participant could listen on a loudspeaker while being filmed. As the camermen had to reload film every nine minutes, and everything had to be coordinated, it was a laborious process and must have been very expensive to produce. Eventually the series was shown on BBC1 and I was impressed by the resulting programmes. In addition I had spent three interesting days at the homes of Sir Norman Birkett (a famous barrister), a world authority on Russian Affairs and the actress Vivien Leigh.

The start of BBC2 meant a further huge expansion as did the coming of Colour, while the senior service branched out into Local Radio and adopted stereo broadcasting for all networks. Not only did the networks of lines constantly grow to meet these needs but new digital techniques were adopted to provide higher reliability and fidelity. BBC Research and Designs engineers came up with 'Sound-in-Syncs' a method of transmitting the sound within the picture, thereby doing away with the need for a separate sound line for television programmes. Similar technology was also developed to provide high quality multi-channel links for Radio, but using wide-band circuits as the carrier.

Telephone systems

In 1961 I moved out of mainstream broadcast engineering into the department's Telephone Systems and Finance section where I became involved in a specialised activity, the planning of large private telephone systems (PABXs). Each system was custom-built and had to be bought from an authorised contractor. There was also a considerable PO involvement and the time-scale for planning, tendering, installation, testing and commissioning was about a year. New systems had recently been commissioned at BH, Bush House and the first stage of the Television Centre, but the expansion of Television meant the acquisition of new premises, especially in London.

The first was a 'Spec-building', Kensington House, on the other side of Shepherd's Bush Green, which was taken over to provide urgently needed offices so my first project was a PABX to serve this building. Others followed at the new TV OB Base (Kendal Avenue), Riverside Studios and Television Film Studios (Ealing) - replacing the old manual switchboard and the Ealing Broadway premises which were acquired for TV Enterprises. The capacities of the BH and Television Centre systems were also significantly expanded and these were probably the largest in the country, with BH serving 4,500 extensions and Television Centre 4,000.

PABXs were also installed in the Regions, firstly Glasgow then in the new Centres at Pebble Mill, Birmingham, Cardiff and Manchester, as well as the older buildings at Bristol and Belfast. Small systems were also provided at the local Radio Stations as these came into being.

The London PABXs were all interconnected to allow desk-to-desk dialling throughout but, due to the then available technology, calls to and from the regions were manually connected by BH operators. It was necessary to book a call and then wait to be called back which wasn't efficient, and was often frustrating.

In 1977 I concluded that the time was ripe to consider modernising the network by adopting new technology to provide desk-to-desk dialling throughout the country. Management approved the idea in principle and work started on the project which clearly would take several years to bring to fruition. However in 1979, nine years from retirement, I decided on a change of direction and left the Corporation to work in telecommunications consultancy. The reins were therefore taken up at a very early stage by my successor who saw through a massive modernisation programme which included improvements such as Direct-Dialling-In, and many extension facilities like Abbreviated Dialling and Automatic Call-back.

Conclusion

Our old Lines Department became 'Networks and Communications' many years ago, but sadly is no more as the breaking of British Telecomm's monopoly, and newer technologies, to say nothing of the massive reorganisations within the BBC, have allowed the provision of Networks and Telephone Systems to be contracted out.

Broadcasting no longer relies on networks of copper wire but can achieve miracles with microwave and satellite links. I recall what was considered as a great leap forward when reporters were given the first 'midget' voice tape recorders, although they had to bring the tape back to the studio. Now they can carry a suitcase satellite terminal and report on-air, in vision, from practically anywhere in the world.

However we can, I believe, be justly proud of our pioneering work and what we achieved, and of our place in the history of British Broadcasting.

Atlantic Relay Station & the Falklands War,
Norman Shacklady

On the 2nd April 1982 the Argentinians invaded the Falkland Islands, and this was to affect Ascension Island and hence the Atlantic Relay Station in no small measure. Ascension being the nearest British possession, albeit nearly 4,000 miles from the Falklands, was to become the 'forward' supply base.

The task force that was hurriedly despatched from the U.K. was only partially loaded, and the plan was for it to stop at Ascension to pick up the rest of its supplies, which had been flown out in the meantime. Apart from a few empty nissan huts, the military had no resources at all on Ascension Island, and such resources that did exist were those of the resident organisations, and then only sufficient to support their own particular needs. The BBC was responsible for the Power Station which, as well as its primary function of supplying the relay station, also supplied domestic power and water (desalinated sea water) to the British side of the island; the Americans had a similar arrangement for their own operation. The population at that time was approximately 1,100, and about to increase dramatically, as was the use of the single airstrip run by the Americans, which normally handled only 3 or 4 flights a week.

The first arrivals, 3 aircraft and about 150 men, arrived two days after the invasion and the organisations on Ascension were asked to provide resources for them. The BBC store was emptied of spare beds, mattresses, bedding etc. and any form of housing was hastily opened up. Arrangements were quickly made to feed the men at various messes on the island, and the BBC fleet of Bedford shift buses was redeployed to provide transport were necessary. At that time no one was aware of just how far the situation would escalate, everyone tended to believe that diplomacy would find an answer, but in the weeks that followed more and more military personnel arrived, and the number of aircraft movements increased day by day. There were times when aircraft were queuing to get in, each carrying cargoes of 'toilet rolls to torpedoes'. With only one runway and nowhere near to divert to, a major concern was keeping the runway accident free.

In the busiest month, the total number of aircraft movements rose to no less than 3,607, this includes helicopter movements 24 hours per day loading the ships anchored off the island. On Easter Sunday it was said that the runway became the busiest in the world, but in spite of all this traffic, it remained open throughout.

Even though the military brought in resources for their own well being, the demand on what the island could provide remained fairly constant. As far as the BBC Relay Station was concerned, the biggest headache was the demand for domestic water. The island population more than doubled, and it was necessary for the desalination plants to continuously provide the maximum amount of water possible. Evaporation type desalination plants do not like long periods of use without maintenance, and they were being pushed to the absolute limit, but despite the storage available on the island, it became impossible to keep up with the demand. The military were advised, and a combination of getting the troops to use less water (difficult in such a hot climate) and their supplying us with a small reverse osmosis plant (troublesome in the beginning), the unthinkable was avoided, but only just. The other unthinkable situation was the supply of beer, for it almost ran out as well!

The BBC's operation on Ascension included a large diesel fuel farm, in which the military showed considerable interest. As it was not known when the next tanker delivery would occur, and to have run out of fuel would have been a disaster for World Service, the amount of help that could be given in this respect had to be limited. Apart from supplies for transport use, there were a number of occasions when the bunkering of two Royal Navy guard ships took place. They moored in English Bay and were supplied by the floating hose which is normally used to pump incoming fuel from tanker to shore. It had to be a gravity feed, and one of the ship's log reads:-

May 11

"........Secure stern to volcanic rubble to fuel from BBC generator stocks! Slow progress."

General help was provided in many ways, workshop facilities, use of transport when required, even down to providing fridges to keep their beer cool. Every old, rusty and broken down fridge was pressed into service and they became valuable assets, capable of being bartered for almost anything!

The island by now was dominated by all this. With so much activity in the air, a further concern was the safety of helicopters flying close to the HF aerial arrays, having their on-board electronics affected by high RF fields; such problems had occurred elsewhere. But apart from one helicopter slicing through a long wire receiving aerial - with its undercarriage fortunately - and the embarrassment of landing with its flotation bags inflated, there were no other problems. It was considered that the Argentinians might possibly attempt a commando raid and attack the Power Station, and this prompted the Army to erect a pill box outside the station - the night shift approached with a certain trepidation! Troops and equipment were brought ashore to take part in exercises and there were times when the beach at English Bay resembled the D-Day landings. During one landing the Power Station main fuel pipeline was ruptured, which caused us a certain amount of concern.

In a matter of a few short weeks what had hitherto been a quiet, remote and lonely island was transformed into a place of incredible noise and hectic activity; the island had become quite unrecognisable. So had the sea, normally it was a vast expanse of empty ocean, but no longer so, it was now full of ships of all types. On shore, troops were sleeping in any kind of shelter, old huts, empty garages, tents - anything with a roof- accommodation was the greatest problem, certainly in the early phases, but there was never enough to cope.

Then occurred a quite unique event. One lunchtime World Service news carried an item:- "Today the British Ministry of Defence has requisitioned one of the BBC's transmitters on Ascension Island......." After some delay (no satellite communication at that time) a telephone call to London confirmed the news. The BBC was not prepared to broadcast particular government material, and as a result, the government under the terms of the BBC's Charter and Agreement, used its powers to requisition one of the transmitters. They then proceeded to transmit programmes of their own in Spanish, twice a day, directed at the Argentinian military on the Falkland Islands, under the station name of 'Radio Atlantico del Sur'.

Without warning, the authorities announced that in the interests of security all telephone and telex links into and out of the island had been cut until further notice. This caused considerable anxieties amongst the families of our staff both on Ascension and at home in the UK - many were in the habit of making weekly calls to families and loved ones. It also resulted in an operational problem. At that time, programme feeds from the UK were by HF i.s.b transmission, and when a particular frequency became unusable a telephone call to London would arrange an alternative feed. The authorities, representatives of the M.O.D. resident on the island, eventually agreed that such calls could be made via South Africa, but only under strict supervision. All calls were monitored and only the business in hand could be discussed. This situation was to continue for several weeks.

Along with others on the island, BBC families played a vital part in providing hospitality to many members of H.M. forces - in fact at that time many friendships were formed. The UK and St Helenian wives ran a forces canteen in Georgetown, which proved to be a huge success with the troops; there was little else there for them. For those not familiar with Ascension, St. Helenians are the 'locally employed', there being no indigenous population on the island. St. Helena is some 750 miles away, and the 'Saints' and their families spend long periods on Ascension under contract of employment to the various organisations.

During the whole period of the conflict, which lasted for some 3 months, BBC Transmission played its part to the full in giving help and support to HM forces, who faced a very difficult task in the setting up of a supply base which was to play a major role in regaining possession of the Falkland Islands.

The Falklands Islands war is a good example of the way in which broadcasts aimed at people trapped under aggression can help to maintain their morale. After the conflict ended, the Falklands Senior Medical Officer related how the World Service 'Calling the Falklands' broadcasts from London via Ascension had kept the residents in touch with the outside world, and of the hope this gave them in spite of the way they were treated by the Argentinians. He paid a memorable visit to the relay station on his way back to the UK.

CRYSTAL PALACE AND THE ROCKETS, IAN BLANTHORN

Following its construction, tests were carried out on the Crystal Palace Tower using rockets.

A large number of people from The National Physical Laboratory, Building Dept., Aerial Unit (P.I.D.) armed with theodolites, wobbulators, scopes etc., a cameraman above the rockets, and even Professor Bronowski, who was nothing whatever to do with the tests, were assembled to witness the firing of four one ton thrust rockets from one face of the tower at about 650 feet. The object was to find out what movement occurred, from which they would then deduce the conditions that could produce oscillations in the structure.

The rockets were assembled and fired by the Army, and nothing much moved except the trace of the oscilloscope attached to the tower via N.P.L.'s van, which the Professor was happily explaining to all and sundry much to the chagrin of N.P.L.

Shortly after the firing an elderly, very irate gent, came walking down the drive with a dead turkey under his arm. He was shouting loudly and demanding compensation for his dead turkey which he was rearing for Christmas, and he claimed that the noise from the firing had caused the turkey to have a heart attack. The BICC riggers took him to one side and negotiated a price (£4-10 shillings) and he went away happy and the riggers had turkey for supper!

IT ALL BEGAN WITH "WHAT'S MY LINE", TIM BURRELL

As a youngster I was fascinated by all things electrical and often scared my mother to death with potentially lethal investigations into the world of electricity. I can't remember the exact date, but I think it was late fifties or possibly early sixties (when I was 8 or 9), I was watching 'What's my line'. One of the contestants was a BBC engineer. At the end of his turn, I can't remember whether he beat the panel or not, he explained how aspiring engineers joined the BBC and were trained. I was hooked. From that moment I was determined to do just that. I wrote to the BBC on many occasions from that point onwards making sure that the educational choices I had to make were in line with entry requirements.

Readers may imagine the overwhelming joy when in 1968 that offer finally came in the post to join the BBC and to start my engineering training at Wood Norton.

It was some 16 years later that I began my association with Transmission. By that time I'd moved from engineering into personnel and become Head of Personnel for Transmission.

One of the notable events in the Transmission calendar was the annual managers' conference at Wood Norton where late night story tellings oiled with a modicum of Scottish wine were not unknown. It was during one of these occasions that I told my account of joining the BBC. To my surprise and delight one of the older members of the group identified that BBC engineer as Geoff Dukes who was then in the process of closing the old MF station at Moorside Edge. As it happened I was due to go and see Geoff shortly before his retirement.

A short time later I duly arrived at Moorside Edge and Geoff showed me round both the old and new stations. Geoff, like all his colleagues round the country, had an excellent pub to go for lunch and I recounted my story to him over a pint and sausage and chips.

Sadly Geoff did not live to enjoy his retirement for very long. I was so glad though that I had both identified and had the opportunity to meet the source of my inspiration to join the BBC.

Sender 3 and "The Apiezion Q", Dick Skyrme

With the introduction into service of Senders 4, 5 and 6 in the late 1930's, the various experimental transmitters were no longer required. Closure of 5GB (MF) at Daventry also released a convenient building in which SD & ID assembled an HF transmitter from units and components from the redundant transmitters and scrap items salvaged throughout Transmitter Dept. It became Sender 3 to be used for some short European services in the late 30's and returned to a regular service from 1942 to 1945 broadcasting the wartime Overseas Forces Programme to Europe and North Africa.

Sender 3 can best be described as a curiosity, as "bitzas" usually are. It is alleged, without record, that the modulator and main rectifier supplies were ex-2LO rotating machines (Motor General MG) converting AC to DC with associated electrical switch-gear from everywhere. The final RF amplifier was similarly alleged to have come from Alexandra Palace where it had broadcast the 1936 competitive tests between the Baird 240 and EMI 405 line television systems, although some authorities do not agree; one states "It could have, if it was finished with in February 1937 as stated later. I never heard that it did; nor, conversely, that it did not".

Sender 3 copied the design of the MF Regional transmitters, where the RF carrier was modulated in the penultimate RF amplifier, with further amplification in the final RF amplifier, (a linear class B amplifier). The penultimate RF amplifier was built on site for the installation, and was the only major unit that had not been in service elsewhere.

Both modulator and rectifier units were cooled with rainwater collected from the building roof and held in outdoor ponds. The water was always warm and at times produced a rich growth of algae. The mineral impurities in the water were deposited as scale on the valve anodes, and required regular de-scaling by immersion in a bath of hydrochloric acid. The rectifier valves having a glass envelope at each end were not so easily de-scaled with this "dipping" process, and thus were more vulnerable to accidental breakages. Having removed the cooling jacket the valve was suspended horizontally across the acid bath, and acid ladled over the anode with a jug. There was no Health and Safety at Work Act in the 1940's and protective clothing was in short supply. De-scaling valves with acid was not a popular maintenance item.

Water cooling of the pen RF and final Amplifiers was "state of the art" for the period - an enclosed system of distilled water stored in a tank, circulated by a pump through the valve anodes, cooled by an air blast cooler and returned to the storage tank.

The final RF amplifier was unique in the annals of BBC transmitter engineering. Built by Metropolitan Vickers it contained a pair of continuously evacuated de-mountable tetrodes. In the event of internal electrode failure (filament, grid, screen grid), the valve could be "opened up", dismantled and the faulty electrodes replaced – that was the easy bit.

The valve assembly was constructed in three sections:-

Bottom, the vacuum pumps; middle, the water cooled anode; and top, the "head" assembly from which hung the filament, grid and screen electrodes. Each section was supported by and insulated from its neighbour by a porcelain cylinder with a precision ground bronze flange cemented to each end, which matched up to an identical flange on the adjacent section. The valve could be opened up at any flange, usually the top one to release the head unit for electrode replacement. The external facing edge of each flange was chamfered to form a Vee groove around the periphery of the matching faces. This groove was filled with a plasticine-like compound (titled Apiezion Q compound), which completed the seal. Application of this sealant was a long and tedious task, forcing the compound into the groove by pressing and stroking with one's thumbs.

When a satisfactory mechanical seal had been produced the vacuum pumps were switched on – then followed the hour of truth. The vacuum pump system was equipped with a series of vacuum relays and discharge tube indicators at the input to each pump, which provided an indication (not measurement) of the state of vacuum achieved. Evacuation pumping was often accompanied by further "thumbing" of the seals if progress was unsatisfactory.

When an acceptable vacuum had been achieved the valve was conditioned, which involved the application of a manually controlled stepped voltage to each of the valve electrodes starting with the filament, the grid, then adding screen grid, then anode. These conditioning supplies were obtained from the service filament generator for the filaments and from a conditioning unit containing auto-transformers, rheostats and all the paraphernalia to produce, measure and protect a series of variable voltages. Often conditioning was accompanied by an adverse vacuum indication, or trips which involved anxiously waiting for restoration of vacuum whilst thumbing away at the seals when the valve was cool enough to touch.

When a valve was showing signs of severe ageing, those "in the know" going to work on the night shift bus and likely to be involved had an edgy look about them. On arrival their first query was "de-mount night?" and if it was then any spare effort was despatched to Sender 3 to knead and roll Apiezion Q compound into strips; then later when the valve had been re-assembled, thumbing the compound into the valve seals. All this resulted in sore hands and blistered thumbs for the rest of the week.

NEW BLOOD AND IDEAS WERE NEEDED, JOHN PACKMAN

Joining the BBC in 1961 was an amazing time. I knew nothing about broadcasting and the final year at university produced the usual round of job interviews. At these interviews, the BBC stood out as an organisation that had a dynamic engineering vision. Pilkington had just reported and there was going to be a new 625-line colour TV, for the first time in the world. The advent of the transistor would mean new work in FM radio and automation. The project and development departments (TCPD, Designs, Research and Equipment) were going to double in size. New blood and ideas were needed. Broadcasting was clearly an exciting place for an Engineer to be. And so it proved for a quarter of a century.

Dozens of us joined straight from university, not realising that we were in a narrow age group – we had no predecessors and few followed us for several years. But in spite of our lack of experience we made the new era of broadcasting happen under the guidance of some enlightened senior engineering staff.

Many years on, most of us are still friends and few of us realised what we were achieving changing the everyday habits of people. The engineering itself was too interesting, there was much to be done and nearly all of it was new. There was the design, manufacture and installation of small unattended transmitters, or transposers, which filled in all the service gaps caused by the line-of-sight propagation of VHF and UHF radio waves. The first one was at Creteway Down near Folkestone and was in a weatherproof cubicle on a hill overlooking the English Channel. The design even included a special tent that could be rigged between the back of a Land Rover and the cubicle to make a waterproof work area. Most of the designs used transistors for the first time and much work had to be done to make RF power transistor design reliable. Although this was the early 1960's, serious problems were still being encountered in the early 1990's with UHF television transmitters so perhaps evolution is slower than we think.

The UHF television requirement was perhaps the most challenging. It had been decided to use the American NTSC[10] (Never Twice the Same Colour) rather than the French SECAM[11] (System Essentially Contrary to American Methods). Both had defects and, rather late in the day, PAL[12] arrived. It was so much better it was dubbed 'Peace At Last' and adopted as the UK standard.

A prototype transmitter was required for Crystal Palace and was built using a remarkable 'Heath Robinson' approach from many different suppliers. The core was the high-power high-gain Klystron which had already been developed for 50cm radar. Existing VHF 405-line and VHF FM radio low power designs were modified and a viable transmitter was built for channel 34. The antenna feeder was an elliptical waveguide which, at this frequency, was of massive proportions.

Soon, every day trade test transmissions were made using the same films. The one about the building of the Kariba Dam seemed to be the most frequent. During this time, industry was developing the colour TV receivers. These were enormous and the most common appeared to be the Decca CTV25. It was a 25 inch design that used countless valves and had a massive cabinet of real wood. It took hours to warm up and 'converge'. It was reputed that many transmitter staff converted them to cocktail cabinets or armchairs in later years!

---

[10] NTSC actually stands for National Television Standards Committee
[11] SECAM actually stands for Sequential Colour with Memory
[12] PAL actually stands for Phase Alternating Line

A second transmitter on channel 44 followed soon, also at Crystal Palace, before the real BBC2 channel 33 transmitter replaced them both. Of course, the first night of BBC2 has been well documented with the massive electricity failure cutting Television Centre out and totally disrupting the first night. This was apparently due to a fault at Battersea power station, which many years later is just a forlorn shell.

During any such period of innovation, many characters are produced and it would be fair to say that all the departments had their fair share, although it was probably the independent types in TMTs (Transmitter Maintenance Teams) that had the most. That is not to say that some colourful types did not exist elsewhere. There was a chap called Geoff Larkby in Designs whose speciality seemed to be difficult OB links. He fitted a UHF transposer into a borrowed RAF Shackleton in order to do a live broadcast from a borrowed Navy minesweeper of Sir Alec Rose's homecoming from his solo circumnavigation from hundreds of miles off Land's End. Each year, he used to do the Cowes to Torquay Power-boat race and he usually borrowed something large from the Royal Navy. One year it was the self-levelling gun-turret – as a camera mount – from the warship used by Harold Wilson for his meeting with Ian Smith about Rhodesian UDI.

A lot of design effort was directed towards the automation of the whole transmission network, although little was done in the field of AM radio which remained much as it had been built.

Some designs were more successful than others but many of the problems were simply down to the lack of the right technology which did not really happen until integrated circuits and microprocessors made it all so much more achievable.

The BBC had always decided that the correct route was automatic operation with remote monitoring. One of the more bizarre designs was an automatic fault reporter using an endless recorded tape. Long before these had become common, the BBC designed its own - and this was in the days when many telephone exchanges were still manual. Eavesdropping on one of these AFRs calling a manual exchange was often quite interesting especially on Fair Isle where there was only one radio link to the island and all the phones were in parallel. The message would state something like "This is an automatic device on Much Binding 250 calling Potton 355." Very often the lady at the exchange could be heard to say "Oh it's that stupid machine again" and put it through to the BBC saying "Your machine wants to talk to you".

Much of the new UHF TV transmitter network had been designed with a hotchpotch of bulky test equipment. This was in no way suitable for mobile use and so a programme of work was started to design suitable devices. Although having designed transmitters for some years, I was despatched into this whole new world of transmitter maintenance to evaluate the requirements. Note that there was no specification as there would be today. My first impressions were of a world of characters brought about by their remoteness from Head Office and the nomadic nature of the job. Some of this work involved the installation staff of TP & ID, later TCPD, and there were quite a few characters there as well. Most of these are still living so the law of libel must be bone in mind! Some memories remain more vivid than others. At one site, Glendocherty, the access involved crossing a peat bog or clambering over a rocky track. Neither of these routes were suitable for transporting a heavy item of equipment. The technique used was to put a very heavy item, a Polyskop, into a machine resembling a motorised tracked wheelbarrow called a Hillbilly which was set off across the bog whilst the engineer clambered round the path and met around the other side! Needless to say, it did not usually arrive in the desired place.

A lot of test gear was shared, and one impression gained of Scottish teams was that the exchange was also used as the reason for a round of golf and a few drams.

However, the more serious engineering impression was that most teams were struggling with designs that had been intended for use in a studio centre and virtually no account had been taken of mobility or RF measurements. The team vehicles seemed to be little better mainly consisting of old Land Rovers and a few Mini vans. However, all over the UK, there was a lot of drive and personality in these mobile teams. So it was back to the laboratory to produce the right design for the job.

Throughout this era, much of the driving force for innovation was coming from within the BBC, although British industry was producing transmitters of 1kW and above, but even here, automation was coming from the BBC. However, the new graduates of a decade ago were now moving into industry and the emphasis started to change. One of the new Design's entry, Ken Barratt, eventually became chairman of Sony Broadcast and many others started their own companies or became senior managers in well-known industry names. So the world was changing, some twenty years before a fashionable BBC word became 'out-sourcing'. The engineers had got there a generation before the accountants.

The UHF television networks, serving much of the UK, had been built in just a few years, using technologies that were still being developed and well ahead of the world. Also, of course, the UHF ITV network had been created at the same time. This involved hundreds of sites, most of which were 'green field' so there was much more to it than putting some equipment into a building extension. At least there did not need to be discussions about the relative merits of final amplifier technology - only a Klystron could deliver the power. Of course, the down side was the economy of the network. All the engineers had made massive strides in savings of operation and maintenance staff, but many of the designs used a lot of electricity as well as having reliability problems. Once the main objective of building the networks had been achieved, the emphasis changed to improving it and reducing the running costs. There were two main thrusts: the first was to improve automatic quality monitoring on site whilst the second was the transmission of fault data to allow remote monitoring at the new MICs (monitoring and information centre). Once again, this was new technology that was ahead of its time, or more particularly, before the microprocessor. It was a long hard route that involved a myriad of productive co-operation between the many departments of engineering division. Private Industry was producing transmitters but the BBC engineers were producing the low power relays and improvements in operating economies as well as managing all the projects.

However, things had started to change in industry. Helped by an influx of BBC and IBA staff, products started to become available designed with commercial market in view as well as the emerging international aspect. Gradually the emphasis had started to change until, many years later, the BBC management felt confident enough to buy in more services from industry.

SNOWTRACS, DE'S MUDDY SHOES AND WINDY SITES, ROY DALRYMPLE

When planning the UHF coverage of the West Highlands & Islands, it was soon obvious that a link station at South Knapdale was necessary to feed the main station at Torosay on the Isle of Mull. As this was only going to be a link site, and only visited on average once every two months, the powers in Head Office decided that it would be a ridiculous expense to build three miles of track up to the site. So the team was presented with a 'Snowtrac'. As its name would suggest, it was designed for use in the snow, but it was also capable of travelling over bog land, its eighteen inch wide tracks only sinking a couple of inches into the bog. However, on many occasions the wretched vehicle got stuck, and there were multifarious spikes and hold parts to help pull the thing out. This of course entailed a couple of lads getting out to drive the spikes into the nearest bit of reasonably dry ground. This was easier said than done. Although the 'Snowtrac' only sat two inches into the bog, the lads with the spikes and rope were invariably over their wellies in foul peaty water. Conversely, during one particularly dry spell, the exhaust set fire to the heather. The boys were half way up the hill before they discovered what had happened, and it took the best part of the afternoon to put it out.

The original estimate of one visit per two months was grossly over optimistic to say the least as the equipment proved to be extremely unreliable (old receivers with dodgy diversity switching, which was extremely tricky to set up). At least once per week was the actual number of visits for the first nine months of the station's operation. However, things steadied down slightly and the then Director of Engineering decided to pay South Knapdale a visit on his tour of Scotland. DE duly arrived (late) and the Rigger Handyman whose expertise with the Snowtrac (both driving and maintaining) was second to none, delivered DE and his entourage to the site. It was the middle of November. When he finished his inspection and decided to return to the comfort of the Torbert Hotel, he stepped out of the station to find that visibility was down to about ten feet due to a thick mist. I believe, the Rigger Handyman, being aware of the situation, had been unsuccessfully endeavouring to draw attention to the problem for the past three quarters of an hour.

They set off and even with the headlights full on, due to the bumpiness of the terrain, the lights were either pointing skywards or six feet in front of the vehicle. After driving for about an hour, the good Rigger Handyman said he was not quite sure exactly where he was, so for safety sake, he decided to stop, walk downhill till they reached the deer fence, and follow the fence till it met with the old mining track and hence to the Snowtrac garage where the Range Rover was waiting to take them down to Torbert.

The next day the Snowtrac was found about sixty yards from a fairly steep bank just above the old mining track. DE's first instruction when he returned to London, I am told, was to build a track up to South Knapdale and in the meantime have the Snowtrac route lined with marker posts every ten yards up the hill.

Rumour has it that DE ruined a fine pair of shoes that day. I find that hard to believe. We always had a spare pare of wellies around for TCPD and visiting dignitaries.

Dychliemore

During Phase II of the UHF engineering programme, the good burghers of Dalmally (there being over two hundred of them) qualified for a UHF transmitting station. However, when Site Acquisition Section went out to do their survey, they discovered there was rather a nasty snag. No site in the immediate environs of Dalmally was found which could receive a signal from Torosay and transmit to Dalmally. A suitable transmitter site was found and it was decided to feed it from Torosay via an active deflector about a mile from the proposed transmitting station. Problem number two. The nearest Hydro Board power line was over a mile away from the proposed receiver site at Dychliemore, and the cost to have a power line installed would put the whole scheme away over budget.

As the receivers only required 24V DC it was decided to power them by means of two heavy duty batteries, one being charged by a wind generator and the other by four solar panels; commonly known as the 'Windy Side' and the 'Sunny Side' with a relay between the two which selected the side with the highest output volts.

In summer the 'Sunny' side took the load, but when the days shortened, the 'Windy' side took over. The first gales of the winter exposed some of the frailties of the system. The method of braking in excessively high winds proved to be rather ineffective, eventually resulting in the propeller whizzing round at such a speed, the armature burnt out and the whole mechanism seized up.

A new braking system was devised using a frequency conscious relay which applied a manual brake when the generator attained a pre-determined speed. This worked well for a while till the fuse to the braking circuit failed and the next gale caused such a vibration in the tower that all the bolts securing the generator slackened off and the whole caboodle landed on the deck wrecking the propeller and not doing much good to the casting of the generator either. A new, much more sophisticated, generator was then installed whose propeller blades feather automatically in strong winds and as far as I know it is functioning well to this day.

This was the first BBC station to be powered by natural resources.

At the end of the day, financially, in the cases of both the South Knapdale Track and the powering of Dychliemore, it would have proved infinitely cheaper to build a track at the outset at South Knapdale and have the Hydro Board run a line to Dychliemore.

A bit of homespun philosophy from RWD to accountants and managers who should pay much heed to them:

"Investing in a little common sense invariably ensures you don't forever more keep paying for your parsimony".

Bagpipes, Grallaching and Goliath, Syd Garrioch

Melvaig TMT was born in the Spring of 1965, under the TTM-ship of Arthur Morris, with Hugh Hart as his second man, to maintain Glendocherty Link Site and Melvaig (Link, 405-TV, VHF Radio). These were approx. 40 miles apart with, in those days, single track road for 35 of them. If two tourist caravans met on a bad corner, with neither driver schooled in the secrets of reversing, it was not unusual for that journey to take 4 hours.

Achievements included learning to play the bagpipes, subsequently displayed by Arthur in Transmitter halls from Eitshal to Droitwich, and acquiring skills in grallaching combating (or abetting - depending on the circumstances) salmon poachers, and driving Goliath (see later).

Changes in the grading system in 1970 led to Hugh's departure to Moel-y-Parc and I became ATTM Melvaig. I did not learn to grallach, or play the pipes, but driving Goliath was obligatory. Goliath was a LWB Land Rover, open back, with tractor wheels all round, and sort of armour-plated body work, top speed 28 mph, whose purpose in life was to transport test equipment and nitrogen cylinders to Glendocherty, over a rocky bog. (When Glendocherty was built, the landowner would not allow a road, and insisted that if a vehicle was able to cross the 300 yds or so, it had to take a different route each trip). Goliath was one of only three ever built, and was originally bought by the BBC to help in the building of Fort Augustus Link Site. Its chief attribute was to frighten the life out of tourist drivers – lay-bys suddenly became much more attractive. It was eventually replaced by the Hillbilly – a sort of motorised, tracked, wheelbarrow, which was great in peat-bog, but would tip over in a second if it went over a rock, and the nitrogen cylinder took a hand. Is it still in use at Westerglen? After suitable experiments, I think its main attribute was transporting feed/fertiliser to the Angling Club Hill Lochs.

The weather in Gairloch is not all that extreme, but there is more than a fair share of wind. It rains a bit as well, but every time the then Supremo Team (?) visited, the weather was splendid. Luckily, the myth of perpetual idyllic conditions was dispelled by Derek East's visit in 1971 when, on one of the worst days of the winter, he got soaked to the marrow running over to Glendocherty. Kenlochare Hotel provided a drying out room for a change of clothes, and suitable inner warmth (soup).

The 405 RBR signal into Glendocherty was plagued from day one by ignition-type interference (2 broad bands) whenever we had a dry, breezy spell which, at the worst, was virtually a shutdown. This was caused by Hydro-Board lines along the path of the received signal, and the number of Service Messages sent could have papered the walls of BH. This problem was not resolved until the new 625 link (SHF) and Standards Converter went on in 1975.

For a few years around 1975 – 1978, we were demoted in title, and administered from Rosemarkie – every week Peter Wilkins (EiC RK) and Arthur would meet somewhere along the 90 miles, and exchange pound notes and pleasantries – but with VHF separation from 1978 onwards, and various boards which restored us to what we had been in the first place, Melvaig became an independent Team again, and Fort William was 'relieved' of the Skye sites. In 1980 the base was moved to Gairloch, and by 1983 the team had increased to 6 (I nearly said the standard 6, but there's no such thing), its area being the largest in Britain – arguably – various bits separated by large lumps of water.

The roads had improved.

As I'm sure is common to all teams, various emergencies punctuated those years. The passive reflector at Glen Marksie was uprooted in a gale in early 1978, cutting the UHF link to the west, but that was a minor wriggle compared to The Big One – the night of November 23rd 1981 – when Skriaig's UHF aerial blew off, and Eitshal was hit by lightning, within about six hours. The ensuing fire at Eitshal was centred in the workshop but the heat, and corrosive fumes from melting plastic trunking etc. in the Transmitter Hall, made the Write-Off Requests a couple of pages longer than usual.

The abiding memory of the next few weeks/months at both sites is of the splendid co-operation of everybody in all departments concerned (that includes the IBA), and if some budding author cared to collect the hundreds of stories from those involved including, especially, the apocryphal, a very interesting volume would ensue - to be made required reading for Trainees, if ever there are any.

In 1983 Arthur Morris departed to become EiC Droitwich, and because nobody else even knew the meaning of grallach, I became TM. The team at this time was Arthur, Syd Garrioch, Pete Lawrence, Keith Gurr, Dave Cowie and Alan Jackson (rigger/handyman). Arthur was a boss whose dedication to the BBC was supreme, extremely loyal to his men, and a character. A few of his entries from the log:-

"Land Rover Gear Box drained. Half a ton of assorted metal work discovered. Reconditioned G/Box recommended".

"Forking sea weed and debris - Windy as all get out, so I did" (When high tides covered the access road to home with all kinds of flotsam).

"Nasal evidence of burn-up in diesel room".

"ACCIDENT. Thumped by a French woman at the end of GDY road. See Accident Report".

To continue punctuating:- In late 1983 one of the passive 12ft dishes blew off the Sgairr Marcasaith system again causing complete cessation of UHF for a time, and in 1990 a large portion of the roof was blown off Skriaig, exposing UHF transmitters to the elements, but working quite happily - they always liked it cool. If the IBA hadn't gone to site that day, we would have had al fresco transmitters for days.

There doesn't seem to have been quite as many incidents over the remaining years, or maybe nobody told me. As elsewhere, FM re-engineering, and NICAM, new FM installations and UHF relay sites kept us going.

Ferry travel is necessary, and the quality of sea-legs varies, but the man least keen on sailing is Arthur Masson, Building Works Supervisor for Scotland. So what happens - Arthur and I spent 11 hours at sea (after a normal 2-hour Lochmaddy - Uig (Skye) trip) to end up back where we started, the last $3^{1}/_{2}$ hours straight into a gale. Arthur spent those $3^{1}/_{2}$ hours studying the porcelain, not happy.

The other epic series of journeys, by Bob Munro and John Higginbotham, was an attempt to install the translators at Borve on Barra. Ferries to and from Barra are at inconvenient times anyway -

there were gales for the whole week, timetables were disrupted, and they spent 5 days, getting to digs at 02.00 or leaving digs at 05.00, generally enjoying themselves in this fashion. The trip was abortive anyway, and to cap it all on the final leg of the home run, the Kyle ferry broke down, and there was a roadworks hold up half an hour out of Gairloch. John had over 26 hours overtime and 29 hours penalty payments.

The team after gradual, then total, emigration to Inverness, ceased to exist on 26 May 1994.

All who worked at Gairloch/Melvaig had to put up with certain disadvantages, but these were outweighed by the bonuses - magnificent scenery being only one – use your imagination for the rest, and I thank all with whom I worked from far and near, for their dedication, support and friendship.

Sadly, Arthur Morris did not enjoy many retirement years. He died in 1994, cheerful to the end.

(Note: To GRALLACH – what is done to a deer after it has been shot).

"The Quality Street Gang", Jim McPherson.

The Clerk of Works described the team maintaining the transmission system in the North Isles and the Northern coast of Scotland as 'The Quality Street Gang', all different and all contributing something beyond the confines of a job description.

The part-time clerk, Pat Smith, could not be idle and as soon as the Unisys computer appeared she had the cash sheet on it and in the non printing columns there was a running total of the budget lines. This allowed her to take over the area inventory which also went on the database. And all before empowerment!

The year Christmas day fell on a Friday and Keelylang Hill in Orkney had a shut down on BBC1 she again came up trumps, or rather her husband did. No ferries till Monday, no Loganair charter since they were saving the pilot's hours in case of an ambulance flight. Over the Pentland Firth on his fishing boat, fault fixed and back home in time for tea. He was quite happy to do it for the universal currency of the

North, a bottle of whisky, but he was paid the same rate as a charter flight, oh and the bottle of whisky!

Pat's main claim to fame was her hand bag. The Transmitter Manager was based at Thrumster near Wick on the mainland with engineers on Orkney and Shetland. When a new major piece of test equipment or new transmission equipment was introduced the head office engineer responsible would be convinced to come and give a run down on the various features to the whole team assembled in Orkney. Pat would stuff the appropriate cash to cover the T&DE and a fistful of Cash Advance forms in the hand bag and as people arrived at Netherbutton it was "Sign here", but the money stayed in the hand bag.

Then it was down to the Lynnfield where seven or eight men would order up with the adjoinder "And she's paying." After the technical lecture, demonstration and discussion there would be further exercising of the hand bag and when it was empty every one went home.

Jackie Miller came to the BBC by a circuitous route. A time served electrician, he was working for Finlayson's who had the contract for the electrical work on the LPTV stations. This was the Band I, 405 line, black and white service from places like Thrumster and Orkney. The Orkney site was an old RAF radar station at Netherbutton and the masts were on the flight path to Kirkwall airport. Not too sure about installing the anti-collision lights on the masts, Jackie thought of getting the riggers from J.L.Eves to do it for him but they convinced him to come up with them. Jackie took to the work like a duck to water so when Thrumster was put into service Jackie applied for and got the job as the rigger.

Many an installation engineer must have wondered in later years why, instead of getting the drawings out, the local team got the rigger out instead.

A good maintenance engineer is a man who works himself out of a job. There were ongoing problems with lightning strikes especially at Bressay in Shetland. At one time handfuls of integrated circuits would be killed off in one strike and in some cases the plastic encapsulation would be blown apart, revealing the chip and the gold wires running to the pins. The local team, Derri Cameron and John Waters, carried out an investigation and by strategic placing of Transorbs and other devices developed a protection system which became pretty standard throughout Transmission.

A good maintenance engineer is also a man who regularly updates maintenance practice. After one of the Orkney meetings when the modern H.P. Spectrum Analyser was introduced it was apparent that it could be interfaced with a portable PC and so a performance test programme was written. To prove the system the handyman was sent off to carry out a performance test on a relay station. This was successful but although the system was ready for Transmission, Transmission was not ready for the system.

For Team working line management was simple, big boss at headquarters, area boss at Blackhill and local boss.

One of the final phases of television relay station provision was known as Phase IIE, where the cost of the station per head of population in the service area was not to exceed that of the previous Phase II. Such a relay could only be provided at a site in the North of the mainland if there was no track to the station. This was accepted by the local boss on the understanding, agreed by area boss and big boss, that contrary to current practice it may be that a shutdown of a service could not be attended because of access difficulty.

It was less than two months after the station was in service when the call came. The crofter who had an apportionment of the common grazings on which the station was built had made a wee improvement to the access and would we share the cost? How much? £15,000!

The local boss just had to see the wee improvement so on the appointed day he, the crofter and the contractor , oh yes there was a contractor by this time, ended up looking at a mini motorway. 4 inch base, 2 inch down rolled as a top coat, lovely culverts to take the water away, the lot.

The conversation went something like this. "Is there no one else sharing this access ?" "Oh just an old widow woman who cuts a few peats and I don't know about you boys but I wouldna be bothering the poor old soul" "Oh right enough to be sure, right enough, and what kind of a grant would be on a thing like this?" "Grant. Oh I don't know about grant, Mr Contractor do you know about grant?" "Oh now I'm no' too sure about grant." "Never mind, I'll be passing the Department on the way home so I can just pop in." "Ah now that will not be necessary." The keen student of the vernacular will have noticed that 'Oh' had become 'Ah'. "Well if it was done under CAGS it would be 80 per cent." "Yes." "So we are talking half of £3,000." "Yes."

Area boss agreed that this kept the station under Phase IIE costs and half was paid.

Now in the North you can tell when spring arrives: a visit from Personnel arrives with it. But big boss is smarter, he waited till summer. On the way up to the site which had created a precedent from lack of access he remarked on the fine road only to have it explained that it was not a road, which we could not have, but a bargain. The reply was a wry smile and that explains much of why it was such a pleasure to have been a part of Transmission in the best of times.

CROSSED LINES, POWER, CHRISTMAS TREES, SPIDERS & DIESELS, PETER CONDRON

Haverfordwest late 60's.

Period was late 60's, before Sound-in-Syncs when vision was distributed by PO links and sound by Private Wires. On the Wenvoe team we saw in a Sunday paper (guess which one) that TV viewers in Pembrokeshire were getting telephone conversations instead of TV sound. Some of the conversations were (for the 60's) very fruity!! We didn't for a minute think of our unattended transmitter at Haverfordwest (Band I Ch.4) but found to our mortification that there had been a fault in a telephone exchange and the resulting fault repair crossed wires so that telephone calls were being routed to the Tx. instead of programme sound! The fault was not reported for a considerable time because the viewers probably liked the private telephone conversations better than the programmes!

Tywyn 1965

Wenvoe team called out on Christmas Eve (Dave Jagger and Pete Condron) to attend a fault at Tywyn medium wave Tx. A long way to drive (about 150 miles) in a farmer's type Landrover with no creature comforts or any motorways in those days.

The reserve Tx. was OK but we couldn't get air pressure on the main Tx. After much head scratching we found the problem.

There had been a mains failure previously and the board had reconnected the supply with 2 phases reversed - result blower motor on main Tx. running backwards. The reserve Tx. was single phase.

Since the blower was hidden in the bowels of the Tx. there was no easy way of diagnosing the fault.

The journey back home in the early hours of Christmas day was interesting, one of the sights was the local bobby in Aberdovery wearing a chamber pot instead of his helmet and carrying a large glass of whisky.

Wenvoe 1965 (Christmastime)

The station at Wenvoe used to make routine telephone calls to check the state of unattended transmitters using a Telephone Indicator Panel (T.I.P.) which gave dots for good condition and dashes for abnormal.

One evening the transmitter at Haverfordwest (4 x 500W, valve Band I amplifiers) indicated 2 Tx's off. The S.M.E. on shift attempted to telephone the team (only 3 people) but got no reply. He decided to send a TA down to where the team leader (Dave Jagger) lived but as this was a new estate the houses were not numbered. Someone at Wenvoe had been down to the house a few weeks ago and remembered an (early) Christmas tree with lights in Dave's window so the directions were "you'll easily find it, it's the house with the lit Christmas tree in the window." Unfortunately it was now December 23rd so every house had an illuminated tree. The irony was that in fact the Christmas tree lights at Dave's house had failed so his tree wasn't even illuminated in the mass of others.

Kilvey Hill Mid 70's

This BBC 2 Tx. had a 1kW Marconi amp driven by a primitive LPT with a parametric up-converter to give 50mW of UHF. One evening I was called out to attend a fault (accompanied by Eifion Williams, TA on shift at Wenvoe) which proved to be a transposer fault. Since any transposer fault involved component changes and subsequent re-alignment with a Polyskop (usually a 3 hr job) a spare transposer was kept on site. All interconnecting leads had to be changed and these were put on the floor. Unfortunately the leads were kicked into the incoming BT telephone duct (pipe in floor) so we had to get on the floor to retrieve them. Fishing around in the duct unveiled a cornucopia of spiders and other creepy crawlies which ran up our hands and all over the floor. We were glad to retrieve all the leads and get the spare transposer into use!

At the same site a diesel was ordered to cover a lengthy mains failure. This was arranged by the Board so no attendance was made. We got a call from the dealer to say the service was coming on for a few seconds then off for 10mins. On approaching site we saw puffs of black smoke then nothing. What was happening was that the totally inadequate diesel was OK during Tx. run up (klystron filament delay 10 mins) but as soon as the 10kV EHT came on this was too much for the diesel which shuddered to a halt in clouds of black smoke.

LIFE ON A MAINTENANCE TEAM & IN TCPD, ROY SHARP

During the winter of 1986 I was attached to the Stockton Team as Transmitter Manager. For the duration of my attachment I stayed in B&B accommodation in Yarm. One evening whilst eating the main course of dinner with my hosts the telephone rang. It was duly answered and I was told it was for me. The STE was phoning me from a public house in Frosterley close to the bottom of the track down from the Weardale site. He explained that the maintenance team, including a trainee, had just walked down in the snow from the site because the Range Rover could not be started. The driver had left the vehicle parked facing uphill with the lights on when they arrived earlier on their fault-finding visit. Coming out of the building to return home they found it was dark and it had been snowing. They had tried to push the vehicle to bump-start it but found it impossible to do in the snow. They decided to walk down from the top of the hill, a distance of about one mile and were now warming themselves supping ale and eating snacks in the pub. He asked me to come and collect them.

I finished my meal, including coffee, and set off in the team Cavalier along snow and ice-covered roads sometimes travelling as slow as 10 mph on winding lanes and occasionally getting up to 50 mph where the roads were clear.

There was also the occasional snow shower to contend with. I eventually arrived at the pub well over an hour later where I found them sitting by a blazing log fire and drinking their beers. I refused an offer of a beer, settling for a pineapple juice instead. When all had finished we set off back to Yarm.

Just on the outskirts of Yarm we were stopped by police manning a checkpoint who asked where we were going. (It was a good thing I had not been drinking!) We were advised that the way ahead (along the road I had previously driven very slowly) was blocked by an articulated lorry which had jack-knifed. We detoured and thankfully arrived safely back home in Yarm later that night.

Next day the team went back to Weardale, walking up to the site, the hillside still covered in snow, towing a replacement battery on a children's sledge.

Life in TCPD

In 1976 the first 'Blue Streak' UHF transposer was installed by Gordon Bowhay and me at Gunnislake, Cornwall. On the Monday following the handover to maintenance staff I was travelling up in the lift in Henry Wood House with Frank Beresford who at the time was Assistant Head of Information Department. I said that I had just completed the installation at Gunnislake to which he replied that EID were going to do the coverage survey and visit the local dealers the following week. "Oh, I wouldn't mind being in on that" I said.

"Well, if you can persuade your boss to let you go I will make arrangements."

Permission having been given I met up with John Pinneger of EID at the office on the following Monday morning and set off in the EID survey vehicle. The field-strength survey was also to include the Tavistock service area, the transposers for which were installed during the same week as those at Gunnislake. Accommodation had been arranged for us at a recommended hotel, The Cherrybrook, right in the heart of Dartmoor. The electricity was provided by a diesel generator, and its backup, from a barn at the back of the hotel. The first to switch on the lights or use an electric razor in the morning would start the generator. The meals were superb and visiting their little bar was very relaxing after a day's work.

On the following day we commenced our field-strength survey of the Gunnislake area which was situated on one side of steep valley screened from the main transmitters. The thing that I remember most was the number of people who took an interest in what we were doing and warmly shook our hands, thanking us most heartily for providing them with decent pictures after all the years of very poor reception of either Band I or III signals. It made one feel very proud and the job worthwhile.

Later that week we had to defend the BBC and ourselves verbally against an irate man (who most likely did not have a TV licence) that we were not seeking out those who did not have a licence.

RIGGING SERVICES: A BRIEF HISTORY AND SOME MEMORIES, CLIVE HOSKEN

Rigging teams have always been an integral part of the HF/MF transmission service. They were very labour intensive due to the physical effort required to raise and lower the arrays, this before the advent of mobile power winches. When the TV and VHF service was introduced in the early 50's one rigger was allocated to each of the new TV stations. He was basically employed for general mast maintenance and station duties. The major antenna maintenance or modifications were carried out by a team of TV riggers assembled under the supervision of a Head Office engineer or by a team of TCPD riggers. This system worked well whilst there were only a few HP or MP TV and VHF stations and the antenna systems were new and the maintenance required was minimal. However, with the proliferation of Band I and Band II stations and UHF in the mid to late 60's the workload of some of the riggers at HP TV stations increased dramatically and a greater degree of skill was required to maintain these antennas. TV rigging staff were given the opportunity to take a trade test and to upgrade to rigger mechanic. Although having a base station, most rigger mechanics at the HP TV stations were released for prolonged periods to work in teams at other sites on mast or antenna maintenance or for installation work with TCPD. They were also required to work with Research Department for new site surveys. By 1974 the workload had increased to such an extent that it, was deemed necessary to divide the TV VHF network into 4 areas for rigging purposes, each with an antenna maintenance supervisor and a team of rigger mechanics. As rigger mechanic effort was reduced at their base station, due to the time taken up with these extra duties away from base, a new category had to be introduced at the base station. These rigger handymen posts were created for first line basic antenna fault finding and cleaning effort for the increasing number of relay stations being installed. In the early 1980's the workload was becoming very heavy and problems recruiting trained rigging staff were experienced. At this point a training programme was introduced to retrain the large pool of HF rigging staff to TV VHF maintenance techniques. These trained staff would then combine with the existing rigging staff and the total transmitting network would be divided into 8 rigging areas, each area with an antenna engineer and Antenna Maintenance Supervisor. This involved less traveling time and made the maintenance programme more efficient.

1988/89 saw the amalgamation of transmitter engineers and TCPD engineers with the demise of TCPD rigging teams. Some of the TCPD rigging team leaders and riggers were absorbed into the existing 8 area rigging teams which then took on the responsibility of relay station antenna installations.

With the expansion of commercial telecommunications the rigging teams undertook the installation and maintenance of antenna systems for various commercial companies. This become a big money earner for Transmission.

During the above mentioned times there have obviously been many incidents, some hilarious, some tragic. They are too numerous to mention but here are a selected few.

Rigging with cradles

Imagine a dark and windy night some time in 1964. 6 1/8" diameter feeders for the new UHF were to be installed through the VHF cylinder at Wenvoe. This work had to be completed at night so as not to disrupt the VHF transmissions. (The HSE has since restricted the working at heights during darkness). In those days the luxury of RTs was still some way away and communication was by whistle signals or a loud voice! The contractor for the work was BICC (British Insulated Callendars Cables) now known as Balfour Beatty and the Site Engineer for the BBC was a young Noel Sudbury. The contractors had a winch with a man carrying cradle which landed staff at the 600 ft platform. There was no laid down amount of men that could be safely carried by this cradle (now it would be a maximum of 4), about 8 persons were either in or hanging on the outside of this cradle as it ascended. When the cradle reached a height of about 500 ft it stopped! Due to the lack of communication nobody in the cradle knew the cause of this stoppage (it was in fact winch failure). The wind was having the effect of swaying the cradle in a circular motion, sometimes quite close to the mast and then 30 ft or so away. The men on the outside of the cage decided that as the cage came close to the mast they would transfer to the mast. As each person left the cage it made the cage lighten and its circular motion diminished so that it didn't come quite so close to the mast. I decided to get onto the mast before the distance became too great. Unfortunately I ended on the leg of the mast furthest from the ladder with no direct access to the ladder. It was pitch black with a distance of about 8'6" to the ladder with no way back into the cage. Eventually the ladder was reached with some difficulty. The two men left in the cage, Noel Sudbury and BICC Safety Officer, decided that discretion was the better part of valour and remained there. Two hours or so later, when the winch had been repaired, all ended relatively happily.

Another dark and stormy night on the Isles of Scilly

The coastguard station, which was not far from our station, observed that the 36 ft fibre glass cylinder housing the UHF antenna at the top of the 200 ft tower was swaying alarmingly. Eventually the fibre glass cylinder sheared at its junction with the top of the tower. The cylinder ended up lying head down, flat alongside the tower. It was being held there by a nylon rope, normally used to lower the antenna from the cylinder for maintenance purposes. The two 7/8" feeders were bent through 180° and rather flattened. It was rather daunting when we arrived the following day to see this huge cylinder with its lightning spike pointing directly at the building and only held by the slim nylon rope. Amazingly the feeders were not completely shorted out and programmes were still being transmitted. The rumours that the Scillonians had to turn their television sets upside down to watch the programmes were not proven!

DAVENTRY REMEMBERED, NORMAN TOMLIN

(More information can be found in 'Daventry Calling the World' written by Norman, ISBN 0905355 46 6)

First Impressions

For the many thousands of staff and visitors to the Station on Borough Hill, the first impressions were probably of a wind swept plateau with a landscape and buildings dominated by lattice steel masts, aerials and feeder wires. Then perhaps to glance at the mural inscription 'Quaecunque' (whatsoever) placed between the white stucco pillars leading to the Main Building entrance doors, allowing access to the vestibule. All quiet, to recover from the wind outside, before passing through further swing doors into the cavernous West transmitter hall, lined with grey panelled transmitter units, with inspection windows and large chromium rimmed electrical meters. Probably the feeling and atmosphere of a hospital ward – gleaming clean, with polished floors and shining panels. Then to hear unusual sounds, noise of motor generators, pumps, hiss of steam, sounds of programme, and for some newcomers, the all enveloping sound of high pressure cooling air passing through transmitter cabinets. To remember the two large clocks placed at either end of the transmitter hall, ticking away the seconds in GMT (Daventry's schedule operated in 24 hours GMT).

Making The Station Tick

The station staff complement was divided into two categories. Management, Office Maintenance and support staff working a conventional 9 to 5 five day week, and shift operational engineers working a three shift system – Day, Evening and Night every day of the year.

The four printed schedules, produced by the Schedule Unit in Bush House, The Strand, London, were the 'raison d'etre'. They set out the Daventry daily work load. Complications of urgent schedule changes to meet reception difficulties, or transmissions operating on particular days made life complicated. Additionally, the eleven year sun-spot cycle, and the ever increasing competition from other broadcasters for space in the congested frequency bands, meant the playing field for Short Wave broadcasting was never settled. When the sun-spot cycle called for higher frequencies to be used up to 26 MHz, transmitter components were stretched and tuning some transmitter radio frequency amplifiers needed patience and experience. Spectacular flashovers in the output stages of transmitters, particularly during winter storms and icing of feeders and aerials, were a common experience of shift engineers, necessitating swift action to clear the fault. The ever-increasing demand for higher transmitter powers to compete in the crowded market place meant that Short Wave technology nudged at the edge of component strength and development design.

Clocks dominated the lives of all staff on the Hill, particularly engineers and technicians who maintained the 24 hour operational schedule, transmitting programmes all over the world. Memories of programmes might well include World Service jingle 'Lily Bolero', sound of 'Big Ben', time signal pips, the Victory 'V' signal with drums, and then the announcement "This is London." Of the thirty-five or more foreign languages broadcast in a day, only a few would be recognised by the ardent linguist - Arabic, Russian, French, German, Spanish, Mandarin, Urdu and Hausa! Maintaining the daily schedule, with its many changes in a week, brought the possibility of mistakes being made, some small, some large! Fortunately, or unfortunately, a 'big brother' watchdog receiving station was employed to monitor both World Service and Domestic Service transmissions. This was Tatsfield Monitoring and Receiving Station based in Kent, later relocated to Caversham, near Reading. The dreaded sound of a Control Room voice saying "hello Tats" would herald a telephone enquiry from Tatsfield which raised the heartbeat of many shift staff! Could it be a query relating to wrong frequency, wrong programme, wrong day, wrong aerial, sender 'off' or 'on' in error?; the permutations were endless! It meant the inevitable enquiry, written report and admonishment.

Historic Event

In October 1982, the Station celebrated the 50th anniversary of Short Wave Broadcasting. The distinguished gathering of guests included the Lord Lieutenant of Northamptonshire Lt.Col T. Chandos-Pole, the Director General Alistair Milne, and the Director of Engineering Bryce McCrirrick. Visitors came from a wide cross-section of society: from Daventry Town and District, County and many places in England, representing Local Government, Education, Utilities, Manufacturers, different professions and BBC management. To commemorate the occasion, a plaque was unveiled at the entrance to the vestibule in the Main Building.

The 50th Anniversary effectively marked a water-shed in Daventry's technical development and staffing. At that time the total staff under Senior Transmitter Manager Maurice Williamson numbered 61, made up of shift, aerial, maintenance, administration and support staff. The team effort enabled a daily output of 37 languages, totalling 240 hours. A daily power bill to maintain 15 transmitters ran to £2,000, with an annual overall cost of £1.7 million. Over the site area of 220 acres were 18 lattice steel masts ranging from 150-500 feet, 4 steel towers from 115-356 feet and 22 tubular masts from 80 to 150 feet. A total of 47 aerials hung between the masts covering 4 to 26 MHz, all directional with reversible reflectors, giving the station the capability of broadcasting to every country in the World. Daventry was the biggest Short Wave station operated by the BBC.

From 1982 to the closure in 1992, significant technical changes took place. At that time, four Marconi transmitters installed in 1939 still required manual movement of pre-set inductance trucks for frequency changing. Manual operation was also needed to change pre-set channels on one Standard Telephone and Cable 1940 transmitter, and four Marconi transmitters installed in 1962. But the most labour intensive work involved inductance changing on four Marconi 250kW transmitters installed in 1965. At the closure in 1992, the station had been re-equipped with six totally automatic Marconi 300kW transmitters, with micro-processor control of their operation, change of frequency, programme and aerial. Transmission schedule changes took place in twenty seconds instead of 15 minutes, and operational staff were reduced to three on shift, compared to a wartime peak of twenty!

Characters

Memories of wartime and World events were intermingled with the great mix of people who came to Daventry from all parts of Britain, and many overseas countries for short and long periods. The comedians, who kept a shift alive, with stories and jokes to help periods of inactivity pass more quickly. One such person, Stanley Unwin, later 'Professor' Stan Unwin of gobble-de-gook fame, together with other colonial recruited staff, created a legend of jokes played on other staff, particularly fresh faced youth from school!

Station Rituals

For the many thousands of staff who came to Daventry, they would probably recall the twice weekly 'mopping out' in every station building, by station attendants, with mops and buckets. Cleaning also had to be carried out in high voltage equipment areas, where for staff safety, all voltage supplies had to be removed. This was done by operating an auxiliary isolator switch to the 'off' position, which changed warning lights from red to green, indicating that it was safe to enter an area. Additionally, in some transmitter enclosures mechanical door interlocks coupled to earthing switches had to be operated.

Operational shift staff were involved in many routine tasks. Each year Bush House originated four new schedules, involving frequency and aerial changes, to take account of changes in the ionosphere due to the seasons, and the 11 year sun spot cycle. The preparation work involved power testing transmitters on each new frequency and aerial. For the Senior Maintenance Engineer (Aerials) and his rigging staff, it meant a great deal of hazardous work in all weathers, to carry out re-routing of feeders and switch changes in the open wire "Gantry'. For many years, until the early sixties, when automated aerial switching was installed, the scramble to complete the work during the one hour maintenance break was ongoing and demanding, fraught with the possibility of error. Transmitters also had to be prepared to operate on new frequencies. The work varied with each transmitter type. Without doubt, the four 100kW Marconi transmitters, installed in 1938 and still operational in 1982, presented the biggest challenge! Re-building the moveable truck pre-set inductances by altering the layout of tubular copper coils and tubular capacitors was fiddling and time consuming! Then the transmitter had to be tuned through on its new frequency and stabilised (to prevent self-oscillation). The twin channel 100kW Marconi transmitters installed in 1962, and the 250kW Marconi transmitter installed in 1965, presented less of a challenge. Sender 7 (later S17), the Standard Telephone and Cable twin channel 100kW transmitter introduced in 1940 needed qualities of patience, perseverance and hard work to change the channel frequency. To set up the inductances and capacitances required was one thing – to stabilise the transmitter was another. Sender 7 would be remembered by many shift engineers for a variety of reasons!

Transmitter Daily Routines

From the beginning, Long, Medium and Short Wave transmitter circuit design incorporated electrical meters to indicate not only circuit performance, but critically, to enable the mains, high voltage, bias and filament supplies to be adjusted to their correct value. The routine taking of meter readings at regular intervals during transmission was a necessary chore. The readings did have value to the extent of indicating incipient fault conditions, some minor some catastrophic! Short Wave transmitters at Daventry, as with other stations were completely dependent on the aerial 'load' (ability to absorb transmitter power). In high wind and severe winter conditions, which brought damage to aerials and feeders due to freezing fog, transmitter output amplifier stages could react alarmingly. Some more than others, but all relying on meters to help engineers to make tuning adjustments, which would reduce the risk of severe flashovers (often accompanied by speech and music), that could damage capacitors and valves.

Other Routines

In 1982, Daventry's annual power bill came to £800,000. Taking the weekly meter readings in the EMEB (East Midlands Electricity Board) sub-stations, was an important ritual. Too high or too low, explanations were demanded. Should the maximum power demand exceed the negotiated figure with the Electricity Board, it would effectively be the 'crime of the century' – the air would be blue in the front office!

Diesel Alternators

From the mid thirties until the station closure, the two English Electric ship diesel alternators (located in the Power House), played an important role in providing standby power in the case of mains failure. Although they provided less than a quarter of the station load, it nevertheless enabled an emergency restricted service to operate, invaluable during the war and during the severe power restrictions in the post war period. In the bleak winter of 1946/47, when the Industrial Midlands was shutdown for weeks, the diesels pounded away to feed power into the National Grid. For many years, the routine testing of the diesel-alternators was a feature of Daventry. Paralleling the output of the alternators by the closure of an oil circuit breaker at precisely 'twelve o'clock' on the phase meter, would be remembered by many engineers who carried out the task! Easy to get it wrong, and suffer the wrath of the diesel mechanic tentatively watching developments through the diesel room door.

Distilled Water

All visitors, students and new staff posted to Daventry would inevitably be taken down the steps leading to the crypts under the Main Building transmitter halls. Faced with an over-whelming collection of massive cylindrical tanks, pumps, meters, interconnecting pipes and other equipment in wire mesh enclosures, they might be excused if their senses became deadened by sight, noise and heat! As described before, valves work inefficiently, and their anodes can glow cherry red, and need to be cooled. This was achieved in older transmitters by pumping high pressure distilled water around the valve anodes placed in water jackets. Large fan assisted external water cooling radiators ensured the water temperature in the transmitter cylindrical tanks was controlled. Every transmitting station that used water-cooled valves had a similar array of 'plumbing' equipment. In the course of their careers many Daventry engineers and other staff could relate to transmitter shutdowns involving a variety of water problems. Leaks, large and small, some flooding the crypt to several inches (all hands to the pump), or other incidents involving the replacement of large valves.

For many years, until the early sixties, high grade water was produced by two distillers (periodically checked by Customs and Excise!). Operating 24 hours a day, they supplied a trickle of water into the central storage tanks in the two crypts, to replace leaks and losses. The introduction of the 'Elgastat', which used a chemical de-ioniser process to produce high grade water, replaced the distillers, and thus ended another part of Daventry history.

Valves

It would be well beyond the scope of this book to detail every part of Daventry's technical history, but the valve has a unique place in Broadcasting. Over 67 years Daventry Station used diode, triode, tetrode and pentode (two, three, four and five electrodes) valves. Small valves used in the Programme Control Room and Central Drive Room (where the carrier signal was generated) low power amplifiers produced little heat. Water cooled valve anodes present a problem, as anodes can reach potentials of 20,000 volts, and because of impurities, tap water conducts electricity and cannot be used – hence the requirement of distilled water. The manufacturers Marconi and Standard Telephone and Cable had different approaches to the problem. Marconi pumped distilled water at high pressure to the valve anodes, through coiled rubber hoses. Standard Telephone used ceramic tubes and flat pancake ceramics to feed water to the valve anodes. New type Marconi 100kW, 250kW and 300kW transmitters employing vapour phase valve boilers were insulated from ground by the use of small bore PTFE tubes through which distilled water was supplied from gravity controlled tanks. Each system met the design technology of the day, but water systems do have ongoing problems. Unfortunately they leak, suffer from corrosion, and have high levels of maintenance.

Over the years three designs of water cooled valve/jackets were used, plus the unique de-mountable valve manufactured by Metropolitan Vickers installed in Sender 3 transmitter (installed in the old 5GB building).

S T & C valves had an integral envelope and water jacket. Marconi valves and jackets were manufactured separately, which reduced cost and made valve replacement easy. With the installation of Marconi 100kW, 250kW and 300kW transmitters, the valve jacket was replaced by the valve boiler - steam cooling had arrived!

It is of historical interest to note that the highest power 500kW transmitters currently used in the BBC and other countries use vapour phase cooling, but with hyper-vapourtron valve anodes developed by the French Thomson Co.

Valves are a weak link in high power transmitters – the higher the power, the shorter the life! They need to be handled with great care and attention - no prizes for breakages! For many years the routine of power testing new valves, and the hurried replacement of large faulty valves in shut-down conditions was a vivid memory of shift life. Large valves came to the Station in wooden crates fitted with large coil springs, to reduce transit shocks. Then after checking for damage, were carefully placed in valve cupboards for later power testing. The electrode connections and protrusions on valves brought the possibilities of breakage. The smaller Standard Telephone valves were manhandled into position, but the larger valves in Sender 7 (S17), employed a three wheel truck, which gave the feeling of instability, and was treated with caution!

Changing the Final Stage valves in the Marconi 100kW transmitter was an engineering exercise! The manufacturer designed an ingenious tailor-made truck, with four pram type wheels, the rear two moveable. It incorporated a platform that could be moved backwards and forwards and raised a few inches. To remove a valve from its transmitter unit pedestal an empty truck would be inserted into a location channel. An interlock would then allow a hand operated wheel to move the valve platform forward into the unit using a worm drive. Once the platform was correctly positioned under the valve flange, it could be raised a few inches by a lever, allowing the valve to be withdrawn from the unit. A valve change in shut down conditions might take ten to fifteen minutes - or longer!

In vapour phase transmitters valve changing was mechanically simpler. To lift the valve from its boiler a detachable hoist with four hooks was used. The hoist, placed on a unit frame runner would be positioned above the valve, allowing the hooks to be fitted around the valve corona ring. A handle on the hoist would then be turned to winch the valve from its boiler, after all connections had been released. It sounds to be an easy exercise. In fact the unit temperatures in steam cooled transmitters made it hazardous through scalding water and very hot metal work – protective arm length leather gloves had to be used. If problems were met with water sealing gaskets a valve replacement could run to thirty minutes.

Spanner in the rigging[13], Rex Boys

After 4 years in Research Department, I was getting restless. Promotion had slowed down and it slowly dawned on me that it was vacancies rather than ability that would determine my future progress. Although I'd produced one idea that got patented, I began to feel that my career prospects would be brighter elsewhere. Relief came in the form of a work experience scheme under which selected junior engineers were given the opportunity to move around the Specialist Departments until they found a niche where they might hope to get a permanent job through the normal procedure.

In September 1951 I said goodbye to cycling home for lunch and working in the stately laboratories of Kingswood Warren to join the commuter trail, via London Bridge and Oxford Circus, to a desk in Bentinck House where I became a founder member of the Aerial Unit of Planning and Installation Department.

Nearly all the installation work was done by contractors and a whole year elapsed before I was sent out to put up an aerial with my own hands. This was the reserve aerial for the new television transmitting station at Wenvoe, near Cardiff and was, effectively, a simpler version of the main aerial on a separate, smaller mast.

Helped by the local rigger, Charlie, I got the eight dipoles bolted into place and hoisted up the combining unit. This was a cylindrical structure that filled the middle of the mast, taking up so much space that, for the first time, I had to get off the ladder, ease myself out between the struts and crawl up the outside of the mast for a couple of yards. Terrified at first, I soon found myself performing the manoeuvre with a stylish grace that could only have been inherited from a treetop ancestry.

At the top of the combining unit there were eight outlets, each of which had to be connected to a dipole, using a new type of cable that I had never previously handled. Taking the form of an aluminium

---

[13] From an article published in Ariel (Sept 1993) under the title "Spanner in the Rigging."

tube nearly an inch in diameter, it was more of a plumbing job than an engineering one. There was a special tool for bending it but this was so big and heavy it could not be used up the mast. The cable could just about be bent by hand but it kinked easily and that meant scrapping the piece and starting again.

The first four dipoles were connected without too much difficulty but, for technical reasons, extra length had to be incorporated in the cables to the other four dipoles and this is where the real trouble started.

Imagine the situation. Two points, 10 feet apart, have to be joined by a piece of aluminium tube 13'-7" long, the extra 3'-7" being absorbed in bends and elbows. Four such lengths have to be installed inside a galvanised steel mast, barely two feet square, at a height of 200 feet above the ground: this space also has to accommodate the person doing the job. The designer (not me) has left it to the installer (me) to improvise the routing of the cables, bearing in mind the need to clamp them to the mast at frequent intervals. It is December.

It was a nightmare of a job, some of the loops had to project outside the mast and the kindest thing that could be said about the result was that it was untidy. Indeed, that was the exact word used by the Head of Department, Mr. A.N. Thomas, when he came down for the opening ceremony - and he could see it from ground level.

On the Friday afternoon, before going home for the weekend, I decided that I really ought to go up and see if I could find a few more places to clamp the cables to the mast. This would not be easy because the devious route they followed did not coincide too frequently with the mast structure itself.

It was one of those cold, dark days before Christmas with a sharpish East wind and the nuts on the clamps were too small to be handled with gloves. Without gloves, though, the fingers quickly became numb and had to be constantly tucked inside my clothes to thaw out. I didn't mind dropping nuts but I had only one spanner and didn't fancy the 400 ft return trip to recover that if I dropped it.

There had been an incident a couple of weeks previously when I had asked Charlie to pop down to the base of the mast to fetch something. When he was about halfway down, I heard a clanging noise but thought nothing of it. Looking down a few moments later, I could see Charlie heading for the transmitter building so I called to ask where he was going. "My 'ead's cut open", was the terse reply. When I next reached into my windcheater pocket for a spanner, all I found was a hole; then I realised what the clanging noise had been.

As I worked, I recalled a conversation I'd had with my wife some months previously when the BBC introduced an improved insurance policy for people working on masts. Discussing our financial plight, we had speculated on how much she would get if I could somehow fall off a mast and land on her mother!

It was when it began to snow that morale really plummeted. They were not the big gentle flakes that you see on Christmas cards but the heavy wet ones that travel horizontally, hit you in the neck and trickle down inside the collar. They blotted out the ground and the cold, cramped steel cage became a very lonely place.

That was when I had a sort of moment of truth and resolved that, come what may, I was going to get a job sitting at a desk and only going out of doors at times of my own choosing. It was about a year before the right advertisement appeared, a post calling for a qualified engineer to work in Engineering Buying. My friends all said I was being shunted into a siding and they were right, but I had a whale of a time there for 25 years.

FAREHAM AND THE ELECTRICITY BOARD, DICK STIBBONS

The Transmitter Maintenance Team at Crystal Palace was responsible for all un-attended transmitters on the Dover, Fareham, Mildenhall, Oxford patch. The station at Fareham was a small 'Home Service' local medium wave station, technically interesting because of its wartime RCA transmitter which used Doherty Modulation. However, that's not the point of the story.

Fareham had been reduced from a full time staff of seven to nil and it was so reliable that we sometimes wouldn't need to visit it for months on end. One day we received a report that it was off the air and I was dispatched to investigate. Beating my way in through the cobwebs, I found three postcards on the doormat, all from the local Electricity Board.

The first said "Dear Sir, Your electricity bill is overdue" The second said "If you don't pay it we'll cut you off." The third said "We did."

I rushed along to the local office of the suppliers and explained that this was the BBC they were dealing with. Unmoved, they refused to reconnect until they had the money, whereupon I promptly wrote them a personal cheque for six hundred and twenty pounds. I remember the amount because it was then the biggest cheque I had ever written and represented half a year's pay! Having seen the transmitter safely back on air, I raced to BH to recover the money before the cheque bounced.

Anyone who worked on Mobile Maintenance in those days will have dozens of stories to tell of the way we rose to the call of duty, frequently using the most unconventional and cavalier tactics. Our inspiration for this approach came largely from the Team Leader at Brookman's Park. His name was Bert Gallon. I wonder what became of him…?

STARTING WITH THE BBC IN 1941, DON BOWMAN

On July 13th 1941 I joined the BBC at Sheffield 'H' Group transmitter at Manor Lane School, or what was left of the school after the blitz the previous November, with the grand title of 'Youth Transmitters'.

The transmitter was located in the former cloak-room of the abandoned school where the roof had been reinforced, and for an air raid shelter we had a steel 'Bell Shelter' standing outside. The mast for the aerial was stuck in the middle of the playground. The transmitter, as I remember, was designed by a man called Webb and had an output of 100 Watts, sufficient power to reach all-round the city. The drive unit was the old faithful CP17E using a 'Post Office' crystal and the operating frequency was 1474kHz or 203.5 metres.

I am told that there were 60 'H' group stations throughout the country and they radiated the Home Service. One of these 'H' Group stations in Reading was hit by a bomb during the war. As lads our main duty was monitoring the programme and conferring with 'Control' in Manchester by private telephone line if there were clicks or interruptions to the programme. We also were required to regularly contact the local police in order that they knew we were alright.

The idea of the 'H' groups was, in war time, to provide communication to the people in the large cities in the event of an invasion or the appearance of German Paratroops. So each station had a microphone and some means of creating a makeshift studio so that instructions could be broadcast by well known local people or politicians should the need arise. I remember one night testing the microphone as we were required to do but failed to disconnect a feed to a Radio Relay Company which was used to distribute BBC programmes by wire. Perhaps all the subscribers had gone to bed as there were no repercussions afterwards.

The BBC management were very keen that we should be proficient in Morse code, both sending and receiving, up to 25 words per minute. We had a gramophone and Morse practice recordings which we had to use frequently. The shift hours were long, within a few days of joining I spent a week on night shift starting at 10.00 p.m. and ending at 9.00 am plus a double tram journey on each end, and seven, eleven hour long night shifts in a row! I still remember coming home after my first week at work and gave my mother about 30 shillings (£1.50p). She couldn't believe they would pay a lad of sixteen years old all that money and she wanted to know where I had obtained it.

One incident for which I was very unpopular was having Diphtheria within a week or so of getting a 'flu injection. I was in an isolation hospital for three weeks and both the house and the transmitting station had to be fumigated. In those days Diphtheria was still a serious illness. Within a year we were faced with interviews in Manchester to become Junior Maintenance Engineers (Unestablished) and this meant the transfer to a large station. I suppose this was in an effort to replace staff from the large stations who had been called up into the armed forces. So in June 1942 I was sent on a course at Maida Vale studios in London followed by a week's course at Daventry. I have no memory of air attacks whilst we were in London so it was probably a quiet period of the war. During the Daventry based course we were billeted in Long Buckby and ferried daily the six miles to Daventry by bus.

At the end of the course my three colleagues, Peter Dyson, Ken Jackson and Alan Slater and myself (all ex Sheffield Junior Technical School) were posted to Daventry transmitting station. At that time the Engineer in Charge was Douglas Birkinshaw who previously had been on the engineering staff at Alexandra Palace from where the pre-war Television had been broadcast. The Assistant Engineer in Charge (A.EiC) was L.F.Ivin, who seven years later, was back at Daventry involved in Television Interference research.

In those 1942 early days the station, on Borough Hill, had fields all the way down to the town, across a railway line which ran from Northampton to Blisworth, via Weedon and Daventry to Leamington Spa, a railway line which no longer exists. I worked on the two short wave senders 1 & 2 as I can clearly recall taking my oral TA1 examination, during the war, on senders 1 & 2 with D.C. Birkinshaw. By the way the Borough Hill site was bought in 1925 for £2,670.

I spent quite a lot of the next two years on shift on the old 1925 5XX transmitter.

My contact with 5XX started in 1942 when the 17 year old 25kW transmitter was in use once more, transmitting to Europe on 1,500 metres. 5XX had the distinction of being the first transmitter designed to transmit to a national audience, compared to the few low power 1kW local transmitters currently in use in major towns with a range of 25 miles.

5XX radiated the National programme said to reach about 85% of the population. The red brick building housing 5XX was not quite at the summit of Borough Hill, and in those days a metal concentric feeder, which tended to arcle and sparkle a bit, ran above ground, except where it went under the concrete drive, and connected the RF output to an ATH and thence to a 'Tee' aerial supported by two 500 ft masts. Memories of walking up to the ATH carrying the hut key on a large ring made of copper to take the two hourly ATH meter readings; notwithstanding the size of the key ring I managed one day to get it into my pocket and to inadvertently take it home.

5XX was very spread out and the 'transmitter works' were surrounded by a protective wire netting fence about six feet high with an interlocked access gate. Photographs taken in the early days of 5XX showed only a waist high rail around the transmitter enclosure, showing safety wasn't that important in 1925. The Radio Frequency side consisted of one air cooled valve (ACT9), followed by the Pen RF stage using two Marconi MR9 valves, which glowed cherry red, and, for the final RF stage, four Marconi water cooled CAT1 valves operating in parallel. By the time I arrived, the tuning fork, which had been used to control the carrier frequency, had been replaced by the CP17E crystal drive unit. There was a clever gadget in the drive room which received a very accurate 1,000 cycle tone which was used to check our carrier frequency. It was the same as the 'L' Group of transmitters which included the very powerful Ottringham transmitters.

Unlike operating a short wave transmitter, tuning 5XX called for the S.M.E. at least, or even the A.EIC! The AF side ended up with eight water cooled Marconi CAM1 valves in parallel.

The EHT dc supplies (11kV) were derived initially from two motor alternators, each producing about 3,000 volts at 300 cycles, then via oil filled step up transformers to water cooled CAR2 valve rectifiers. EHT smoothing used oil filled chokes and a line of $0.1\mu F$ condensers in pot jars connected to a copper HT rail by thin wire fuses. Touching a condenser terminal where the fuse wire was broken could be a very 'moving' experience (failure to use 'earthing wands' comes to mind). Filament supplies were produced from two 10kW motor-generator sets with a third 25kW MG set producing auxiliary supplies.

Starting the MG sets was a lengthy and very noisy operation usually performed about 5.30 am. in preparation for 6.00 service.

I recall the noisy job of 'hand starting' all the 5XX rotating machinery, the 10kW filament machines, then the 25kW and finally the two 70kW machines for high tension. You were about deafened after 15 minutes in the MG room. Ringing in the ears afterwards was an understatement!

The control desk with red bulbs in glass domes on top was the only indication the 'excitation' on the machines had been established. Winding up the transmitter filaments on the rectifiers, valve filaments and other motor generator derived supplies kept one busy and hopeful that it would all work. Then during the war hearing the Trumpet Voluntary blaring out about 6.00 am at the start of a transmission in German.

Valve cooling, compared to modern standards, was a bit of a joke, nevertheless very effective with good insulation figures. None of your rubber hose coils but instead spray units to insulate the valves using hard tap water! Outside were two ponds, one with cold water the other one containing the hot water discharged from the valves. Cold water was pumped up to a large header tank inside the building from whence water flowed by gravity to the water cooled units. Each unit had a rectangular top tank into which the water was sprayed, water then was admitted to the bottom of the valve jackets by rubber hoses. Warm water left the top of the valve jackets and via individual insulating sprays into a lower tank and thence out to the 'hot' pond. Finally water found its way from the hot to the cold ponds.

One daily maintenance chore, which was carried out during an afternoon break in transmission, was dipping valve copper anodes in acid to remove hard tap water scale.

I don't recall many breakdowns; generally once you had got 5XX going it stayed on the air; the main tasks were recording meter readings and adjusting voltages following variations in the mains power supply. However I remember one day after the water header tank had been cleaned out, one by one steam issued from valve jackets as dirt, dislodged from the tank, had blocked the valve spray units. This involved taking the transmitter off the air several times in order to disconnect valve filaments!

Being in 5XX during a thunderstorm was a rather frightening experience, as well as the transmitter tripping, we often watched lightening dancing down the control panel. 5XX had its own electrician, maintenance and cleaning staff and a coke boiler which had to be tended correctly by the shift staff after office hours otherwise the night shift, in particular, would be cold. During the war I got the nickname 'Bobby' from the 5XX staff, a name that stuck with me for many years.

In wartime there was a shift of three, but one had to man an Air Ministry transmitter, known as AM1, located in an adjoining room. This spent its odd hours on the air as required by signals received in Morse code from some unidentified place! On night shift we awaited the welcome signal "GNOM" which was an acronym for 'Good night old man'.

One drawback was the absence of a flush toilet just a smelly 'Elsan'. One plus, particularly on evening and night duty, was the 'billiard room' along the main entrance passage, where the Club snooker table resided.

With the 5XX building being perched on top of a 600 ft high hill the lights from its windows could of course be seen at night. Quite often in the war, during hours of darkness, we were told to douse the lights at the time of an air raid warning. Sometimes we also received urgent messages to take the transmitter off the air to prevent its use by aircraft for direction finding. One night we lost the aerial due to a low flying aircraft clipping it with its gun turret (whose's aircraft I don't know) and we were unable to radiate our programme in German at 5.45 am.

There is also the apocryphal story (during a period when paratroops were expected) that the military guard, consisting of 'Blue Caps' - Corps of Military Police, whose guard hut was close to 5XX, turned out in force one night when loud voices were heard from the aerial field in German! Only to discover that it was a corona on a feeder carrying a German language broadcast!

One tale I must tell concerning the 5XX communal 'Lilo' we used during the war for a rest during a night shift. There wasn't a pump so one had to blow it up. Unfortunately there was a small hole in it and if you didn't drop off to sleep within a few minutes you found yourself on the hard concrete floor! Often one could spend the whole rest hour blowing it up. I never discovered why someone hadn't the sense to mend the leak with a bike puncture outfit!

I also remember the guards stopping the oncoming shift bus, near their guard house, and coming on board to check that we all had our BBC passes. Never mind us vouching for a colleague - no pass - he was sent back to get it! The shift bus was a Morris with the entrance door at the rear, with long side facing seats. It was always crowded but sometimes we had some light relief as a man called Batty used to entertain us with his fiddle.

Not only 5XX but what about Sender 3 in another building on the top of the hill, with its de-mountable output valves? Only one story comes to mind about Sender 3. One night a de-mountable valve had been stripped, possibly to replace an electrode, and very close to transmission time there was the usual problem of removing air and establishing the necessary internal vacuum. One youngster [not me] was shouted at for suggesting to the S.M.E. that a cup of tea was in order! For many years afterwards there was a cartoon depicting the incident displayed on the wall in the building. Sender 3 building was later used for the 'Ampliphase' transmitter to start the Third Programme, the building later became the station workshop and in the early 1960's was demolished to make way for aerial feeders.

Post War, 5XX was replaced by T3, a modern twin air cooled 100kW transmitter which carried the Third Programme. Finally, in 1992, 5XX building became home to the Tape Reclamation Unit.

My wartime Daventry experiences were cut short by the war and papers calling me up for army service in June 1944.

Finishing with the BBC in 1997, Martin Ellen

When I joined the BBC in 1966 and started as a TA at Daventry, little did I know that I would be playing a part in selling BBC transmission 30 years later! In 1996, along with Nigel Turner and John Ward, and led by Alan Rees, we gave presentations about BBC Transmission to prospective buyers and we spent much of the year burning the midnight oil answering hundreds of questions. The City of London also became quite familiar. We had a farewell lunch with the Director General during which he read a nice speech about BBC Transmission and then we all moved to Castle Transmission International (later to become Crown Castle International).

In the same month as privatisation it became clear that digital terrestrial television would become a reality and having spent a year helping to sell BBC Transmission we launched straight into bidding for six DTT multiplex contracts. We went through a baptism of fire and won 4-2 against our competitors, but that's another story, for another book. Suffice to say that this, followed by developing a whole new business in third generation mobile telecoms meant there was little time for looking back.

Nevertheless, I think that our heritage is important so, around the time of privatisation, I wrote a 26 page note on the history of BBC Transmission and I am delighted that Norman Shacklady together with all the other contributors have gone much further to make this book possible.

Daventry has featured a lot in this book. It's obviously been very important in terms of its function and in terms of its influence on very many people who passed through it. I enjoyed my time at Daventry, but only for the first year! After that I tired of the constant moaning from bored colleagues and eventually got a job in Designs department, which was a wonderful place. I spent 15 years there but nearly always working on designs for Transmission, so I rubbed shoulders with many people at team bases and in TCPD. It was quite interesting to observe the various relationships: team bases versus MICs versus HF stations; all versus HQ; Transmission HQ versus

TCPD etc. Everyone wanted to do it their way, and indeed tended to be promoted if they showed the right amount of self-sufficiency and 'steel', which was no bad thing. (Some, including me, found it difficult to determine what 'the right amount' was.) Tactics included stealth, currying favour with the boss (not the normal expression used), arguments which bordered on warfare and, I'm pleased to say, reasoned discussion. Through good times and bad, (nearly) everyone was bound together through an innate collective desire to do a first class professional job.

Designs Department at Western House (next to BH in London) was closed down in the mid 1980's and a smaller Design Group was merged with Equipment Department in Chiswick to form D&ED. This change was made in the context of increasing availability of equipment from outside industry. It was initiated by a decision that was dubbed 'Black Spot', and it marked the beginning of major changes to BBC Engineering Division. D&ED closed down in 1994 and the Design Group then merged with Research Department at Kingswood Warren. Luckily for me I was asked to move to Communications Department just before Black Spot and I enjoyed a couple of years at Duchess Street responsible for communications projects.

Despite this background it was not my idea to include sections in this book on the 'specialist departments', although I'm glad it has happened because they all played a vital role in building BBC Transmission. I am sorry that the contributions are not more complete. Many of the achievements from Designs, Research, Communications and Equipment Department are covered, but more on Engineering Training and other areas such as Valve Section and Site Acquisition would have given a more balanced picture.

Up until the mid 1980's Transmission HQ, Communications Department and part of TCPD were in central London and the other part of TCPD was based at Brookmans Park. For years there had been discussions about moving to lower cost and more strategically placed premises outside London and in 1986 it started to happen. These departments were merged to form 'BBC Transmission' and the search started for new premises. Towards the end of the search a number of senior people (of which I was the most junior) went on a memorable coach trip to two sites in Redditch and one in Warwick. Despite being given a rather nice tape measure by the council people at Redditch I voted for the patch of muddy ground at Warwick and it was good to see our new headquarters being built there. I saw it being built because a number of us moved to temporary accommodation in the office of a nearby factory. My abiding memory of this place was seeing all the workers gather behind a line in the road waiting for the whistle to blow so they could go home. It made me realise that Daventry in the 1960's perhaps wasn't such a bad place after all.

We moved into the new Headquarters on 5 September 1989 and, although it was sad to say goodbye to the people who didn't move from the London area, overall it was a great success.

By this time the number of people working in transmission had reduced considerably from its peak, but the constant drive for efficiency and the feasibility of introducing new technology meant that this process continued. It is unfortunate that this book does not have a contribution about working in a Monitoring and Control Centre, because five communities built up around the MICs at Crystal Palace, Wenvoe, Sutton Coldfield, Holme Moss and Blackhill. These operations were state of the art when they started in the 1970's, but advances in technology enabled us to replace them all from one 'Technical Operations Centre' in Warwick (plus an unattended backup elsewhere). Everyone understood the realities, but it was sad to see them close down and for the communities including cooks, admin staff and engineers, to be lost. It was offset though by seeing the tremendous enthusiasm of the people who created and ran the TOC. Initially, the TOC was also responsible for managing wide area telecom networks for the entire BBC and this demonstrated very well the innate ability of able and well trained transmission engineers to take on new skills very quickly!

I've tried to fill in a few gaps that exist in the book and I'm tempted to go on, but I think that's enough. Perhaps the most notable absence is from some of the most senior people in BBC Engineering who had a profound influence on Transmission. I guess that they all have other priorities, and now, so have I.

INDEX

2LO, 1, 2, 3, 4, 5, 97, 131, 172
A.R.S. Ascension, 38
achievement, 5, 91, 163
Alexandra Palace, 19, 23, 30, 50, 51, 57, 60, 61, 62, 79, 92, 98, 100, 102, 105, 111, 131, 159, 160, 172, 209
America, 12, 29, 30, 38, 39, 41, 42, 61, 63, 81, 100, 101, 140, 156, 157, 163, 175
Architectural and Civil Engineering Department, 93
Ascension, 38, 39, 41, 42, 43, 166, 167, 168, 169
Ashkirk, 20
Aspidistra, 12
automatic control, 32, 37, 41, 45, 69
Automatic Fault Reporter, 70
B.E.M.R.S. Cyprus, 44, 45, 46
B.E.R.S. Masirah, 47
Bagley Croft, 19, 79
Baird, 50, 64, 172
Band I, 51, 52, 54, 55, 61, 62, 63, 83, 88, 186, 188, 189, 192, 193
Band IV, 62
Bartley, 13, 14, 71
BBC engineer, 125, 142, 170, 171
BBC Engineering, 77, 151, 215, 217
BBC1, 64, 65, 67, 163, 185
BBC2, 64, 65, 67, 162, 163, 176
Blue Streak transposer, 67, 90, 191
Bluebell Hill, 23
bomb, 11, 14, 111, 208
British Telecom, 22, 152
Brookmans Park, 4, 5, 6, 7, 8, 10, 11, 13, 14, 17, 21, 50, 97, 98, 143, 215
Brougher Mountain, 14
Burghead, 6, 13, 19
Carnane, 59
Ceefax, 66

Chelmsford, 4, 24, 98
Chief Engineer, 3, 5, 77, 78
Clevedon, 6, 9, 13, 14, 28
Collapsed structures, 11, 13, 36, 41, 65, 121, 125
colour, 35, 57, 62, 63, 64, 65, 67, 80, 81, 82, 89, 130, 174, 175
Communications Department, 77, 83, 91, 92, 215
Coronation, 54, 55, 57, 58, 80, 96, 98, 124, 151, 160
Crowborough, 12
Crystal Palace, 21, 23, 60, 61, 62, 63, 64, 68, 70, 72, 81, 82, 84, 85, 96, 170, 175, 176, 206, 216
Daventry, 4, 5, 7, 11, 24, 25, 27, 28, 29, 30, 33, 34, 37, 39, 45, 69, 96, 98, 99, 100, 102, 103, 104, 105, 108, 109, 110, 113, 114, 115, 116, 120, 171, 195, 196, 197, 198, 199, 200, 201, 202, 209, 213, 214, 216
Designs, 22, 32, 53, 73, 78, 79, 82, 83, 88, 143, 146, 150, 164, 174, 176, 214, 215
Designs Department, 22, 67, 79
diesel, 5, 11, 12, 29, 35, 78, 128, 135, 138, 167, 184, 190, 192, 200
diesel engines, 5, 78
digital, 19, 22, 23, 65, 66, 81, 82, 83, 84, 85, 86, 87, 90, 164, 214
Diplomatic Wireless Service, 34, 44, 45, 47
Director of Engineering, 55, 56, 83, 95, 117, 132, 133, 197
Divis, 14, 56
Dodford, 69
Domino, 50
Douglas, 59, 109, 120, 122, 209
drives, 7, 8, 26, 29, 99, 137

Droitwich, 4, 6, 10, 11, 13, 19, 69, 79, 98, 112, 113, 120, 134, 136, 139, 182, 184, 189
DTT, 68, 214
Eckersley, 3, 5
Edinburgh, 1, 3, 53, 69, 141, 143, 144
efficiency, 14, 17, 33, 67, 68, 73, 130, 216
EMI, 50, 62, 64, 92, 158, 172
Empire, 24, 97, 98, 100, 101, 117, 131
Equipment Department, 56, 73, 78, 79, 91, 142, 143, 144, 150, 174, 215
Europe, 1, 12, 13, 30, 80, 82, 136, 139, 171, 209
Evesham, 79, 122, 135
experimental transmissions, 4, 24, 50
F.C. McLean, 55
Falklands, 38, 96, 166, 169
Farnley, 14, 69
feeder, 26, 27, 53, 54, 69, 99, 109, 115, 116, 118, 132, 141, 175, 195, 210, 212
flash-over, 28
Force, 47, 107, 112
Forces, 9, 12, 30, 38, 40, 42, 112, 138, 166, 169, 171, 178, 209, 212
Foreign Office, 34, 45
G5SW, 24, 98, 99
Glasgow, 1, 3, 53, 69, 141, 148, 164
Glencairn, 56
Group H, 9, 13
Guildford, 23, 83
Harthill, 53
Holme Moss, 21, 52, 58, 59, 70, 72, 122, 123, 124, 125, 127, 128, 129, 130, 131, 216
Home, 5, 13, 20, 58, 80, 109, 111, 120, 132, 206, 208
Home Service, 13, 109, 206, 208
Hong Kong, 32
icing, 52, 104, 196
interference, 1, 9, 19, 58, 59, 112, 130, 148, 149, 183
Isle of Man, 58, 60
ITA, 64, 65
jamming, 11, 30, 50, 51
King George VI, 53
Kingswood Warren, 61, 79, 80, 144, 151, 204, 215
Kirk o'Shotts, 53, 54, 56, 70, 72, 96, 141, 151
klystron, 64, 67, 68, 190
Kranji, 36, 37
Lady's Mile, 45, 46, 47
Langham, 79, 158
Light, 13, 14, 20, 21, 80, 112
Lines Department, 78, 91, 92, 96, 151, 152, 165
Lisnagarvey, 6
Llandrindod Wells, 20
Local Radio, 21, 22, 163
Maintenance, 20, 61, 71, 72, 96, 100, 103, 105, 120, 131, 152, 162, 176, 190, 193, 196, 199, 206, 207, 208
Marconi, 1, 4, 11, 14, 24, 25, 28, 29, 31, 32, 34, 35, 36, 37, 38, 45, 46, 47, 53, 56, 98, 99, 101, 102, 108, 117, 142, 190, 198, 199, 202, 203, 210
Masirah, 47
Meldrum, 58
Meriden, 21
MIC, 70, 216
Microprocessors, 32, 70
Moorside Edge, 6, 10, 11, 12, 13, 19, 30, 71, 121, 122, 127, 132, 171
Morecambe Bay, 20

Newcastle, 1, 3, 55, 56, 69, 143, 148
NICAM, 22, 66, 84, 85, 90, 184
North Hessary Tor, 58
Norwich, 13
ntl, 64, 67
NTSC, 61, 63, 81, 82, 85, 175
Orkney, 20, 185, 186, 187
OSE1 Daventry, 25
OSE2 Daventry, 25
OSE3 Rampisham, 29
OSE4 Start Point, 28
OSE5 Ottringham, 11, 117, 118
OSE6 Droitwich, 11
OSE7 Lisnagarvey, 29
OSE8 Skelton A, 29
OSE9 Skelton B, 29
OSE10 Woofferton, 29
Ottringham, 11, 13, 117, 121, 210
Oxford, 4, 19, 20, 131, 156, 204, 206
PAL, 63, 82, 83, 85, 89, 175
PCM, 21, 22, 38, 125
Penge, 60
Penmon, 6, 9, 13, 20
Plessey, 37
Pontop Pike, 20, 56, 64, 83, 151
Post Office, 1, 21, 24, 53, 65, 78, 81, 88, 91, 129, 130, 152, 153, 155, 159, 160, 161, 162, 208
Postmaster General, 51
propaganda, 25, 119, 121
propagation, 20, 24, 62, 64, 66, 175
Punggol, 37, 38
Racal, 35, 37
radar, 24, 30, 57, 175, 186
Radio 1, 17, 21
Radio 2, 21
RAF, 8, 30, 47, 59, 163, 176, 186
Rampisham, 12, 28, 30, 32, 33, 101, 102, 106, 107, 109, 110, 111, 113, 114, 115, 116, 117, 120, 121, 131

RCA, 12, 31, 46, 54, 55, 62, 112, 206
RDS, 22, 83, 84
Redmoss, 6, 9, 13, 14, 58
Redruth, 13, 20
Regional Programme, 5, 6, 7, 13
Regional Scheme, 5, 6
Reigate, 23
Research, 19, 22, 61, 65, 66, 77, 78, 79, 80, 81, 82, 83, 84, 86, 89, 105, 144, 147, 150, 164, 174, 193, 204, 215
Richard Dimbleby, 52, 109, 124
rockets, 30, 50, 61, 170
Rosemarkie, 20, 183
Rowridge, 21, 57
Sandale, 58
SECAM, 63, 175
Service Planning, 16, 86, 93
Seychelles, 32
Shetland, 20, 186
sideband, 51, 60, 63, 88
Silver Streak transposer, 67, 90
Singapore, 34, 35, 36, 37, 38
Site Acquisition, 93, 215
Site Sharing, 64
Skegness, 20
Snaefell, 58, 59, 60
Sound-in-Syncs, 65, 66, 81, 82, 125, 164, 188
ST&C, 24, 25, 28, 29, 98, 99, 101
St. Helena, 43, 169
Stagshaw, 6, 13, 71, 96, 119, 151
standards converter, 65, 80, 81, 82
Start Point, 6, 10, 13, 28
Station Design and Installation Department, 78, 93
stereo, 21, 22, 66, 82, 83, 84, 85, 158, 164
Sutton Coldfield, 21, 52, 64, 70, 80, 122, 129, 189, 216

Swains Lane, 21
SWB18, 25, 28, 29, 35, 36
synchronisation, 7, 156
Tacolneston, 58
Tanglin, 38
TCPD, 51, 53, 55, 92, 96, 141, 174, 177, 180, 190, 191, 193, 214, 215
Tebrau, 34, 35, 36, 37
Technical Assistant, 72, 118, 121
Technical Operations Centre, 216
Telephone Indicator Panel, 70, 189
Teletext, 66, 82
tetrode, 55, 68, 202
Third, 13, 14, 20, 69, 80, 213
Thorpe Lodge, 21
Tick Hill, 21
TMT, 20, 69, 71, 72, 90, 182
Transmitter Capital Projects Department, 51, 77, 79
Transmitter Department, 29, 77, 90
Transport, 73, 78
Truleigh Hill, 57
UHF TV, 66, 69, 177
unattended, 14, 20, 32, 69, 71, 72, 73, 75, 174, 188, 189, 216

VHF/FM, 19, 20, 21, 22, 23, 51, 52, 60, 79, 80
War, 8, 12, 30, 33, 43, 44, 51, 54, 59, 79, 96, 120, 132, 134, 139, 153, 161, 166, 213
Washford, 6, 7, 10, 13, 72, 98, 131, 143
wave change, 25
Wenvoe, 54, 70, 72, 188, 189, 190, 194, 204, 216
West Indies, 24, 40
Westerglen, 6, 10, 12, 13, 19, 30, 140, 182
Whipsnade, 21
Whitehawk Hill, 57
Wigtown, 58
Wine Press transposer, 67
Woodleigh, 35, 36
World Service, 35, 38, 42, 73, 84, 90, 167, 168, 169, 197
Wrotham, 20, 21, 60, 80, 81, 83
Wychwood Hill, 21
Y-Gerat, 50
Zyyi, 44, 45, 46, 47